Day Trading For Canadians

2nd Edition

**by Bryan Borzykowski
and Annie Logue, MBA**

for
dummies®

A Wiley Brand

Day Trading For Canadians For Dummies®, 2nd Edition

Published by: **John Wiley & Sons, Inc.,** 111 River Street, Hoboken, NJ 07030-5774, www.wiley.com

Copyright © 2021 by John Wiley & Sons, Inc., Hoboken, New Jersey

Published simultaneously in Canada

For general information on our other products and services, please contact our Customer Care Department within the U.S. at 877-762-2974, outside the U.S. at 317-572-3993, or fax 317-572-4002. For technical support, please visit https://hub.wiley.com/community/support/dummies.

Wiley publishes in a variety of print and electronic formats and by print-on-demand. Some material included with standard print versions of this book may not be included in e-books or in print-on-demand. If this book refers to media such as a CD or DVD that is not included in the version you purchased, you may download this material at http://booksupport.wiley.com. For more information about Wiley products, visit www.wiley.com.

Library of Congress Control Number: 2020948814

ISBN 978-1-119-73671-4 (pbk); ISBN 978-1-119-73672-1 (ebk); ISBN 978-1-119-73674-5 (ebk)

Manufactured in the United States of America

SKY10022089 103020

Contents at a Glance

Table of Contents

Introduction

A lot has happened since the first edition of *Day Trading For Canadians For Dummies* came out a decade ago. Mobile apps, tax law changes, new investments accounts and an entirely new asset class — cryptocurrency — have changed the work of day trading. The world also feels more uncertain than ever before, in part because, as we're writing this, in the summer of 2020, COVID-19 is wreaking havoc on the world. Stock market volatility is higher than it's been in years, and while that's not great for the average investor, it's good news for day traders, who love market ups and downs.

There will always be people who try to make money off daily stock price movements, but whenever there's market uncertainty (like the tech bubble and burst in 2001, the Great Recession in 2008, and now the novel coronavirus crisis in 2020) more people want to try their hand at day trading. So if you're looking to learn more about how all of this works, you've come to the right place. Our second Canadian edition will help steer you straight.

It may be obvious, but it's worth saying out loud: Day trading is a business in which you use real money to take on the markets. If you love the thrill of market ups and downs and have the patience to sit and stare at a screen for hours, waiting for the right moment to get in and get out of securities, then day trading may be a great career option. But it has many risks too. Any day can be your best day, but it can also put you out of business forever. For that reason, day trading requires the right psychological makeup. Good day traders are patient and decisive, confident but not arrogant. They most certainly are not gamblers, although day trading attracts gamblers who discover it's a great way to *lose* money from home.

Day Trading For Canadians For Dummies, 2nd Edition, is for people who are looking to get into the trading business or who simply want to supplement their investment returns with new techniques. In this book, you can find all the information you need to determine whether you're cut out for day trading, from laying out your home office, to researching and planning trades, and more. (And even if you decide day trading isn't for you, you can still find lots of sound general advice about markets, trading, and investing strategies that you can benefit from. Plus, you'll have saved all the money you would have otherwise invested on research and training, not to mention the trading losses!)

A lot of people make a lot of money selling services to neophyte day traders, claiming to be the best thing going. And maybe so — for some people. In this book, we give you a wider perspective. Instead of telling you to use a particular trading strategy, for example, we help you research and evaluate the different day trading methods available so that you can find one that works for you. Still, as comprehensive as this book may be, it shouldn't be your only guide.

About This Book

First, let us tell you what this book is not: It's not a textbook, and it's not a guide for professional investors. Several of those are on the market already, and they are fabulous — but often dry and assume underlying knowledge.

This book assumes you don't know much about day trading, but that you are a smart person who is thinking about doing it. It contains straightforward explanations of how day trading works and how to get started. Of course, we also talk about the pitfalls and cover some of the alternatives for your portfolio and for your career. If you really want to read some textbooks, we list a few in the appendix.

Foolish Assumptions

In writing this book, we made some assumptions about you, the reader:

>> You're someone who needs to know a lot about day trading in a short period of time.

>> You may be considering a career change, looking for a productive part-time retirement activity, or bored and looking for a challenge. Maybe you just want to know if day trading is a good way to supplement your current investment program. Whatever your reason for considering day trading, you want to know how to decide whether it's the right option for you.

>> If you already know that day trading is right for you, you want to know how to get started, from opening an account to setting up your computer monitors. (And yep, that's plural.)

>> You have extra money to trade (whether it's yours or not) and you want to try day trading techniques to enhance your portfolio returns.

>> You have some understanding of the basics of investing, so you know about mutual funds and brokerage accounts, for example. If you don't feel comfortable with that much, you may want to peruse some personal finance books first. It's okay. We'll be here when you're done.

Icons Used in This Book

As you read this book, you'll see icons scattered around the margins of the text. Each icon points out a certain type of information, most of which you should know or may find interesting about day trading. Here's what they mean:

REMEMBER

This icon notes something you should keep in mind about day trading. It may refer to something we covered earlier in the book, or it may highlight something you need to remember for future investing decisions.

TIP

Tip information tells you how to invest a little better, a little smarter, and a little more efficiently. The information can help you make better day trades or ask better questions of people who want to supply you with research, training, and trading systems.

WARNING

We've included nothing in this book that can cause death or bodily harm, as far as we can figure out, but plenty of things in the world of day trading can cause you to lose big money or, worse, your sanity. These points help you avoid big problems.

TECHNICAL STUFF

We put the nonessential (but often helpful) academic stuff here. By reading material marked by this icon, you get the detailed information behind the investment theories or, sometimes, some interesting trivia or background information.

Beyond the Book

Along with the material in this book, there is also a free Cheat Sheet that you can access on the web. The Cheat Sheet includes additional day trading information that you should find useful. To view the Cheat Sheet, go to www.dummies.com and type "Day Trading For Canadians For Dummies Cheat Sheet" in the Search box.

Where to Go from Here

Well, open up the book and get going! It's a good idea to read it from front to back, but if you know nothing about day trading, then certainly start with Chapter 1 so that you can get a good sense of what we're talking about. If you want to know more about getting started — like how to set up your office — then read Chapter 2. You'll definitely need to learn how to read charts and why technical analysis is important for day traders, which you can find in Chapter 9.

If you have a particular area of interest, use the index and table of contents to go to the topic you want. If you're not sure, you may as well turn the page and start at the beginning.

1
Day Trading Fundamentals

Chapter **1**

All You Need to Know about Day Trading

Make money from the comfort of your home! Be your own boss! Beat the market with your own smarts! Build real wealth! Tempting, isn't it? Day trading can be a great way to make money all on your own. It's also a great way to lose a ton of money, all on your own. Are you cut out to take the risk?

Day trading is a crazy business. Traders work in front of their computer screens, reacting to blips, each of which represent real dollars. They make quick decisions, because their ability to make money depends on successfully executing a large number of trades that generate small profits. Because they close out their positions in the stocks, options, and futures contracts they own at the end of the day, some of the risks are limited. Each day is a new day, and nothing can happen overnight to disturb an existing profit position.

But those limits on risk can limit profits. After all, a lot can happen in a year, increasing the likelihood that your trade idea will work out. But in a day? You have to be patient and work fast. Some days nothing seems good to buy. Other days it feels like every trade loses money. Do you have the fortitude to face the market every morning?

REMEMBER

There are also other forces at play that can mess with your day trading abilities, namely high-frequency algorithms programmed by hedge funds and brokerage firms that have no emotions and can make trades faster than even the speediest human can.

In this chapter, we give you an overview of day trading. We cover what exactly day traders do all day, go through the advantages and disadvantages of day trading, cover some of the personality traits of successful day traders, and give you some information on your likelihood of success.

You may find that day trading takes advantage of your street smarts and clear thinking — or that the risk outweighs the potential benefits. That's okay: The more you know before you make the decision to trade, the greater the chance of being successful. If it turns out that day trading isn't right for you, you can apply strategies and techniques that day traders use to improve the performance of your investment portfolio.

It's All in a Day's Work

The definition of day trading is that day traders hold their securities for only one day. They close out their positions at the end of every day and then start all over again the next day. By contrast, *swing traders* hold securities for days and sometimes even months, whereas *investors* sometimes hold for years.

The short-term nature of day trading reduces some risks, because no chance exists of something happening overnight to cause big losses. Meanwhile, many investors have gone to bed thinking their position is in great shape, then woken up to find that the company has announced terrible earnings or that its CEO is being indicted on fraud charges.

But there's a flip side (there's always a flip side, isn't there?): The day trader's choice of securities and positions has to work out in a day, or it's gone. There's no tomorrow for any specific position. Meanwhile, the swing trader or the investor has the luxury of time, as it sometimes takes a while for a position to work out the way your research shows it should. In the long run, markets are efficient, and prices reflect all information about a security. Unfortunately, it can take a few days of short runs for this efficiency to kick in.

REMEMBER

Day traders are speculators working in zero-sum markets one day at a time. That makes the dynamics different from other types of financial activities you may have been involved in. When you take up day trading, the rules that may have helped you pick good stocks or find great mutual funds over the years will no longer apply. This is a different game with different rules.

Speculating, not hedging

Professional traders fall into two categories: speculators and hedgers. Speculators look to make a profit from price changes. Hedgers want to protect against a price change. They're making their buy and sell choices as insurance, not as a way to make a profit, so they choose positions that offset their exposure in another market. For example, a food-processing company might look to hedge against the risks of the prices of key ingredients — like corn, cooking oil, or meat — going up by buying futures contracts on those ingredients. That way, if prices do go up, the company's profits on the contracts help fund the higher prices that it has to pay to make its products. If the prices stay the same or go down, it loses only the price of the contract, which may be a fair tradeoff to the company.

The farmer raising corn, soybeans, or cattle, on the other hand, would benefit if prices went up and would suffer if they went down. To protect against a price decline, the farmer would sell futures on those commodities. Then, his futures position would make money if the price went down, offsetting the decline on his products. And if the prices went up, he'd lose money on the contracts, but that would be offset by his gain on his harvest.

REMEMBER

The commodity markets were intended to help agricultural producers manage risk and find buyers for their products. The stock and bond markets were intended to create an incentive for investors to finance companies. Speculation emerged in all of these markets almost immediately, but it was not their primary purpose.

Day traders are all speculators. They look to make money from the market as they see it now. They manage their risks by carefully allocating their money, using stop and limit orders (which close out positions as soon as predetermined price levels are reached) and close out at the end of the night. Day traders don't manage risk with offsetting positions the way a hedger does. They use other techniques to limit losses, like careful money management and stop and limit orders (all of which you can read about in Chapter 2).

Knowing that different participants have different profit and loss expectations can help a day trader navigate the turmoil of each day's trading. And that's important, because in a zero-sum market you only make money if someone else loses.

Understanding zero-sum markets

A zero-sum game has exactly as many winners as losers. No net gain exists, which makes it hard to eke out a profit. And here's the thing: Options and futures markets, which are popular with day traders, are zero-sum markets. If the person who holds an option makes a profit, then the person who *wrote* (which is option-speak for *sold*) that option loses the same amount. No net gain or net loss exists in the market as a whole.

Now, some of those buying and selling in zero-sum markets are hedgers who are content to take small losses in order to prevent big ones. Speculators may have the profit advantage in certain market conditions. But they can't count on having that advantage all the time.

So who wins and loses in a zero-sum market? Some days, it all depends on luck, but over the long run, the winners are the people who are the most disciplined. They have a trading plan, set limits and stick to them, and can trade based on the data on the screen — not based on emotions like hope, fear, and greed.

Unlike the options and futures markets, the stock market is not a zero-sum game. As long as company profits will grow, share prices will grow. Over the long run, there are more winners than losers; otherwise no one would put their retirement money into stocks. However, that doesn't mean there will be more winners than losers today. In the short run, the stock market should be treated like a zero-sum market.

If you understand how profits are divided in the markets you choose to trade, you'll have a better understanding of the risks you face as well as the risks that are being taken by the other participants. People do make money in zero-sum markets, but you don't want those winners to be making a profit off of you.

REMEMBER

Some traders make money — lots of money — doing what they like. Trading is all about risk and reward. Those traders who are rewarded risked the 80 percent washout rate. Knowing that, do you want to take the plunge? If so, read on. And if not, read on anyway, as you might get some ideas that can help you manage your other investments.

Keeping the discipline: Closing out each night

Day traders start each day fresh and finish each day with a clean slate. That reduces some of the risk, and it forces discipline. You can't keep your losers longer than a day, and you have to take your profits at the end of the day before those winning positions turn into losers.

And that discipline is important. When you're day trading, you face a market that doesn't know or care who you are, what you're doing, or what your personal or financial goals are. No kindly boss who might cut you a little slack today, no friendly coworker to help through a jam, no great client dropping you a little hint about her spending plans for the next fiscal year. Unless you have rules in place to guide your trading decisions, you will fall prey to hope, fear, doubt, and greed — the Four Horsemen of trading ruin.

So how do you start? First, you develop a business plan and a trading plan that reflect your goals and your personality. Then, you set your working days and hours and you accept that you will close out every night. Both of these steps are covered in Chapter 2. As you think about the securities that you will trade (Chapters 4 and 5) and how you might trade them (Chapters 6 and 7), you'll also want to test your trading system (Chapter 14) to see how it might work in actual trading.

In other words, you do need to prepare and have a plan. That's a basic strategy for any endeavour, whether it's running a marathon, building a new garage, or taking up day trading.

Committing to Trading as a Business

Many people are attracted to day trading because they can set their own hours and, hopefully, make money at the same time. They think they'll trade when their baby is napping, or on their lunch break, or in between games of golf and tennis. Well, if you plan on day trading for a few minutes here and there per day, then you can might as well burn your money in a fire pit instead. At least you won't have spent money on monitors and computers.

Day trading is a business, and the best traders approach it as such. Like any good entrepreneurs in any business, they have a business plan, which, in this case, will include what they will trade, how they will in invest in their business, and how they will protect their trading profits. Much of this book is about this business of trading: how to create a business plan, how to set up your office (both in Chapter 2), tax considerations (Chapter 18), and performance evaluation (Chapter 14). Day trading can be a lot of fun, but if you want that fun to last, you have to dedicate your time and your energy to the enterprise to make it work.

Trading part-time: An okay idea if done right

Can you make money trading part-time? You can, and some people do. But they still treat it like a job, not something to do in between hockey game periods. A part-time trader may commit to trading three days a week, or to closing out at noon instead of at the close of the market. A successful part-time trader still has a business plan, still sets limits, and still acts like any professional trader would, just for a smaller part of the day.

Part-time trading works best when the trader can set and maintain fixed business hours. Your brain knows when it needs to go to work and concentrate on the market, because the habit is ingrained.

The successful part-timer operates as a professional with fixed hours. Think of it this way: Bryan's wife's kindergarten teaching partner only works half days. She shows up when she's scheduled and, when she's there, she's doing as much work as any of the other educators. She commits her attention to her job when she's in the classroom; when she's not there she's teaching spin classes and is as focused on getting people into shape as she is getting children to learn. She doesn't pop into school to teach an extra lesson during a break from her spin class gig, nor does she sneak around setting up meetings with parents while she's helping people exercise. If she worked on one job while she was at the other, her work would suffer. And what parent wants their children to be taught by someone who won't dedicate themselves to the kids, even if it's just for a few hours a day?

TIP

If you want to be a part-time day trader, approach it the same way that a part-time teacher, part-time lawyer, or part-time accountant would approach work. Find hours that fit your schedule and commit to trading during them. Have a dedicated office space with high-speed Internet access and a computer that you use just for trading. If you have children at home, you may need to have child care during your trading hours. And if you have another job, set your trading hours away from your work time.

WARNING

Trading via an app during your morning commute is a really good way to lose a lot of money (not to mention your life if you try it while driving).

Trading as a hobby: A bad idea

Because of the excitement of day trading and the supposed ease of doing it, you may be thinking that it would make a great hobby. If it's a boring Saturday afternoon, you could just spend a few hours day trading in the forex market (foreign exchange), and that way you'd make more money than if you spent those few hours playing video games! Right?

Uh, no.

WARNING

Trading without a plan and without committing the time and energy to do it right is a route to losses. Professional traders are betting that there will be plenty of suckers out there, because they create the situations that allow the pros to take profits in a zero-sum market.

WARNING

The biggest mistake an amateur trader can make is to make a lot of money the first time trading. That first success was almost definitely due to luck, and that luck can turn against a trader on a dime. If you make money your first time out, take a step back and see if you can figure out why. Then test your strategy, using Chapter 14 as a guide, to see if it's a good one that you can use often.

Yes, we have two warnings in this section, and for good reason: Successful day traders commit to their business. Even then, most day traders fail in their first year. Brokerage firms, training services, and other traders have a vested interest in making trading seem like an easy activity that you can work into your life. But it's a job — a job that some people love, but a job nonetheless.

Working with a Small Number of Assets

Most day traders pick one or two markets and concentrate on those to the exclusion of all others. That way, they can learn how the markets trade, how news affects prices, and how the other participants react to new information. Also, concentrating on just one or two markets helps a trader maintain focus.

And what do day traders trade? Chapter 3 has information on all of the different markets and how they work, but here's a quick summary of the most popular assets with day traders right now:

>> **Derivatives:** Futures, options, and CFDs (contracts for difference) allow traders to profit from price changes in such market indexes as the TSX/S&P Composite Index in Canada, or the Dow Jones Industrial Average in the U.S. They give traders exposure to the prices at a much lower cost than buying all of the stocks in the index individually. Of course, they tend to be more volatile than the indexes they track, because they are based on expectations.

>> **Forex:** *Forex,* short for *foreign exchange,* involves trading in currencies all over the world to profit from changes in exchange rates. Forex is the largest and most liquid market, and it's open for trading all day, every day except Sunday. Traders like the huge number of opportunities. Because most price changes are small, they have to use *leverage* (borrowed money) to make a profit. The borrowings have to be repaid no matter what happens to the trade, which adds to the risk of forex. (Leverage isn't unique to forex — investors can borrow money to trade derivatives and stocks too.)

>> **Common stock:** The entire business of day trading began in the stock market, and the stock market continues to be popular with day traders. They look for news on company performance and investor perception that affects stock prices, and they look to make money from those price changes. Day traders are a big factor in some industries, such as technology. The big drawback? Stock traders can get killed at tax time if they are not careful. (See Chapter 18 for more information.)

Managing your positions

A key to successful trading is knowing how much you're going to trade and when you're going to get out of your position. Sure, day traders are always going to close out at the end of the day — or they wouldn't be day traders — but they also need to cut their losses and take their profits as they occur during the day.

Traders rarely place all their money on one trade. That's a good way to lose it! Instead, they trade just some of it, keeping the rest to make other trades as new opportunities in the market present themselves. If any one trade fails, the trader still has money to place new trades. Some traders divide their money into fixed proportions, and others determine how much money to trade based on the expected risk and expected return of the security that they are trading. Careful money management helps a trader stay in the game longer, and the longer a trader stays in, the better the chance of making good money. Chapter 2 has more information on this.

To protect their funds, traders use *stop* and *limit orders*. These are placed with the brokerage firm and kick in whenever the security reaches a predetermined price level. If the security starts to fall in price more than the trader would like, *bam!* It's sold, and no more losses will occur on that trade. The trader doesn't agonize over the decision or second-guess herself. Instead, she just moves on to the next trade, putting her money to work on a trade that's likely to be better.

REMEMBER

Day traders make a lot of trades, and a lot of those trades are going to be losers. The key is to have more winners than losers. By limiting the amount of losses, the trader makes it easier for the gains to be big enough to generate more than enough money to make up for them.

Focusing your attention

Day traders are often undone by stress and emotion. It's hard, looking at screens all day, working alone, to keep a steady eye on what's happening in the market. But traders have to do that. They have to concentrate on the market and stick to their trading system, staying as calm and rational as possible.

Those who do well have support systems in place. They are able to close their positions and spend the rest of the day on other activities. They do something to get rid of their excess energy and clear their minds, such as running or yoga or meditation. They understand that their ability to maintain a clear mind when the market is open is crucial.

Traders sometimes think of the market itself, or everyone else who is trading, as the enemy. The real enemies are emotions: doubt, fear, greed, and hope. Those four feelings keep traders from concentrating on the market and sticking to their systems.

REMEMBER

One of the frustrations of trading is that some days, there will be more opportunities to trade than you have time or money to trade. Good trades are getting away from you. You simply don't have the resources to take advantage of every opportunity you see. That's why it's important to have a plan and to concentrate on what works for you.

Working with risk capital

WARNING

Pay attention to the words that follow this sentence: Do not use your grocery or your retirement money to day trade. Now read that line again.

Day traders lose money, and some lose everything that they start out with. Even savvy traders can have terrible days and lose a lot. The most responsible traders work with *risk capital*, which is money that they can afford to lose. They might start with $10,000 that they wouldn't care much about it if all disappeared. If you need to pull money from your RRSP to day trade, then first, think twice about whether day trading is for you, and second, be prepared to live more frugally in retirement.

Personality Traits of Successful Day Traders

Traders are a special breed. They can be blunt and crude, because they act fast against a market that has absolutely no consideration for them. For all their rough exterior, they maintain strict discipline about how they approach their trading day and what they do during market hours.

The discipline begins with a plan for how to start the day, including reviews of news events and trading patterns. It includes keeping track of trades made during the day, to help the trader figure out what works and why. And it depends on cutting losses as they occur, reaping all profits that appear, and refining a set of trading rules so that tomorrow will be even better. No, it's not as much fun as just jumping in and placing orders, but it's more likely to lead to success.

Not everyone can be a day trader, nor should everyone try it. In this section, we cover some of the traits that make up the best of them.

Independence

For the most part, day traders work by themselves, usually at home, alone, stuck in a room with nothing but some computer screens for company. It can be boring, and it can make it hard to concentrate. Some people can't handle it.

But, just like some people prefer working from home over the office, many traders thrive on being by themselves. They know their trading depends on them alone, not on anyone else. The trader has sole responsibility when something goes wrong, but he also gets to keep all the spoils. He can make his own decisions about what works and what doesn't, with no pesky boss or annoying corporate drone telling him what he needs to do today.

If the idea of being in charge of your own business and your own trading account is exciting, then day trading might be a good career option for you.

TIP

And what if you want to trade but don't want to be working by yourself? Consider going to work for a brokerage firm, a hedge fund, a mutual fund, or a commodities company. These businesses need traders to manage their own money, and they usually have large numbers of people working together on their trading desks to share ideas, cheer each other on, and give each other support when things go wrong. (If you do want to work at a professional investment firm, you will need some education beyond this book first, like a chartered financial analyst designation, among potentially other designations and degrees.)

REMEMBER

No matter how independent you are, your trading will benefit if you have friends and family to offer support and encouragement. That network will help you better manage the emotional aspects of trading. Besides, it's more fun to celebrate your success with someone else!

Quick-wittedness

Day trading is a game of minutes. An hour may as well be a decade when the markets are moving fast. And that means a day trader can't be deliberative or panicky. When it's time to buy or sell, it's time to buy or sell, and that's all there is to it.

Many investors prefer to spend hours doing a careful study of a security and markets before committing money. Some of these people are enormously successful. Warren Buffett, the CEO of Berkshire Hathaway, amassed $54 billion from his careful investing style. But Buffett and people like him are not traders.

Traders have to have enough trust in their system and enough experience in the markets that they can act quickly when they see a buy or sell opportunity. Many brokerage firms offer their clients demonstration accounts or backtesting services that allow traders to work with their system before committing actual dollars, helping them learn to recognize market patterns that signal potential profits.

A trader with a great system who isn't quick on the mouse button has another option: automating trades. Many brokerage firms offer software that will execute trades automatically whenever certain market conditions occur. For many traders, it's a perfect way to take the emotion out of a trading strategy. Others dislike automatic trading, because it takes some of the fun out of it. And let's face it, successful traders find the whole process to be a good time.

Decisiveness

Day traders have to move quickly, so they also have to be able to make decisions quickly. There's no waiting until tomorrow to see how the charts play out before committing capital. If the trader sees an opportunity, she has to go with it. Now.

But what if it's a bad decision? Well, of course some decisions are going to be bad. That's the risk of making any kind of an investment — and no risk, no return. Anyone playing around in the markets has to accept that.

But two good day trading practices help limit the effects of making a bad decision. The first is the use of stop and limit orders, which automatically close out losing positions. The second is closing out all positions at the end of every day, which lets traders start fresh the next day.

If you have some downside protection in place, then it's psychologically easier to go ahead and make the decisions you need to make in order to make a profit. And if you're one of those people who has a hard time making a decision, day trading probably isn't right for you.

The Difference between Trading, Investing, and Gambling

Many people equate gambling and day trading, and poorly prepared traders are basically doing the former. But really, day trading is a cousin to both investing and gambling. Day trading involves quick reactions to the markets, not a long-term consideration of all the factors that can drive an investment. It works with odds in your favor, or at least that are even, rather than with odds that are against you.

Many day traders also invest, and some came to trading after years of watching the markets as an investor. In addition, day traders have claimed that good poker skills are useful for understanding market psychology, and many day traders can point to a winning trade that was made for no particular reason at all. To help you keep straight the differences between day trading, investing, and gambling, this section explains which is which so that you can better understand what you're doing when you day trade. After all, you can increase your chances of success if you stick to the business at hand.

Investing is slow and steady

Investing is the process of putting money at risk in order to get a return. It's the raw material of capitalism. It's the way that businesses get started, roads get built, and explorations get financed. It's how our economy matches people who have more money than they need, at least during part of their lives, with people who need it in order to grow society's capabilities.

Investing is heady stuff. And it's very much focused on the long term. Good investors do a lot of research before committing their money because they know that it will take a long time to see a payoff. That's okay with them. Investors often invest in things that are out of favour, because they know that, with time, others will recognize the value and respond in kind. There are also many ways to invest, whether it's through buying a mutual fund that you hold for 20 years or purchasing stocks that you may rotate in and out of your portfolio annually. However you do it, the aim is grow your wealth over time.

TIP

One of the best investors of all time is Warren Buffett, chief executive officer of Berkshire Hathaway. His annual letters to shareholders offer great insight and are a great introduction to the work that goes into choosing and managing investments. You can read them at www.berkshirehathaway.com/letters/letters.html.

What's the difference between investing and saving? When you save, you take no risk. Your compensation is low; it's just enough to cover the time value of money. Generally, the return on savings equals inflation and no more. In fact, a lot of banks pay a lot less than the inflation rate, meaning that you're paying the bank to use your money.

In contrast to investing, day trading moves fast. Day traders react only to what's on the screen. There's no time to do research, and the market is always right when you're day trading. You don't have two months or two years to wait for the fundamentals to work out and the rest of Bay Street to see how smart you were. You have today. And if you can't live with that, you shouldn't be day trading.

Trading works fast

Trading is the act of buying and selling securities. All investors trade, because they need to buy and sell their investments. But to investors, trading is a rare transaction, and they get more value from finding a good opportunity and selling it at a much higher price sometime in the future. But traders are not investors.

Traders look to take advantage of short-term price discrepancies in the market. In general, they don't take a lot of risk on each trade, so they don't get a lot of return on each trade, either. Traders act quickly. They look at what the market is telling them and then respond. They know that many of their trades won't work out, but as long as they measure proper risk versus reward, they'll be okay. They don't do a lot of in-depth research on the securities they trade, but they know the normal price and volume patterns well enough that they can recognize potential profit opportunities.

Trading keeps markets efficient because it creates the short-term supply and demand that eliminates small price discrepancies. It also creates a lot of stress for traders, who must react in the here and now. Traders give up the luxury of time in exchange for a quick profit.

Speculation is related to trading in that it often involves short-term transactions. Speculators take risks, assuming a much greater return than may be expected, and a lot of what-ifs may have to be satisfied for the transaction to pay off. Many speculators hedge their risks with other securities, such as options or futures.

Gambling is nothing more than luck

A *gambler* puts up money in the hopes of a payoff if a random event occurs. The odds are always against the gambler and in favour of the house, but people like to gamble because they like to hope that, if they hit it lucky, their return will be as large as their loss is likely. It's a zero-sum game with one big winner — the house — and a whole bunch of losers.

Some gamblers believe the odds can be beaten, but they are wrong. (Certain card games are more games of skill than gambling, assuming you can find a casino that plays under standard rules. Yeah, you can count cards when playing blackjack with your friends, but doing so is a lot harder in a professionally run casino.) They get excited about the potential for a big win and get caught up in the glamour of the casino, and soon the odds go to work and drain away their stakes.

There is some evidence that day traders are gamblers. For example, in 2016, some researchers at the University of Adelaide published the paper "Day Traders in South Australia: Similarities and Differences with Traditional Gamblers." They found that almost 91 percent of the day traders in their survey were also gamblers, and that 7.6 percent of those also had a problem with gambling, significantly higher than among people who were not day traders. The authors concluded that many day traders are actually gamblers who have added the financial markets to the games that they play.

WARNING

Trading is not gambling, but traders who aren't paying attention to their strategy and its performance can cross over into gambling. They can view the blips on their computer screen as a game. They can start making trades without any regard for the risk and return characteristics. They can start believing that how they do things affects the trade. And pretty soon, they're using the securities market as a giant casino, using trading techniques that have odds as bad as any slot machine.

REMEMBER

If you lose money day trading, you won't get free drinks or comped tickets to the Celine Dion show in Vegas.

Busting Some Day Trading Myths

Much mythology exists about day trading: Day traders lose money. Day traders make money. Day traders are insane. Day traders are cold and rational. Day trading is easy. Day trading is a direct path to alcoholism and ruin.

There are plenty of day trading myths, some of which we've busted already — day trading is not investing and it's not gambling — and others we'll tackle in the following sections.

Myth #1: I can make millions

One big myth is that you can get rich by trading. Like any business, some will be wildly successful and make a mint. Others will crash and burn. Then there's everyone in between who works hard, sticks to their plan, and makes enough to live a decent middle-class life. If you're able to make money at day trading, then you'll likely fall somewhere in between riches and ruin. If you go into it purely to make millions, you'll fail. The goal, at least to start, should be to make enough so that you don't have to go into a boring 9-to-5 job. If you find that you are successful, then like any entrepreneur, you can work growth into your business plan.

Myth #2: Profits are guaranteed

While it's true that long-term investors have, over time, come out ahead (though that doesn't mean they will in the future), as we've said, many day traders can lose a lot of money and quickly. Bryan once interviewed someone who made and then lost a million dollars over the course of a few months.

You also only hear about the winners. No one is going to go on the speaking circuit for losing money; only the ones who make money say how great trading can be. In fact, the research into whether day traders make money is mixed. Some studies have said, some have said no. See the sidebar "Crunching the numbers: The data on day trading success rates" for links to a few related reports.

Myth #3: Day trading is dangerous

We're repeating ourselves a bit here, but day trading is only dangerous if you're unprepared and if you put your retirement or day-to-day money at risk. Make sure you're only using money that you can afford to lose and use tools and tech to help you minimize losses. For instance, many traders use stop and limit orders to reduce losses (which we cover later in the book). Understand the risk and rewards of trading and you'll be safe.

REMEMBER

Many day trading strategies rely on *leverage,* which is the use of borrowed money to increase potential returns. That carries the risk of the trader losing more money than is in his account. However, the brokerage firm doesn't want that to happen, so it will probably close a leveraged account that's in danger of going under. That's good, because it limits your potential loss.

Myth #4: It's easy

Some people think day trading is easy. Get in front of the computer and then buy and sell Apple and Amazon all day long. Here's the truth: Day trading has a relatively low rate of success, and it can be really stressful. It takes a lot of energy to concentrate on the markets, knowing that real money is at stake. The profit amounts on any one trade are likely to be small, which means the trader has to be persistent and keep placing trades until the end of the day.

Some traders can't handle the stress. Some get bored. Some get frustrated. And some can't believe that they can make a living doing something that they love.

A lot of other worthwhile activities are stressful too

Day trading is tough, but many day traders can't imagine doing anything else. The simple fact is that a lot of occupations are difficult ways to make a living, and yet they are right for some people. Every career has its advantages and disadvantages, and day trading is no different.

When you finish this book, you should have a good sense of whether or not day trading is right for you. If you realize it's the career you have been searching for, we hope it leaves you with good ideas for how to get set up and learn more so that you are successful.

And if you find that maybe day trading isn't right for you, we hope you get some ideas that can help you manage your long-term investments better. After all, the attention to price movements, timing, and risk that is critical to a day trader's success can help any investor improve their returns. What's not to like about that?

CRUNCHING THE NUMBERS: THE DATA ON DAY TRADING SUCCESS RATES

Academic researchers like to work with data from the financial markets because there is so much of it. They are always looking at who makes money and how they are able to do it. Here we review some of the literature to show you the current state of day trading success rates. Note that they are low. Few people who take up day trading succeed, in part because few people who take it up are prepared. And even many of the prepared traders fail.

- *Do Individual Currency Traders Make Money?* In 2014, Boris Abbey and John Doukas looked at the performance of 428 foreign exchange accounts from 2004 to 2009. They found that it was indeed possible for traders to do well; half of the traders studied earned positive returns even considering transaction costs, although only a quarter of the traders that they looked at had positive returns after adjusting for risk. You can see the abstract at www.sciencedirect.com/science/article/pii/S0261560614001624.

- *Do Individual Day Traders Make Money? Evidence from Taiwan:* This paper, written in 2004 by Brad Barber, Yi-Tsung Lee, Yu-Jane Liu, and Terrance Odean (and available at http://faculty.haas.berkeley.edu/odean/papers/Day%20Traders/Day%20Trade%20040330.pdf), found that only 20 percent of day traders in Taiwan tracked between 1995 and 1999 made money in any six-month period, after considering transaction costs. Median profits, net of costs, were $4,200 (USD) for any six-month period, although the best traders showed semi-annual profits of $33,000. The study also found that those who placed the most trades made the most money, possibly because they were the most experienced traders in the group. This paper is one of the most cited on the subject, and the authors have found similar results looking at other time periods and in other markets.

- ***Overconfident Individual Day Traders: Evidence from the Taiwan Futures Market:*** Researchers Wei-Yu Kuo and Tse-Chun Lin looked at the results of 3,470 traders between October 2007 and September 2008 and found that most of them had significant losses after transactions costs were considered. The biggest problem seemed to be that traders over-estimated the quality of the news they received as well as their ability to evaluate it. This led to excessive trading — especially for those that ended up with the largest losses. The abstract is available at www.sciencedirect. com/science/article/pii/S0378426613002331.

- ***What Do Retail FX Traders Learn?*** Simon Hayley and Ian Marsh of City University in London collected data from a retail trading platform that had 95,000 individual investors over 30 months. Not all of these people were day traders, although many of them were and are. They found that traders didn't necessarily learn to trade in order to get better over time, but they did learn how to manage risk and position sizes based on their own skill and results. In addition, those who had an unsuccessful trading day were more likely to trade less, trade smaller amounts, or take a break from trading all together. They also found that even experienced traders often lose money. You can see an article about their findings at www. cass.city.ac.uk/faculties-and-research/research/cass-knowledge/2017/november/what-do-retail-fx-traders-learn.

Chapter **2**

The Business of Day Trading

Before we get into the nuts and bolts of day trading, it's important to understand how to get started and what it really involves. You're committing real money, so you should set yourself up in order to increase your chances of success. The stakes aren't only financial. You're committing your time and your energy, which is worth something. Honour that time and energy by figuring out how to use them effectively.

In fact, protecting your energy is a key reason to have a plan. Trading can be extraordinarily stressful, which is good for many people who function best under pressure. (For example, we know a couple of book authors who leave a manuscript alone until two days before it's due. Maybe you know who they are? Hint: Check the cover of this book.) People like this find that the weight of the endeavour pushes everything else out of the way so that they can get down to business.

This chapter looks at how to get your trading operation up and running as well as possible.

A Day in the Life of a Trader

What's it like being a day trader? We spoke to one Toronto-based day trader who once sold a business to Research in Motion (the makers of BlackBerry), about what he does and why he does it. He wanted to remain anonymous, but was still happy to share his secrets. "I wake up before 4 a.m. to watch Europe's open and see what happens in Asia. If things are exciting enough, I'll stay awake and concentrate on the markets until 11 a.m. That may sound like a ridiculous schedule, but it works out well for me," he says.

Q: What do you trade, and how long have you been trading?

My trading focuses on futures contracts and options on futures contracts. I began with stocks, then moved to options, then to forex before finally coming up with a formula that works best for me. The futures contracts I trade are on high-liquidity assets such as the S&P 500 Index, U.S. treasuries, the euro, the yen, the Australian dollar, gold, and sometimes oil and natural gas.

I trade the Canadian dollar to compensate for cycles of weakness in my home currency, but I try to avoid trading it for short-term gains as it's hard to view it in a truly objective fashion. However, the Canadian dollar is a great indicator on risk sentiment, and even if I don't trade it, I always watch it. If a Canadian dollar trade is brewing, then I'm more likely to execute the same trade on the Australian dollar or crude oil instead, since those assets usually move with the Canadian dollar. I don't know why it seems to work better than a plain old Canadian dollar trade, but for me it does.

Q: How did you get started trading?

I was an entrepreneur in the technology sector. In 1997, I started a small software company; when I went to my accountant to file my first corporate return, I learned that there was this thing called an RRSP that would give me more money on my personal tax return. Then I found out that some banks would lend you money to put in an RRSP so you could save on your taxes even if you didn't have money to put in the account yourself. I was young and thought I knew what I was doing and it sounded like a great deal, so I signed up. This particular RRSP was "self-directed," which gave me a chance to learn how to lose money in the stock market all on my own.

My bank offered me a non-RRSP account that would allow me to trade options and I thought, wow I can play the upside of a stock that costs $100 and only have to put up $5 to do it? Pretty quickly the money I made from my consulting company ended up in someone else's hands.

I decided to take the markets more seriously and enrolled in the Canadian securities course, a great introductory program that gave me a solid foundation of financial knowledge.

I took a break from trading to focus on my company, but always planned to get back to it. In 2006, my company was purchased by Research in Motion, and all of the sudden, I was no longer in debt and had some free cash on hand. Although I was required to work at RIM full-time for the next two years, I opened an Interactive Brokers account and started ramping up my trading as well. I learned how to set up and use the more complicated options strategies available through the IB system. Things started going well, but then, in 2008, the financial crisis hit, and it wasn't the best time to cut your teeth on complicated options strategies. I didn't "trade myself into the ground" as they say, but I learned some tough lessons. The biggest lesson was a refresher on what I had learned a decade earlier: If you are going to trade, take it seriously.

After my contract at RIM was up, I became a full-time independent trader. I read a lot of different books, watched videos, read online articles, tried different strategies, and set up the rule that for every week I lost money, my punishment would be to read another textbook or research another trading topic. That helped with learning technical aspects of trading.

Q: Do you close out trades every day, or do you carry some over?

I don't close out trades every day. Since I mostly trade on the U.S. futures markets, there is essentially only one market close a week. The markets open Sunday night and close end of business day on Friday, and I do not go more than a few hours without checking on them during the entire week. Many of my trades involve options contracts, which usually expire once a month. I do close parts of trades leading into that monthly expiry, but it's unusual for me to exit a position just because the New York markets are closing.

Q: What trading strategy do you swear by?

The Elliott Wave Principle for sure. It's a technical analysis method developed by Ralph Nelson Elliott in the 1930s. It's a remarkably elegant mathematical concept that provides a framework to analyze price action on multiple time frames in a fractal approach, building on concepts taken from Dow Theory.

Another tool that is a close second for me is what traders call "intermarket analysis," which is the study of the relationships between the four main asset classes: stocks, bonds, currencies, and commodities. By viewing the market through these two lenses, I have all I need to trade regardless of what software or brokerage I am using.

Q: What is a typical day like? How easy is it to quit at the end of the day?

My week starts at 6 p.m. on Sunday. I log in to the markets, check Bloomberg.com, Dailyfx.com, and other sites to find out what happened over the weekend. I skim through Sunday talk shows like NBC's *Meet the Press* and ABC's *This Week* and watch *Fareed Zakaria GPS*. I also examine the charts and then wait for Asia to open. It's usually pretty slow until Europe opens in the middle of the night, but this is when I get my head around the big events for the week and what price actions on the main four asset classes are saying about where things will go.

At some point, I'll go to sleep and wake up, without an alarm clock, before 4 a.m. to watch Europe's open and see what happened in Asia. If things are exciting enough I'll stay awake and concentrate on the markets until around 11 a.m. when most of the U.S. economic data has been released for the day and the market has had its opening direction set. I have around three hours from 11 a.m. to 2 p.m. where I concentrate on other things that need to be addressed during local business hours — like grocery shopping — but I like to be back focusing on the markets by 3 p.m. at the latest. Once the trading day ends in New York at 4 p.m., or sometimes by 6 p.m. if the after-market has anything to offer like an earnings release, my day is over. I watch CNBC's *Fast Money* and then repeat that same 24 hours four more times until the week is over.

That may sound like a ridiculous schedule, but it works out well for me. I may sleep four hours a night for five nights in a row (some nights even less), but if I am tired and my positions are set, then I can sleep as much as I need. If I have something that demands my attention for, say, a week at a time, I don't need to ask for vacation. I just do it. And there is a lot of down time as a trader. Sometimes the markets can be very quiet for days on end. Even on busy days there are usually quiet times, often something like 90 minutes of working on the markets and 90 minutes working on something else while watching the markets with my one eye. That something else is usually working on my charting and automated trading system. This keeps me productive in software development but also keeps me from overtrading. If it was just me and a trading terminal locked in a room for hours on end, my itchy fingers would probably get me into trouble.

I admit that it's not easy to quit at the end of the day. If the markets are open, I'm probably trading, or at the very least watching them. When I first got into forex trading I found myself waiting for the weekends to come to an end so I could get back into the markets. A friend of mine told me that when he leaves work at the end of a Friday, he says to the other traders on the floor, "Only three more days till Monday!"

Q: What is your secret to managing the stress of trading?

Managing stress is an important part of trading. My goal is to set up a trade as best I can and then stick to the plan. If it works, great; if it fails and I did everything according to plan, I try to learn what I can from the situation and improve the next trade plan. If it fails because I went off plan or made another mistake, I take a timeout from the market based on how big the loss was and force myself to study a trading-related topic as my punishment. I try to make sure I'm making the best of both successes and failures by turning my monetary losses into clear gains of both knowledge and experience.

Elliott Wave also really helps with stress by defining stop-loss and profit-taking exit points as well as giving you a solid framework to continually evaluate your trading hypothesis. I learned Elliott Wave as a punishment for a really bad week of trading about a year ago, and it has literally changed my life as a trader.

Q: What's your best piece of advice for someone considering day trading?

Your mission is to find the trading methodology that will work for you in a sustainable way before you run out of money to trade with. You need to be able to make good decisions and commit to those decisions all while still being flexible and challenging your beliefs when it appears they may be in error. You need to be relentless in learning new concepts and information, disciplined in your execution and risk management, and humble and respectful of the market's ability to alter your financial situation in either direction very quickly. The easiest way to succeed at something is to enjoy doing it. That way the effort it takes to excel doesn't feel like work. I never get tired working towards a goal if I enjoy the journey, and trading will be a lifelong journey for me.

Setting Up Your Trading Laboratory

Did the preceding section give you a good sense of what trading is really like? The ups and downs? The drama? The boredom? We hope so. Now it's time to get your own day trading office set up.

It used to cost thousands, if not millions, to buy all the equipment and network connections you'd need to successfully day trade. Now you can have a full setup for less than a trip to Mexico. "But wait," you say. "I have an iPhone, so I can do it for free." Not so fast.

Successful day traders approach trading as a professional activity. That means starting with an adequate workspace and dedicated equipment.

Where to sit, where to work

Start by finding an area to work. If you can't give up an entire room in your house, find a corner or hallway where you can put a desk and a computer just for day trading. Going to an area dedicated to day trading will clear your mind so that you can focus on the work at hand. Instead of borrowing a chair from the dining room, get a good desk chair that swivels and that you can adjust as necessary while you work. You also need a shelf and a cabinet of some sort to hold your files and documents.

Although no rule stipulates the proper layout of your equipment, the more you can see and do without getting up from your chair, the better off you'll be. If you find yourself getting sore at the end of the day, investigate ergonomic products such as special keyboards, contoured mice, wrist pads, and foot rests, all of which are readily available at office supply stores. In other words, set up your day trading home office like you would a home office for a law firm, accounting service, or content agency. (You should see Bryan's sweet home office.)

Count on your computer

You can't day trade without at least one computer, and some traders use both a desktop and a laptop computer. Almost every personal computer on the market today has the power to handle day trading activities, so you don't need to sweat over the details. In general, faster processing speeds are better than slower ones, and more memory and storage are preferable to less.

What about the manufacturer? Well, you may not want an Apple computer for day trading, because you may discover that not all the software packages you need will be Mac-compatible. If you are one of those die-hard Mac heads, though, be sure to ask brokers and software vendors about compatibility. Other than that, the manufacturer doesn't matter much.

See it on the big screen

Do yourself a favour and spend money on at least one big flat-screen monitor. If you need to look at more than one window at a time — to see charts and Level II quotes at the same time, for example — consider using two or more monitors hooked to the same PC. This arrangement gives you a clear view of necessary data. Most traders work with at least two monitors, often extra-large ones (you can also look for ultra-wide monitors), because the information they need is too valuable to be hidden by overlapping windows during a work session.

Connect to the Internet

Most people have Inernet these days, but even in 2021, not all connections are created equal. If you're day trading, you'll need as much bandwidth as possible. Ask around to find out the fastest service in your area. Your Internet service provider may charge more for faster performance, but most day traders find the extra cost worth it. If the Internet goes down, have a phone handy with a good data plan to hotspot your computer to. If market prices are changing quickly, a delay of half a second can be costly.

REMEMBER

You need fast service, but don't base your strategy on speed. Even if you pay up for the fastest service in your area, the brokers and hedge funds of the world will probably have faster service. In the U.S., NYSE Technologies, the data-services business of exchange-operator NYSE Euronext, allows brokerage and trading firms to put their servers on the floor of the exchange. This colocation can reduce trade execution times to fractions of a second, allowing more trades to be executed in less time than if the server were in, say, midtown Toronto or Manhattan. NYSE Euronext colocation isn't cheap, but if you make thousands of trades per day, it may be worth it.

Some people, though, may want to consider connecting their trading computer to their Internet service provider's wire rather than using WiFi. If you want to go wireless, shop around for a good wireless router. If other people in your household want Internet access, consider getting two Internet lines so that your child downloading videos in the family room doesn't slow down your data feeds.

Fix hours, vacation, and sick leave

Like with most businesses, it's possible to trade around the clock. The markets are open more or less continuously. Although many exchanges have set trading hours, you can find traders working after hours who are willing to sell if you want to buy. Some markets, such as foreign exchange, take only the briefest of breaks over the course of a week, which gives day traders incredible flexibility. No matter what hours and what days are best for you to trade, you can find something that works for you. If you're sharpest in the evenings, for example, you may be better off trading Asian currencies, because those markets are active when you are. However, an always-open market can be a disadvantage, because no one is setting limits for you. You need to set hours and stick to them, take breaks, and commit to spending a week or two by a lake or on a ski slope instead of in front of a screen. Everyone need vacations and time away from work. It's the same if you're a doctor or day trader.

AVOIDING THE ALL-NIGHTER

Some traders get so caught up in the excitement of the job that they end up working around the clock. Do not do this. Yes, there's always another trade you can make, but remember, day trading shouldn't be gambling where you can pull the slot lever all day and all night. Plenty of research has shown that not getting enough sleep impacts one's cognitive abilities, increases stress, hinders focus, and more. Doing day trading right means paying careful attention to the markets, having a clear head in order to act quickly, and staying calm. You can't do any of that if you're staying up all night to trade.

Stay virus- and hacker-free

No one wants to get hacked, but especially a trader with potentially a lot of money in the bank. Fortunately, most operating systems have built-in firewall and virus protection that can handle most likely threats with aplomb. The discount brokerage firms you're using should also have air-tight security. You can also subscribe to different virus protection services. No matter which way you go, be careful how you set these up. Some pointers:

>> **Check compatibility.** Check with your brokerage firm to make sure that its system is compatible with the virus protection package you choose; some are not. (That potential problem increasingly makes the built-in options more practical.)

>> **Determine whether there's a trade-off in access speed.** Some types of antivirus software protect your system at the expense of data speed, which will hurt your trading execution.

>> **Keep your system updated.** Operating-system companies send out updates all the time. It can be a big hassle, too — you turn on your computer and it takes 30 minutes to get everything set up. It's tempting to skip these updates entirely, but doing so can lead to problems down the line. You may not have time to update when your system sends out the notice, but do so as soon as possible.

>> **Set your system to upgrade outside of market hours.** Whether you go with the built-in software or buy an outside package or are a Mac or a PC, be sure to set automatic downloads, software upgrades, and background scans to take place after market hours. You don't want to be slowed down because of an operating system update.

The department of redundancy department: Back up your systems

When you day trade, you're intentionally looking at volatile markets and fast-moving securities because that's where you have the most opportunity to make money in a short time. If you're in a position that moves against you and you can't get out, you're sunk.

Not being able to get out because the markets are melting down due to some kind of global catastrophe (pandemic anyone?) is bad enough. But suppose you can't get out because the batteries in your wireless mouse have died and a member of your household absconded with the AAs in the junk drawer? What if you spill your drink and short out your keyboard — or your PC? What if the developer building a McMansion next door accidentally knocks out your phone line and your DSL service? All these little workaday calamities happen — and they're downright annoying even if you aren't trading. If you *are* trading, they can be ruinous. If you're serious about making money as a day trader, build in redundant systems as much as possible:

>> Load your broker's mobile app on your phone so that you can switch to it should something odd happen to crash your computer.

>> Keep extra batteries on hand.

>> Invest in an uninterruptible power supply (UPS) backup for your PC so that if the power goes down, your computer stays up. The backup doesn't have to last for hours, just long enough that you can close out your positions. You don't need a backup generator, though — unless you think that you'd still want to trade after your town was devastated by an ice storm or a flood. (Hey, crisis creates opportunities!)

>> Back up your computer regularly. You don't want to lose your tax records! Several services let you do online backups, either to the cloud, to a proprietary server, or to an external hard drive connected to your PC. Most backup systems can be set up to work automatically — but don't back up during trading hours! It'll slow you down.

Planning Your Trading Business

Now that you have your office and schedule set up, it's time to come up with a good day trading business plan. Always keep in mind that a day trader is an entrepreneur who has started a small business that trades in securities in hopes of making a return. With a plan, you know what your goals are and what you need to do to achieve them.

You can find a lot of sample business plans in books and on the Internet, but most of them are not appropriate for a trader. A typical business plan is designed to not only guide the business but also to attract outside financing. Unless you're going to take in partners or borrow money from an outside source, your day trading business plan is only for you. No executive summary and no pages of projections needed.

So what do you need instead? How about a list of your goals and a plan for what you'll trade, what your hours will be, what equipment you'll need, and how much to invest in the business? The following sections have the details.

Setting your goals

The first thing you need in your plan is a list of your goals, both short term and long term. Here is a sample list of key questions to get you started:

>> Where do you want to be with your career and your life in the next three months, six months, nine months, year, three years, five years, and ten years?

>> How many days a year do you want to trade?

>> What do you need to know to trade better?

>> How much do you want to make?

>> What will you do with your profits?

>> How will you reward yourself when you hit your goals?

Be as specific as possible when you think about what you want to do with your trading business and don't worry if your business goals overlap with your personal goals. When you are in business for yourself, the two often mix.

WARNING

You may be tempted to say, "I want to make as much money as I possibly can," and forget the rest, but "as much as I can" isn't a quantifiable goal. If you don't know that you've reached your goal, how can you go on to set new ones? And if you don't meet your goal, how will you know how to make changes?

Finding volatility

You can day trade so many different securities and derivatives! Sure, you want to trade anything that makes money for you, but what on earth is that? Each market has its own nuances, so if you flit from futures to forex, you may be courting disaster. But if you know what markets you want to trade, you have a better sense of what research services you need, what ongoing training you may want to consider, and how to evaluate your performance.

Chapters 3, 4, and 5 cover different asset classes in great detail and discuss how you may use them. For now, the little cheat sheet in Table 2-1 lists asset classes that are most popular with day traders. Think about your chosen markets in the same way: What do you want to trade, where will you trade it, what is the risk and return, and what are some of the characteristics that make this market attractive to you? (Canadian exchanges are listed first.)

TABLE 2-1   ## Popular Things for Day Traders to Trade

Item	Main Exchange	Risk/Reward	Characteristics
Stock index futures	MX, CME	Zero sum/leverage	Benefits from movements of broad markets
Bond futures	MX, CBT	Zero sum/leverage	Best way for day traders to play the bond market
Foreign exchange	OTC	Zero sum/leverage	Markets open all day, every day
Corn	ICE, CBT	Zero sum/leverage	An agricultural market liquid enough for day traders
Large-cap stocks	TSX, NYSE, NASDAQ	Upward bias	Good stocks for day trading; large and volatile
Exchange-traded funds	TSX, NYSE, NASDAQ	Depends on the fund's structure	Offer plays on indices and different market strategies

Key: CME = Chicago Mercantile Exchange, CBT = Chicago Board of Trade (a subsidiary of the CME Group),
MX = Montreal Exchange, OTC = Over the counter, NYSE = New York Stock Exchange, TSX = Toronto Stock Exchange

What do *zero sum, leverage,* and *upward bias* mean? Well, *zero sum* means that for every winner, there is a loser. The market has no net gain. *Leverage* is the use of borrowed money, which increases potential return as well as risk. *Upward bias* means that, in the long run, the market is expected to increase in price, but that doesn't mean it will go up on any given day that you're trading.

The characteristics of the different markets and assets affect both your business plan and your trading plan. The business plan should include information on what you'll trade and why, as well as what you hope to learn to trade in the future. The trading plan looks at what you want to trade each day and why so that you can channel your efforts.

Many day traders work in several different markets, depending on their temperament and trading conditions, but successful traders have narrowed the field down to the few markets where they want to concentrate their efforts. Start slowly, working just one or two different securities, and consider adding new markets as your experience and trading capital grows.

Investing in your business

You won't have the time and money to do everything you want to do in your trading business, so part of your business plan should include a list of things that you want to add over time. A key part of investing in your business is continuous improvement: No matter how good a trader you are now, you can always be better. Furthermore, the markets are always changing. New products come to market, new trading regulations are passed, and new technologies appear. You need to continuously absorb new things, and part of your business plan should consider that. Ask yourself

>> What percentage of your time and trade gains will go into expanding your knowledge of trading?

>> Do you want to gain this additional knowledge by taking seminars or by allocating the time to simulation test? (Refer to Chapter 13 for more on that.)

>> What upgrades will you make to your trading equipment? How about to your programming capabilities?

>> How are you going to set yourself up to stay in trading for the long haul?

It takes money to make money — another cliché. This maxim doesn't mean, however, that you should spend money willy-nilly on any nifty gadget or fancy video seminar that comes your way. Instead, it means that an ongoing, thoughtful investment in your trading business will pay off in a greater likelihood of long-run success.

Evaluating and revising your plan

One component of your business plan should be a plan for revising it. Things are going to change. Since the first edition of this book came out, exchanges have merged, the market has crashed, and high frequency trading has become the norm. You may be more or less successful than you hope, market conditions may change on you, and you may simply find out more about how you trade best. So set a plan for updating your business plan to reflect where you are and where you want to be as you go along. At least once a year, and more often if you feel the need for a change, go through your business plan and revise it to reflect where you are now. What are your new goals? What are your new investment plans? What are you doing right, and what needs to change?

Getting Mobile with the Markets

A growing number of brokerage firms and software developers are coming up with applications that let you trade from a smartphone or a tablet computer. At the time we're writing this, we think these options are a bad idea for most day traders. Even with 4G service, mobile networks can be slow and drop out, and you can't get enough information on a little screen to trade well.

However, technology changes fast, so maybe by the time you're reading this, mobile speeds have become as fast as wired ones. This may be especially true if you live in a rural area without reliable high-speed Internet service. The different brokerage firms (including those listed in Chapter 15 and others) are adding new and better mobile capabilities, and the mobile providers are investing in 5G upgrades.

Still, we remain skeptical that mobile trading is a good idea for an active day trader. If you're a business traveler who gets a great idea on the road and who wants to place one order to buy and hold, then great! Use your phone. If you are a swing trader or an investor who trades more than average, using a mobile device when exit or entry points happen to be great but you are out of the office may be fine. But if you're going to be a day trader, get traditional service, a big screen, and an actual keyboard.

Controlling Your Emotions

You can't plan your emotions, unfortunately. They crop up in response to whatever is happening in your world. And yet, the key to successful day trading is controlling your emotions. After all, the stock doesn't know that you own it, as equity traders like to say, so it isn't going to perform well just because you want it to. This can be infuriating, especially when you are going through a drawdown of your capital. Those losses look mighty personal.

TECHNICAL STUFF

Traditional financial theory is based on the idea that traders are rational. In practice, however, most of them are not. In fact, traders and investors are often irrational in completely predictable ways, which has given birth to a growing area of study called *behavioural finance.* It's a hot area generating Nobel Prize winners, and it may eventually help people incorporate measures of investor behaviour into buy and sell decisions.

TIP

If you can't figure out a way to manage your reactions to the market, you shouldn't be a day trader. Almost all day traders talk about their enemies being fear and greed. If you panic, you'll no longer be trading to win, but trading not to lose. That's an important distinction: If your goal is not to lose, you won't take appropriate risk, and you won't be able to respond quickly to what the market is telling you.

Controlling your emotions is all much easier said than done. Human beings are emotional creatures, constantly reacting (and sometimes overreacting) to everything that happens in their lives. Knowing the emotions that affect trading and having some ways to manage them can greatly improve your overall performance.

Dealing with destructive emotions

In trading, the big emotions can take over and mess up your strategy and your returns. The enemies are doubt, fear, and greed; like any bullies, they have their toadies, including anger, anxiety, boredom, and depression. At this point in your life, you may already know whether you have tendencies toward any of these moods. If so, trading can exacerbate them. If you've never experienced them, you may for the first time. The following sections explain these emotions as they relate to day trading so that you know what you're up against and can plan accordingly.

REMEMBER

We include some tips that can help you deal with destructive reactions, but if you are really in the throes of an emotional crisis that affects your trading, seek professional help. And by all means, walk away from the trading desk.

Doubt

Day traders have to act fast. They have to place their buy and sell orders as the opportunities present themselves. The market doesn't give anyone time to second-guess the decisions, but many traders start to do just that. Did the signal really flash? Is this pattern going to continue or reverse? Will waiting a few seconds lead to a better price? Would closing out for the day just be better?

We don't know. And neither do you. That's why traders need to stick to their plans, which isn't always easy. Backtesting (refer to Chapter 14) can help build confidence in a plan, and the use of automated trading tools can help overcome the tendency to hesitate before clicking on the mouse button.

TIP

Most brokerage firms that offer services to day traders have automated trading capabilities to help you follow your plan. And all brokers can execute stop and limit orders, which can help you get out of positions based on your plans rather than your emotions.

Fear

Fear is one of the worst emotional enemies of the day trader. Instead of trying to make money, the fearful trader tries hard not to lose it. She is so afraid of failing that she limits herself, doesn't take appropriate risk, and questions her trading system so much that she no longer follows it, no matter how well it worked for her in the past.

By the way, failure isn't the only thing that traders fear. Many fear success, sometimes for deep-seated psychological reasons that we are in no position to address. A trader who fears success may think that if she succeeds, her friends will treat her differently, her relatives will try to take her money, and that she will become someone she doesn't want to be.

TIP

One way to limit fear is to have a plan for the trading business. Before you start trading, take some time — maybe half a day — to sit down and think about what you want, what will happen to you if you get it, and what will happen to you if you don't. For example, if you lose your trading capital, then you'll have to live on your walk-away fund (see the section "Watching your walk-away money" later in this chapter) until you find another job. If you make a lot of money, then you can pay off your mortgage, and your friends will be none the wiser.

Greed

Greed seems like a silly thing to have on this list. After all, isn't the whole purpose of day trading to make money? This isn't charity; this is capitalism at its purest. Ah, but there's a popular saying down at the Chicago Board of Trade: "Pigs get fat, but hogs get slaughtered."

Traders who get greedy start to do stupid things. They don't think through what they're doing, and they stop following their trading plans. They hold positions too long in the hope of eking out a return, and sometimes they make rash trades that look an awful lot like gambling. The greedy trader loses all discipline and eventually loses quite a bit of money.

If your goal is simply to make more and more money, you may have a problem with greed. Sure, everyone wants to make more, but there are also a basic *need-to-make number* (enough to cover your costs and your basic living expenses) and a *want-to-make number* (enough to cover costs, basic expenses, and extras that are important to you). Your want-to-make can be open ended (as in "as much as possible"), but your need-to-make should be a key component of your risk management. If you know what those numbers are, you're well on your way to preventing the problem.

TIP

Limit orders, which automatically close out positions when they hit set prices, are one way to force discipline in the face of greed.

Anger

The markets can be maddening. They don't do what you want them to, and that often costs you real money. And no one wants to lose money. Your rage at the markets can cause you to stop seeing straight.

TIP

When anger makes it impossible to think clearly, your best bet is to call it a day, close out your positions, and go somewhere far from your trading screen. Leave your phone at home if you're using your broker's mobile apps, too! Take a long walk and wait for your anger to subside. Otherwise, your rage will interfere with your plans and your profitability. The only way to psych out the market is to be just as mechanical and unemotional as the blips that cross your screen.

Anxiety

Anxiety is the anticipation of things going wrong, and it often includes a physical response: perspiration, clenched jaws, tense muscles, heart palpitations, and so on. Anxious people worry, agonize, overanalyze, and generally stress out. And then they avoid whatever it is that makes them upset. That means that a trader may not make an obvious trade but instead hesitate and miss a market move. He may hold on to a losing position too long because he's worried about the effect that selling it will have on his portfolio. He becomes too nervous to trade according to his plan, and his performance suffers.

Boredom

An ugly truth about day trading is that it can be really dull. In an eight-hour trading session, you may spend seven and a half hours waiting for the right opening. A flurry of trades, and it's all over. To keep yourself entertained, you may start making bad trades, spending too much time in chat rooms, or letting your mind wander away from the task at hand. None of those things is conducive to profitable trading.

TIP

One way to reduce the temptations brought on by boredom is to block access to social media on your trading computer. Several companies make software that will keep you from using Facebook, Pinterest, or Candy Crush when you should be trading! A few to consider are Freedom (www.freedom.to), Cold Turkey (www.getcoldturkey.com), and Inbox When Ready (www.inboxwhenready.org). Keep in mind that they may slow down your system — and that your phone may need a social media blocker, too.

Depression

Depression is a severe downturn in your mood, especially one that causes you to feel inadequate and lose interest in things you used to like. Although everyone is susceptible to depression, the ups and downs of the market can make traders particularly vulnerable. At best, depression can make it hard for a trader to face a day with the market. At worst, it can lead to alcoholism, alienation, and even suicide.

WARNING

If you think you may be depressed, go to your doctor. Doctors have heard it all before and can give you the right diagnosis.

Having an outlet

Successful day traders have a life outside the markets. They close out their positions, shut off their monitors, and go do something else with the rest of the day. The problem is that a market is always open somewhere. Undisciplined traders work overnight and after hours through electronic communications networks and sometimes move the action to exchanges in other parts of the world. Without something to mark a beginning and an end to your trading day, and without other things happening in your life, the market can consume you in an unhealthy way.

So as you plan your life as a day trader, think about what else you're going to do with your days. Exercise, meditation, socializing, and having outside interests are keys to maintaining balance and staying focused on the market when you have to be.

Friends and family

Day trading is a lonely activity. You work by yourself all day. It's just you, your room, and your screen. This job is really isolating. If you don't get other human contact, you run the risk of personalizing the market in order not to feel so lonely. That's bad, because the market isn't a person; it's an agglomeration of all the financial activity taking place, and it has no interest in you whatsoever.

No matter what you do in life, you want to have the support of the people you know and love. And you need to make time for them, too. Start and end your trading day at regular times and be sure to make plans to see people who are important to you. Going to your kid's ball game, having dinner with your spouse, and seeing your friends for a few beers on a regular basis can go a long way to keeping your life in balance — and that will keep your trading in balance.

If you like pets, consider getting one to keep you company during the day. There's nothing like a dog that needs a walk to force you to close shop for the night.

Hobbies and other interests

A lot of people get into day trading because they have long had a fascination with the market. Trading goes from being a hobby to being a living. In many ways, that's perfect. Going to work is so much easier when you have a job that you love.

But if the market is your only interest, then you're going to be too susceptible to its gyrations, and you're going to have trouble sticking to your trading discipline. Plus, whatever upsets you during the trading day is more likely to carry over. So find a new hobby if you don't have one. Maybe it's a TV show, a sport, or knitting, but whatever it is, you need to have something going on outside of your trading.

Trading is just one part of your life.

Setting up support systems

Exercise and friends and family and hobbies and the like are all well and good, but they don't directly address the mindset of trading. Fortunately, a veritable industry supports traders, and you can tap in to it easily. Many day traders find that reading books, hiring a coach, or finding other day traders helps them get through the day.

Books

A library full of books has been written on the psychology of trading itself. In addition, many traders rely on other self-help and history books for inspiration and ideas. (Every trader we've ever known owns a copy of Sun Tzu's *The Art of War*, which is about military strategies and tactics. They find that this book helps them prepare their minds to face the market — or at least gives them something interesting to talk about.) We list several books in the appendix that may help you organize your mind and keep your enthusiasm for the market.

Counseling and coaching

Because handling big losses — and big gains — takes a lot of mental toughness, many traders find professional support. They use counselors, psychologists, or life coaches to help them deal with the challenges of the market and understand their reactions to it. You can ask other traders or your doctor for a referral, or check the online directory at *Psychology Today*'s website, www.psychologytoday.com/ca, or the International Coach Federation, www.coachfederation.org. When interviewing coaches or counselors, ask whether they have experience with traders or others who work in finance.

Many day trading training and brokerage firms also offer coaching services that specialize in helping people learn and follow day trading strategies. Some day traders find these people to be invaluable, whereas others find they are just glorified salespeople.

Finding other traders

To offset the loneliness of trading alone, many day traders choose to join organizations where they will meet other traders. These may be formal or informal groups (we list a few in the appendix) where traders can socialize, learn new things, or just commiserate.

Many day traders also get together through Internet message boards and chat rooms, such as on Reddit or Stockaholics.net. These groups are less formal, more anonymous, and sometimes as destructive as supportive.

Most day traders lose money and give up their first year. You may find that spending too much time with other traders is more depressing than supportive.

Watching your walk-away money

A lot of traders have a secret that lets them get through the worst of the markets. It's something called *walk-away money*, although traders sometimes use more colourful language to describe it. Walk-away money is just what its name implies: enough money to let the trader walk away from trading and do something else.

And just exactly how much walk-away money does a trader need? Well, the exact amount varies from person to person, but having enough money to pay three months' worth of expenses on hand and in cash is a good place to start. If you know that you can pay the mortgage and buy the groceries even if you don't make money trading today, you're better able to avoid desperate trading. You won't have to be greedy, and you won't have to live in fear.

The more money in your walk-away fund, the better. Then you have more time to investigate alternative careers should day trading prove not to be your thing, and you can relax more when you face the market every day.

Most day traders quit after a year or so. There's nothing wrong with deciding to move on and try something else. If you have some money saved, then you're in a better position to control when you stop trading and what you do next.

If all your trading capital is gone, you may be tempted to tap your walk-away fund to stay in the game. *Don't.* That's the exactly the time that you should use your walk-away money to *walk away,* if only for a short time to clear your head, rethink your strategies, and build up some new trading capital. Otherwise, your trading losses may become financial ruin.

One way to get your confidence back while still staying in the market is to trade in very small amounts so that your profits and losses don't really matter. Trade 100 shares, not 1,000 shares. You give up the upside for a time, but you can also get out of the cycle of greed and fear that has destroyed many a trader.

Managing the Risks of Day Trading

When you know more about the risks, returns, and related activities of day trading, you can think more about how you're going to run your day trading business. Before you flip through the book to find out how to get started, consider two more kinds of risk that you need to think about:

>> Business risk

>> Personal risk

You need to understand and manage both in order to better manage the risks of the trading day.

It's your business

Business risk is the uncertainty of the timing of your cash flow. Not every month of trading is going to be great, but your bills will come due no matter what. You'll have to pay for subscriptions while keeping the lights turned on and the computer connected to the Internet. Taxes come due four times a year, and keyboards hold a mysterious attraction for carbonated beverages, causing them to short out at the most inopportune times.

Keep track of your business expenses and keep them as low as is reasonable. You should invest in your business, obviously, but only to the extent that you can pay your bills even if you have an off month in the market.

TIP

Regardless of what happens to your trading account, you need cash on hand to pay your bills or you'll be out of business. The best way to protect yourself is to start out with a cash cushion just for covering your operating expenses. Keep this cushion separate from your trading funds. Replenish it during good months. Walk away from trading if it goes down to zero.

It's your life

The *personal risk* of trading is that it becomes an obsession that crowds out everything else in your life. Trading is a stressful business, and the difference between those who succeed and those who fail is often psychological. You need to be on when you are trading and then, at the end of the trading day, close out the emotions the same way that you close out your positions. It's not easy, so you need to have ways to manage your mood. Figure those out before you start trading, and you'll be ahead of the game.

Chapter **3**

Introducing the Financial Markets

The market is the aggregation of all the traders you'll face in a given day. They're placing orders to buy and sell for every possible rational or irrational reason you can imagine. The financial markets are more or less instantaneous these days. They are global, and they operate almost continuously.

Over centuries — yes, centuries — institutions and regulations have been established to keep the markets from disintegrating into chaos. Markets operate more or less around the globe, around the clock, so that money moves and trades clear even if one part is knocked out by a terrorist attack or political crisis. Not a lot of regulations exist, but enough do to ensure that anonymous participants in far-flung locations honour contracts.

As the world's financial markets become more automated and intertwined, day traders have fewer opportunities to do their thing. That's a fact. But, the more you understand about the markets, the more opportunities you'll find and the fewer expensive mistakes you'll be likely to make.

This chapter gives you a high-level overview of supply and demand, exchanges, and zero-sum games. It discusses the basics of commissions and fees while giving you the underlying knowledge you need to get started.

Having a Firm Grasp How Markets Work

In 1776, Adam Smith wrote *The Wealth of Nations,* a still popular book that set forth the basic principles of markets. He said that the markets work like an "invisible hand" that brings together the efforts of countless people to meet the needs of countless others at a price that satisfies both parties.

This basic explanation of how the market works has held up for more than 200 years. No one has improved it. Smith's explanation for how markets work is still genius.

The following sections explain in plain English some important concepts in Smith's book and how they apply today to day trading.

TIP

Wealth of Nations isn't the easiest book to read, but if you're interested, check it out online at www.adamsmith.org/the-wealth-of-nations. Alternatively, you can find good explanation in a 1980 public television series featuring economist Milton Friedman called *Free to Choose,* available online at www.freetochoose.tv/broadcasts/ftc80.php.

Supply and demand

In a free market, *supply and demand* meet at a price where the buyer receives good value for the price paid and the seller makes enough of a profit to stay in business. The *supply* for a given price is the number of goods that sellers are willing to sell at a given price, and the *demand* is the price that buyers are willing to pay for a given number of goods. If demand increases, then sellers are able to raise prices. If demand falls, sellers lower prices. Likewise, if the supply increases, sellers will cut prices to move inventory. If the supply falls, sellers will raise prices.

Consider what happens if supply and demand are out of whack. Say you want a pair of new shoes and have a budget of $50. You go shopping and find that the shoes you want cost $75, so you walk out empty handed. It's possible someone else would find the $75 price fair, but you don't. And in this example, not enough people do, so the shoe store runs a huge sale on its unsold inventory. Everything is two-thirds off! The shoes that were too expensive at $75? They are now $25 a pair, so you leave with two of them.

But at $25 a pair, the shoe store can't make any money and goes out of business. You're better off, but the seller is worse off — nothing's magical about that.

In this example, if the people running the shoe store had been paying more attention, they would have figured out that at $50, they could sell shoes and still make money. In the real world, business owners talk to customers and track what competitors are doing so that they can figure out where to price their products. They also pay close attention to their costs to make sure that they are able to keep customers happy and stay in business.

And this is what happens in the financial markets. Every day, people go shopping for what they want to buy, whether it be shares of stock, an ETF (exchange-traded fund), commodity option, or foreign currency. Some of these buyers have to make a purchase to cover a loan. Others have done research to figure out how much something seems to be worth. And still others are placing their orders based on hunches. The buyers are determining the amount of demand in the market.

At the same time, people are looking to sell the same set of assets. Some of these sellers have mundane interests. Maybe the assets belonged to someone who died, and so they have to be sold so that the cash can be divided among the heirs. Maybe they're looking to hedge a risk but no longer need to do it. Maybe they've done research to show that the item in question is overpriced, or maybe they're acting on pure emotion. These sellers determine the amount of supply in the market.

And, of course, if the price gets high enough, a lot more people will be interested in selling than in buying, and if it gets low enough, traders will be looking to scoop up bargains. Sometimes traders quip that a stock is up in price because there are more buyers than sellers. That's not quite true — someone has to be on each side of the trade — but motivated buyers will have to raise the price they're willing to pay in order to entice the sellers to part with their shares, bitcoins, or futures contracts.

Exchanges versus over the counter

The people who actually place your order to buy or sell securities are known as brokers. *Brokers* are members or shareholders of the exchanges. The *exchanges*, in turn, are organizations designed to bring together groups of brokers representing a number of buyers and sellers. Having a central place to meet, whether in real life or virtually, increases the number of trades taking place and increases the likelihood that the transaction price will match the true value of the asset in question.

Once upon a time, brokers met physically on the floor of the exchange building. Nowadays, of course, most trading happens electronically, and the exchange buildings are often giant server farms. You won't see that when you watch the opening bell on TV, because the servers are hidden in high-security, temperature-controlled rooms.

Some financial assets trade *over the counter* rather than on the exchange. Instead, they trade through networks of brokers or banks. Years ago, these items traded at special desks at banks and brokerage firms or on the street outside the exchange buildings. That's why sometimes market pundits refer to these markets as *the curb.*

For most traders, there is no real difference in the execution of an order placed in an exchange market or an over-the-counter market. Both are now executed on electronic networks. Some markets, like currency, take place almost entirely over the counter. You still need an account with a broker to access over the counter listings.

After all, the broker's reason for being is to guarantee that customers have the items that they want to sell or the cash to pay for the things they want to buy, which ensures that the market works as intended.

Commissions, fees, and spreads

The broker's service isn't free. After all, brokerage firms are run by capitalists subject to their own sets of supply and demand forces. The prices you pay come in three forms: commissions, fees, and spreads.

Counting up commissions

The *commission* is the charge for placing a trade. Some firms charge a flat rate, like $15 per trade; others charge a price per share or per contract. In any event, the lowest commission isn't always the best deal, because it's only one of several fees a broker charges.

Also, most brokers offer more services than simple trade execution, which makes a difference. Chapter 15 has more information about choosing brokerage firms.

Fees aplenty

The exchanges charge *fees* (a cost added to the trade bill) for their services, too. They aren't high but are tacked on to your *trade commission* (the quoted price to execute your trade). You can't get out of these fees if you're trading an asset listed on an exchange.

It's all in the spread

The *spread* is the difference between the price that the broker pays to buy an asset and the price it sells it to a customer. It's the broker's profit on the trade and is often more significant than the commission. Some brokers do a better job working with day traders than others, and the difference tends to show up in the spread.

Understanding zero-sum games

The first thing to know about game theory is that, despite the name, it isn't about why people have fun. The second thing to know is that it classifies different activities based on how much total value is added or created for the people involved. Game theory is often used to describe financial markets, so the three main categories matter:

>> In a *zero-sum game,* each gain is someone else's loss. For every winner, there is a loser. Sometimes the losers are okay with the loss. Maybe they were willing to accept a small loss in order to prevent a bigger loss, for example. The total value is rearranged but doesn't change.

>> In a *positive-sum game*, most participants are better off. Some may lose money, but the total gains exceed the total losses. Total value increases.

>> In a *negative-sum game*, most participants end up losing money. Some value is destroyed.

Day trading is a zero-sum game. Your gain is someone else's loss, and vice versa. To make this work, you have to determine who is willing to lose money.

This isn't as horrible as it may seem. Remember that each of the people in the market have a different reason for being in it. Many people use options to manage risk, for example. They're all right with paying a little bit of money now in order to prevent a big loss in the future.

Likewise, in currency markets, some people are trading because they need one particular currency in order to make a transaction. Sure, they may get a better rate if they could wait a little bit, but they can't wait. That's the point.

REMEMBER

One reason why it's difficult to make money day trading is because day trading is a zero-sum game. A lot of day traders who lose money aren't prepared and don't manage their risks. If you take the time to trade right, you can increase your odds of making money.

Opening an Account and Placing an Order

This section is super basic, but that may be what you need. It goes through the process of opening an account and placing a trade, and sometimes, it's these mechanics that prove to be the highest hurdle to trading. If you already have a brokerage account, you can skip it.

Opening a brokerage account

After you find a broker (see Chapter 15 for ideas), you go to its website, fill out a bunch of forms, and then set up a transfer from your bank account to your new brokerage account. This transfer will be your initial trading capital.

There are no shortcuts here, by the way. The broker is required by a range of international laws to verify who you are and where your money comes from. A compliance officer isn't willing to go to prison because you don't want to share your personal information in exquisite detail.

Placing your initial order

To place an order, log in to your account and fill out the form to place an order. It's almost like online shopping! You tell the broker what you want and how much of it, and then you enter the other details such as whether the trade is long (that is, you're buying) or short (if you're selling). You can pay for it either with the money in your account or by borrowing money from the broker, known as a *trade on margin*. Press enter, and away it goes for the broker to handle.

Closing out your order

If your initial order was a buy, now you need to sell your position. And, once again, it's almost like online shopping. This time, you're doing a return. You log in and place the order, again specifying what and how much. When the broker completes the transaction, the money will be used to pay off any margin and then go into your account.

Taking your cash

If your brokerage account grows beyond the amount you want to risk, transfer some money back into your bank account. It's simple and easy — and is the way you take your trading profits and apply them to everything else in your life.

Defining the Principles of Successful Day Trading

Although you can day trade almost every asset with wild abandon, doing so probably isn't a good idea. Some traders spend their entire careers working with just one or two types of securities. This section covers the basics of success: working with just a few assets in one market, managing positions carefully, and concentrating on the work at hand.

Working with a small number of assets

Most day traders pick one or two markets and concentrate on those to the exclusion of all others. That way they can figure out how the markets trade, how news affects prices, and how the other participants react to new information. Also, concentrating on just one or two markets helps them maintain focus.

And what do day traders trade? Chapters 4 and 5 have information on all of the different markets and how they work. Here's a quick recap, in no particular order, of the most popular assets with day traders right now if you're overeager:

>> **Financial futures:** *Futures contracts* allow traders to profit from price changes in such market indexes as the S&P/TSX Composite Index, the S&P 500, or the Dow Jones Industrial Average. They give traders exposure to the prices at a much lower cost than buying all the stocks in the index individually. Of course, they tend to be more volatile than the indexes they track because they're based on expectations.

>> **Options:** An *option* gives the holder the right, but not the obligation, to buy or sell something in the future at a price agreed to today. Options are similar to futures. They allow people to take larger positions for less money up front, but doing so increases the amount of risk involved.

>> **Forex:** *Forex,* short for *foreign exchange,* involves trading in currencies all over the world to profit from changes in exchange rates. Forex is the largest and most liquid market there is, and it's open for trading all day, every day. Traders like the huge number of opportunities. Because most price changes are small, forex traders have to use *leverage* (borrowed money) to make a profit. The borrowings have to be repaid no matter what happens to the trade, which adds to the risk of forex. *Cryptocurrency,* a relatively new asset class, has characteristics similar to foreign exchange.

>> **Common stock and exchange-traded funds:** The entire business of day trading began in the stock market, and the stock market continues to be popular with day traders. These day traders look for news on company performance and investor perception that affect stock prices, and they look to make money from those price changes. A similar asset is the *exchange-traded fund,* which trades like a stock but is based on a market index or strategy. The big drawback? Stock and ETF traders can get killed at tax time if they aren't careful. See Chapter 18 for more information.

Day traders can, and sometimes do, trade bonds and commodities. Usually, they do so through financial futures or exchange–traded funds.

Managing your positions

A key to successful trading is knowing how much you're going to trade and when you're going to get out of your position. Sure, day traders are always going to close out at the end of the day — or they wouldn't be day traders — but they also need to cut their losses and take their profits as they occur during the day. Specifically, they need to determine the size of the trade and the maximum profit or loss:

>> **Determining what portion of their money they risk for any particular trade:** Traders rarely place all their money on one trade. That's a good way to lose it! Instead, they trade just some of their money, keeping the rest to make other trades as new opportunities in the market present themselves. If any one trade fails, the trader still has money to place new trades. Some traders divide their money into fixed proportions, and others determine how much money to trade based on the expected risk and expected return of the security they're trading. Careful money management helps a trader stay in the game longer, and the longer a trader stays in, the better the chance of making good money. Chapter 7 has more information on money-management strategies.

>> **Protecting their funds by using stop and limit orders:** *Stop and limit orders* are placed with the brokerage firm and kick in whenever the security reaches a predetermined price level. If the security starts to fall in price more than the trader likes — *bam!* — it's sold, and no more losses will occur on that trade. The trader doesn't agonize over the decision or second-guess herself. Instead, she just moves on to the next trade, putting her money to work on a trade that's likely to be better.

REMEMBER

Day traders make a lot of trades, and a lot of those trades are going to be losers. The key is to have more winners than losers. By limiting the amount of losses, you as the trader make it easier for the gains to be big enough to generate more than enough money to make up for the losers.

Focusing your attention

Day traders are often undone by stress and emotion. Keeping a steady eye on what's happening in the market is hard when you're looking at screens all day and working alone. But as a trader, you have to be able to concentrate on the market and stick to your trading system, staying as calm and rational as possible.

Day traders who do well have support systems in place. They're able to close their positions and spend the rest of the day on other activities. They do something to get rid of their excess energy and clear their minds, such as running or yoga or meditation. They understand that their ability to maintain a clear mind when the market is open is crucial.

Traders sometimes think of the market itself, or everyone else who is trading, as the enemy. The real enemies are emotions: doubt, fear, greed, and hope. Those four feelings keep traders from concentrating on the market and sticking to their systems.

REMEMBER

One of the frustrations of trading is that some days offer more opportunities to trade than you have time or money to trade. On these days, good trades get away from you because you simply don't have the resources to take advantage of every opportunity you see. That's why having a plan and concentrating on what works for you are so important.

Understanding Risk and Return

Investors, traders, and gamblers have this in common: They put their money at risk, and they expect to get a return. Ideally, that return comes in the form of cold, hard cash, but if they're not careful, they could get nothing — or worse, end up owing money. Traders should risk no more than they can afford to lose. There is no shortcut to this: Strategies that offer high returns carry more risk with them and don't trust anyone who tells you otherwise.

Risk can't be eliminated in trading, but it can be managed.

REMEMBER

Trading is a business: The more you know about the potential risks and the sources of your potential return, the better off you'll be. Your risk is that you won't get the return you expect, and your reward is that you get fair compensation for the risk you take.

If you don't want any risk, then your return will be really low. The interest rate on a Guaranteed Investment Certificate is an example of a return without risk, and if that's what you wanted, you wouldn't have even picked up this book. Because earning a return requires taking risk, understanding what risk is and how to manage it is a key to day trading success.

Recognizing what risk is

Risk is the measurable likelihood of loss. The riskier something is, the more frequently a loss will occur, and the larger that loss is likely to be. Playing in traffic is riskier than driving in traffic, and skydiving is riskier than gardening. This doesn't mean that you can't have losses in a low-risk activity or big gains in a high-risk one. It just means that with the low-risk game, losses are less likely to happen, and when they do, they're likely to be small.

TECHNICAL STUFF

What's the difference between risk and uncertainty? Risk involves the *known* likelihood of something good or bad happening so that it can be priced. What's the likelihood of your living to be 100? Or of getting into a car accident tonight? Your insurance company knows, and it figures your rates accordingly. What's the likelihood of aliens from outer space arriving and taking over Earth? Who knows! It could happen, but that event is uncertain, not risky — at least until it happens.

The ability to measure risk makes modern business possible. Until mathematicians were able to use statistics to quantify human activities, people assumed that bad things were simply the result of bad luck or the wrath of the gods. But when people understand probability, they can apply and use that to assess the likelihood of an event happening and determine the commensurate compensation for taking the risk. If a sailor agreed to join a voyage of exploration, what was the probability that he would return home alive? And what would be fair compensation to him for that risk? What was the probability of a silo of grain going up in flames? And how much should the farmer charge the grain buyers for the risk that he was taking, and how much should someone else charge to insure the farmer against that fire?

Considering the probability of a loss

Whenever you take risk, you take on the probability of loss. If you know what that probability is, you can determine whether the terms you're being offered are fair and whether you have a reasonable expectation for the size of the loss.

Say that you're presented with this opportunity:

> You put up $10. You have an 80 percent chance of getting back $11 and a 20 percent chance of losing everything. Should you take it? To find out, you multiply the expected return by the likelihood and add them together: (80% × $11) + (20% × $0) = $8.80. Your expected return of $8.80 is less than the $10 cost of this contract, so you should pass on it.

Now suppose you're offered this opportunity:

> You put up $10. You have a 90 percent chance of getting back $11 and a 10 percent chance of getting back $6. Your expected return is (90% × $11) + (10% × $6) = $10.50. This contract would be in your favour, so you should take it.

Here's a third proposition:

> You put up $10. You have a 90 percent chance of getting back $13.89 and a 10 percent chance of losing $20 — even more than you put up. Your expected return is (90% × 13.89) + (10% × –$20) = $10.50. You end up with the same expected return as the preceding proposition, but do you like it as much?

Many people would not like that deal because they are looking at the dollar value of the loss rather than the risk. People who overreact to the risk of loss without considering the facts on hand are probably not going to be good traders.

REMEMBER

When thinking about loss, most people tend to put too much weight on the absolute dollar amount that they can lose, rather than thinking about the likelihood of losing it. The problem is that the markets don't trade on your personal preferences. This is one of the psychological hurdles of trading that those who are successful can overcome. Can you? (You can find some tips on this in Chapter 11.)

WORKING WITH LIMITED LIABILITY (USUALLY)

Securities markets rely on the concept of *limited liability*. That is, you cannot lose any more money than you invested in the first place. If you buy a stock, that stock can go down to zero, but it can't go any lower. If the company goes bankrupt, no one can come to you and ask you to cover the bills. On the other hand, the stock price can go up infinitely, so the possible return for your risk is huge. (At least as we write this, Shopify and Amazon shares seem to have increased by something mighty close to infinity. Can they go up more? Who knows.)

WARNING

Although most day trading strategies have the same limited liability — that is, you can lose what you trade and no more — some strategies have *unlimited liability*. If you sell a stock short (borrow shares and then sell them in hopes that the stock goes down in price, allowing you to repay the loan with cheaper shares, a strategy discussed in Chapter 6), and if the stock goes up drastically, you have to repay the loan with those highly valued shares! Most likely, you're going to close out your position before that happens, but even if you close out your positions every night like a good day trader should, some strategies have the potential to cost you more money than you have in your trading account.

REMEMBER

To protect themselves and to protect you against losing more money than you have, brokerage firms and options exchanges require you to keep enough funds in your account to cover shortfalls (known as *margin*, discussed in Chapter 4). You have to be approved before you can trade in certain securities. For example, anyone trading options has to fill out an agreement that the brokerage firm must first approve and then keep on file.

PLAYING THE ZERO-SUM GAME

Many day trading strategies are *zero-sum games*, meaning that for every winner on a trade, there is a loser. It's especially true in options markets. Of course, the person on the other side of the trade may not mind being a loser; she may have entered into a trade to *hedge* (protect against a decline in) another investment and is happy to have a small loss instead of a much larger one.

The problem for you as a day trader is that a zero-sum game has little wiggle room. Every trade you make is going to win or lose, and your losses may exactly offset your winners. Beating the odds is even tougher when so many traders are using computer algorithms. Backtesting and tracking (see Chapter 14) are important for assessing your changing risk.

Finding the probability of not getting the return you expect

In addition to absolute measures of risk and liability, you also need to consider *volatility*. That's how much a security's price may go up or down in a given time period.

The math for measuring volatility is based on standard deviation. A standard deviation calculation starts with the average return over a given time period. That average is the *expected* return — the return that, on average, you'll get if you stick with your trading strategy. But any given week, month, or year, the return may be very different from what you expect. The more likely you are to get what you expect, the less risk you take in the form of volatility.

TIP

Standard deviation shows up many times in trading, and you can find a detailed explanation of it in Chapter 14. The key thing to know is this: The higher the standard deviation of the underlying securities, the more risk you take with your trade. However, the same volatility creates trading opportunities for day traders to exploit. A security with a low standard deviation isn't going to offer you many chances to make money over the course of a day.

Standard deviation is used to calculate another statistic: beta. *Beta* tells you how risky a security is relative to the risk of the market itself. If you buy a stock with a beta of more than 1, that stock is expected to go up in price by a larger percentage than the market when the market is up, and it's expected to go down by a larger percentage than the market when the market is down.

REMEMBER

The higher the beta, the riskier the stock — but the greater the potential for return.

TECHNICAL STUFF

The word *beta* comes from the *capital assets pricing model,* an academic theory that says that the return on an investment is a function of the risk-free rate of return (discussed in the next section), the extra risk of investing in the market as a whole, and then the volatility — beta — of the security relative to the market. Under the capital assets pricing model, no other sources of risk and return exist. Any other sources would be called *alpha,* but in theory, alpha doesn't exist. Not everyone agrees with that, but the terms *alpha* and *beta* have stuck.

Getting rewarded for the risk you take

When you take risk, you expect to get a return. That's fair enough, right? That return comes in a few different forms related to the risk taken. Although you may not really care how you get your return as long as you get it, thinking about the breakdown of returns can help you think about your trading strategy and how it works for you.

Opportunity cost

The *opportunity cost* of your money is the return you could get doing something else. Is your choice day trading or staying at your current job? Your opportunity cost is your current salary and benefits. You'd give up that money if you quit to day trade. Is the opportunity cost low enough that it's worth your while? It may be. Just because taking advantage of an opportunity carries a cost doesn't mean that the opportunity isn't worth it.

REMEMBER

When you trade, you want to cover your opportunity cost. Your cost will be different from someone else's, but if you know what that cost is up front, you'll have a better idea of whether your return is worth your risk.

Here's another way to think about opportunity cost. When you make one trade, you give up the opportunity to use that money for another trade. That means you only want to trade if you know that the trade is going to work out, more likely than not. That's why you need to plan your trades and *backtest* (run a simulation using your strategy and historic securities prices) and evaluate your performance. By doing these things, you know that you are trading for the right reasons and not just out of boredom.

Risk-free rate of return and the time value of money

The value of money changes over time. In most cases, this change is the result of *inflation,* which is the general increase in price levels in an economy. But the value of money also changes because you give up the use of money for some period of time. That's why any investment or trading opportunity should include compensation for the *time value of your money.*

In day trading, your returns from the time value of money are small, because you only hold positions for a short period of time and close them out overnight. Still, there's some time component to the money you make. That smallest return is known as the *risk-free rate of return.* That's what you demand for giving up the use of your money, even if you know with certainty that you'll get your money back. In practice, investors think of the risk-free rate of return as the rate on Government of Canada bonds or U.S. government treasury bills, which are bonds that mature in less than one year. This rate is widely quoted electronic price-quote systems.

TIP

If you can't generate a return that's at least equal to the risk-free rate of return, you shouldn't be trading because your return wouldn't be appropriate to the risk you're taking.

Risk-return tradeoff

Economists say that there's no such thing as a free lunch. Whatever return you get, you get because you took some risk and gave up another opportunity for your time and money. In that sense, there's no secret to making money. It's all about work and risk.

This concept is known as the *risk-reward tradeoff.* The greater the potential reward, the greater the amount of risk you're expected to take and thus the greater potential you have for loss. But if you understand the risks you're taking, you may well find that they're worth it. That's why you have to think about the risks and rewards up front.

Market efficiency in the real world

The reason a balance exists between risk and reward is that markets are reasonably efficient. This efficiency means that prices reflect all known information about the companies and the economy and that all participants understand the relative tradeoffs available to them. Otherwise, you'd have opportunities to make a riskless profit, and that just won't do, according to the average economist. "You can't pluck nickels out of thin air," they like to say. In an efficient market, if an opportunity exists to make money without risk, someone would have taken advantage of it already.

Here's how market efficiency works: You have information that says that Company A is going to announce good earnings tomorrow, so you buy the stock. Your increased demand causes the price to go up, and pretty soon, the stock price is where it should be, given that the company is doing well. The information advantage is rapidly eliminated. In most cases, everyone gets the news — or hears the rumour — of the good earnings at the same time, so the price adjustment happens quickly.

WARNING

Wouldn't it be great to get the news of a good earnings report before everyone else and make a quick trading profit? Yep. At least until the RCMP show up and haul you off to prison — talk about your opportunity costs. Trading on *material inside information* (information that is not generally known that would affect the price of the security) is illegal. And yes, the Ontario Securities Commission monitors trading to see whether trading patterns suggest illegal trading based on inside information. They want all investors and traders to feel confident that the investment business is fair. Be very wary of tips that seem too good to be true.

The markets may be more or less efficient, but that doesn't mean they work by magic. Price changes happen because people act on news, and the people who act the fastest are day traders. In the example, notice that it was the activity of traders that caused the price of Company A stock to go up to reflect the expected good earnings report.

In economic terms, *arbitrage* is a riskless profit. A hard-core believer in academic theory would say that arbitrage opportunities don't exist. In practice, though, they do. Here's how arbitrage works: Although Company A is expected to have a good earnings announcement tomorrow, you notice that the stock price has gone up faster than the price of a call option on Company A, even though premium should reflect the stock price. So you sell Company A (borrowing shares and selling it short if you have to) and then use the proceeds to buy the option. When the option price goes up to reflect the stock price, you can sell the option (that is, close out your short position) and lock in a riskless profit — at least, before your trading costs are considered. Chapter 5 discusses arbitrage in more detail.

Market efficiency isn't perfect. It can take a while for people to make a logical decision about what an asset is worth, and until that happens, trading can be irrational and inefficient. Whether it's Japanese stocks, Internet stocks, condominiums in Osoyoos, or gold, the markets have pockets of craziness that defy rhyme and reason. In the short term, a wave of panic or euphoria can overtake the market during a single trading day, pushing prices into inefficient territory. On days like that, your ability to keep calm and steer into the trend, rather than getting swept up into an uncontrollable craze, will help you have more winning trades.

REMEMBER

Bubbles and panics happen, and they happen more often than academic economists like to admit. However, most days, trading is efficient. Your edge comes from knowing the markets, having good risk management, and being able to walk away. Don't count on crazy price action every day.

THE OLDEST ECONOMICS JOKE EVER TOLD

After you become wise to the ways of risk and return, this joke should make sense to you:

Two economists are walking down the street. One sees a $20 bill on the sidewalk and stops to pick it up. "Don't bother," says the other. "If it were real, someone would have taken it already."

"Don't be so sure," says the first economist. He picks it up, sees that it is real, then turns to his friend and says, "How about if I buy you a free lunch?"

Chapter **4**

Assets 101: Stocks, Bonds, Currency, and Commodities

Y ou have a myriad of choices of things to trade. From those, you want to find a few things that you can firmly understand. This chapter and the next go into details about the different assets that day traders use. Here, we cover the basics. We cover the more advanced assets in Chapter 5.

You can't trade everything. A day has only so many hours, and your head can hold only so many ideas at any one time. Furthermore, some trading strategies lend themselves better to certain types of assets than others. By finding out more about all the various investment assets available to a day trader, you can make better decisions about what you want to trade and how you want to trade it.

Grasping the Different Things to Trade

In the financial markets, people buy and sell securities every day, but just what are they buying or selling? *Securities* are financial instruments. In the olden days, they were pieces of paper, but now in the digital age they're electronic entries that represent a legal claim on some type of underlying asset. This asset may be a business, if the security is a stock, or it may be a loan to a government or a corporation, if the security is a bond. In this section, we explain different types of securities that day traders are likely to run across and tell you what you need to jump into the fray.

REMEMBER

In practice, *asset* and *security* are synonyms, and *derivative* is a type of asset or security. But to be precise, these three aren't the same:

>> An *asset* is a physical item. Examples include a company, a house, gold bullion, or a loan.

>> A *security* is a contract that gives someone the right of ownership of the asset, such as a share of stock, a bond, or a promissory note.

>> A *derivative* is a contract that draws its value from the price of a security. Examples include options and futures.

Defining a Good Day Trading Asset

In academic terms, the universe of investable assets includes just about anything you can buy at one price and sell at another, potentially higher price. Artwork and collectibles, real estate, and private companies, for example, are all considered to be investable assets.

Day traders have a much smaller group of assets to work with. Expecting a quick, one-day profit on price changes in real estate isn't realistic. Online auctions for collectible items take place over days, not minutes. If you're going to day trade, you want to find assets that trade easily, several times a day, in recognized markets. In other words, you want *liquidity*. As an individual trading your own account, you want assets that you can purchase with relatively low capital commitments. And finally, you may want to use *leverage* — borrowed money — to improve your return, so you want to look for assets that can be purchased using other people's money. The following sections outline the characteristics of good assets for day trading.

Looking for liquidity

Liquidity is the ability to buy or sell an asset in large quantity without affecting the price levels. Day traders look for *liquid assets* so they can move in and out of the market quickly without disrupting price levels. Otherwise, they may not be able to buy at a good price or sell when they want.

At the most basic level, financial markets are driven by supply and demand. The more of an asset supplied in the market, the lower the price; the more of an asset that people demand, the higher the price. In a perfect market, the amount of supply and demand is matched so that prices don't change. This situation occurs if a high volume of people are trading such that the supply and demand are constantly matched or if the frequency of trades is very low, which keeps the price from changing.

REMEMBER

You may be thinking, "Wait, don't I want big price changes so that I can make money quickly?" Yes, you want price changes in the market, but you don't want to be the one causing them. The less liquid a market is, the more likely your buying and selling are to affect market prices, and the smaller your profit will be.

Volume

Volume is the total amount of a security that trades in a given time period. The greater the volume, the more buyers and sellers are interested in the security and the more easily you can get in there and buy and sell without affecting the price.

Day traders also look at the relationship between volume and price. This important technical indicator is discussed in more detail in Chapter 9. Here's the simple analysis:

» High volume with no change in price levels means an equal match between buyers and sellers.

» High volume with rising prices means that buyers outnumber sellers, so the price will continue going up.

» High volume with falling prices means that sellers outnumber buyers, so the price will keep going down.

Frequency

Another measure of liquidity is *frequency,* or how often a security trades. Some assets, like stock market futures, trade constantly, from the moment the market opens until the very last trade of the day, and then continue into overnight trading. Others, like agricultural commodities, trade only during market hours or only during certain times of the year. Other securities, like stocks, trade frequently, but the volume rises and falls at regular intervals related to such things as *options expiration* (the date at which options on the stock expire).

Much of the market is dominated by *high-frequency traders,* which are proprietary computerized systems that enter, execute, or cancel buy and sell orders in the blink of an eye — or less. These traders have thrown a wrench into a few trading days, but they are only partially responsible for the type of frequency being discussed here. That's because high-frequency traders look for securities that already trade frequently to make the programs work better.

Homing in on high volatility

The *volatility* of a security is how much the price of an asset varies over a period of time. It tells you how much prices fluctuate and thus how likely you are to be able to take advantage of that. For example, if a security has an average price of $5 but trades anywhere between $1 and $14, it is more volatile than one with an average price of $5 that trades between $4 and $6.

One standard measure of volatility and risk is *standard deviation*, which is how much any given price quote varies from a security's average price. If you are dying to see it, the math is explained in the sidebar "Finding the standard deviation — the hard way," but you can calculate it with most spreadsheet programs and many trading platforms.

FINDING THE STANDARD DEVIATION — THE HARD WAY

Here's the equation you use to calculate standard deviation:

$$\sigma = \sqrt{\frac{1}{N}\sum_{i=1}^{N}\left(x_i - \bar{x}\right)^2}$$

In this equation, N is the number of price quotes, x_i is any one price quote, and the funky x with the line over it is the average of all the prices over time.

To calculate standard deviation for yourself, you calculate the difference between any given price and the average value. So if the average price is $5 and the closing price today is $8, the difference is $3. (More likely, the research service that you use would calculate the difference for you; you can learn more about research services in Chapter 13.)

After you have all the differences between the prices and the average for the time period in question, you find the square of these differences. If the difference for one day's price is $8, then the square is $64. You add up all the squared differences over the period of time that you are looking at and then find the average of them. That number is called the *variance*, or σ^2. Finally, calculate the square root of the variance, and you have the standard deviation.

REMEMBER

The higher the standard deviation, the higher the volatility; the higher the volatility, the more a security's price is going to fluctuate, and the more profit — and loss — opportunities there are for a day trader.

Standard deviation is also a measure of risk that can be used to evaluate your trading performance. That use of the measure is discussed in Chapter 14.

Staying within your budget

You don't necessarily need a lot of money to begin day trading, but you do need a lot of money to buy certain securities. Stocks generally trade in *round lots,* which are orders of at least 100 shares. If you want to buy a stock worth $40 per share, you need $4,000 in your account. Your broker will probably let you borrow half of that money, but you still need to come up with the other $2,000.

Options and futures trade by contract; one contract represents some unit of the underlying security. For example, in the options market, one contract is good for 100 shares of the stock. It's possible to trade only one contract, but the most traders work in round lots of 100 contracts per order.

WARNING

No one will stop you from buying a smaller amount than the usual round lot in any given security, but you'll probably pay a high commission and get worse execution for your order. Because the returns on each trade tend to be small anyway, don't take up day trading until you have enough money to trade your target asset effectively. Otherwise, you'll pay too much to your broker without getting much for yourself.

Bonds don't trade in fractional amounts; they trade on a per-bond basis, and each bond has a face value of $1,000. Some trade for more or less than that, depending on how the bond's interest rate differs from the market rate of interest, but the $1,000 figure is a good number to keep in mind when thinking about capital requirements. Many dealers have a minimum order of ten bonds, though, so a minimum order would be $10,000.

Making sure you can use margin

Most day traders make money through a large volume of small profits. One way to increase the profit per trade is to use borrowed money to buy more shares, more contracts, or more bonds. *Margin* is money in your account that you borrow against, and almost all brokers will be happy to arrange a margin loan for you, especially if you're going to use the money to make more trades and generate more commissions for the brokerage firm. You want to think about how margin affects your choice of assets for day trading.

The following section gives you more information on how margin works and what you need to consider when selecting assets to trade, but here's what you need to know now: Most stocks and bonds are marginable (able to be purchased on margin), and the Investment Industry Regulation Organization of Canada (IIROC) allows traders to borrow up to 70 percent of their value, though you usually have to put 30 percent down. But not all securities are marginable. Stocks priced below $2 per share, those traded on the TSX Venture Exchange and stocks with a market capitalization of below $250 million USD cannot be traded on margin. Your brokerage firm should have a list of securities that are not eligible for margin.

If leverage is going to be part of your day trading strategy, be sure that the assets you plan to trade are marginable.

Generally, your stock or bond account must hold the greater of $2,000 or 50 percent of the purchase price of securities when you borrow the money. So, for example, if you want to buy $5,000 worth of something on margin, you need to have $2,500 in your account. The price of those securities can go down, but if they go down so much that the account now holds only 25 percent of the value of the loan, you'll get a *margin call*. That means that you have to add cash or securities to your account right then and there. If not, your position will be liquidated.

Excess margin is the amount of money in your account over and above the minimum. For example, if you have $100,000 in your account and need 30 percent as maintenance margin, then you can borrow against an additional $70,000, the amount in excess of the 30 percent used for maintenance.

For derivatives, the margin rules are a bit different. Each contract has its own requirement for the initial margin and maintenance levels that must be kept on account; in the argot of the derivatives markets, margin is also known as a *performance bond*. If you are trading the Chicago Mercantile Exchange's E-mini MSCI Emerging Markets index contracts, for example, your initial margin per contract is $100,000, and your maintenance margin is $8,000. You can find current margin requirements for Chicago Mercantile Exchange and Chicago Board of Trade products at the Chicago Mercantile Exchange's website, www.cmegroup.com. For Canadian information, visit the Montreal Exchange's website at www.m-x.ca.

Margin requirements aren't set by the brokerage firms. Instead, the minimum amount in your account — and thus the maximum amount you can borrow — is set by IIROC. That's because of concerns that if too much borrowing takes place, the borrowers will panic in a financial downturn and drag the market down even further. (Excessive trading on margin was a contributing factor to the stock market crash of 1929, in which the Dow Jones Industrial Average fell 13 percent in one day, and the market did not fully recover until 1954. The financial crisis of 2008 wasn't caused by leverage in the stock market but by excessive borrowing in the real estate market.)

Obeying your brokerage firm's margin policies

IIROC limits the amount that can be borrowed and monitors how member brokerage firms comply. All brokerage firms have to meet those rules, but some set stricter limits for their customers.

The brokerage firms also set the interest rates for margin and the requirements for customers who want to borrow money to trade. The rates can be high; in 2020, brokerage firm Quetrade charged an annual rate of 3.5 percent plus the prime rate on debit balances up to $100,000 in nonregistered accounts and 8.1 percent plus the prime rate on debts in registered accounts. (This is one way that brokerage firms make money, so keep it in mind when you're comparison shopping.)

Day traders have to pay margin interest, even though their loans are of short duration. Because it takes three days for a securities trade to settle, to the accountants, it looks as though you borrowed the money for three full days, not three hours. Some brokerage firms charge you interest for the full three days.

REMEMBER

You won't pay the quoted interest rate each day, however; the quoted rate is almost always annualized. Divide it by 365 to find the daily rate. If the annual rate is 8.825 percent, then the daily rate will be $8.825 \div 365 = 0.024$ percent. Check with your brokerage firm to find out the specifics of the margin interest calculation for day traders so that you understand what you'll be charged before you start to trade.

Taking a Closer Look at Stocks

A *stock*, also called an *equity*, is a security that represents a fractional interest in the ownership of a company. Buy one share of Shopify and you are an owner of the company, just as founder Tobi Lütke is. He may own a much larger share of the total business, but you both have a stake in it. Stockholders elect a board of directors to represent their interests in how the company is managed. Each share is a vote, so good luck getting Tobi kicked off Shopify's board.

A share of stock has *limited liability*, which means that you can lose all of your investment but no more than that. If the company files for bankruptcy, the creditors cannot come after the shareholders for the money that they are owed.

Some companies pay their shareholders a *dividend*, which is a small cash payment made out of firm profits. Because day traders hold stock for really short periods of time, they don't normally collect dividends.

How Canadian and U.S. stocks trade

Stocks are priced based on a single share, but most brokerage firms charge commissions based on a 100-share basis because stocks are almost always traded in round lots of 100 shares. The supply and demand for a given stock is driven by the company's expected performance.

A stock's price is quoted with a bid and an ask.

>> The *bid* is the price that the broker pays to buy the stock from you if you are selling.

>> The *ask* is the price that the broker charges you if you are the one buying.

TIP

You can remember the difference between the bid and the ask this way: The *broker buys* on the *bid*. Let alliteration be your friend! The difference between the bid and the ask is the *spread*, and that represents the dealer's profit.

Here is an example of a price quote:

TD $60.27 $60.30

This quote is for TD Bank (ticker symbol: TD). The bid, listed first, is $60.27, and the ask is $60.30. The spread is $0.03. (The smallest possible spread is just one penny.) The spread here, which we looked at in the middle of the summer of 2020, is tiny as a percentage of the total price because TD is a liquid stock, and no big news events were happening at this time to change the balance of buyers and sellers.

TIP

The brokerage firm makes money from the commission *and* from the spread. Many novice day traders focus on the amount of the commission and forget that some brokerage firms can execute the order better than others, thus keeping the spread narrower. You need to consider the total cost of trading when you design a trading strategy and choose a brokerage firm, and brokers must disclose data on trade execution quality if you request it.

TECHNICAL STUFF

We tend to use the words *broker* and *dealer* interchangeably, but there is a difference. A *broker* simply matches buyers and sellers of securities, whereas a *dealer* buys and sells securities out of its own account. Almost all brokerage firms are both brokers and dealers.

Where Canadian stocks trade

We provide detailed discussion of financial markets in Chapter 3. Here, we examine some specifics for the stock market. In particular, most Canadian and U.S. stocks trade on organized *exchanges* such as the Toronto Stock Exchange, the New York Stock Exchange, and Nasdaq, but they trade more and more on electronic communications networks, some of which are operated by the exchanges themselves.

The old-line exchanges are what you may think about when someone mentions stock exchanges: brick-and-mortar buildings with lots of people running around to execute trades in person. They are still major factors in the market, but they have competition from electronic communication networks, which were created with the theory being that more competition would make markets function even better. It hasn't quite worked out that way. Spreads between bid and ask prices have narrowed, but volatility has increased since they became a factor in the market. On the other hand, volatility creates opportunity for day traders, so that's not necessarily a bad thing.

When you place an order with your brokerage firm, the broker's computer executes that order wherever it can get the best deal. But is that the best deal for you or the best deal for the brokerage firm? It's tough to know the right answer. In general, firms that do more trading and participate in several exchanges and electronic communications networks can get you the best execution.

REMEMBER

The financial markets are in a state of flux, with a lot of mergers and acquisitions among the exchanges. By the time you read the information here, things may have changed again, which I think is fascinating. It wasn't so long ago that these exchanges were staid organizations run like private clubs.

Toronto Stock Exchange (TSX)

The TSX is the main Canadian exchange. If a Canadian company wants the public's cash, it will usually list on the TSX. However, not all companies can trade on the exchange — you definitely won't see the corner store take out an IPO, and even larger businesses can't automatically list. More than 1,600 companies are listed on the exchange, with a total market cap — the total dollar market value of a company's outstanding shares — of more than $3.1 trillion.

All the companies listed on the exchange paid a fee to be there. Depending on the size of the company, businesses have to pay between $10,000 and $200,000 to list. In many cases companies are assigned a three-letter ticker symbol, but not always. Shopify, the largest company by market cap on the TSX at the time of writing, has the symbol SHOP (very appropriate!), and Toronto Dominion Bank can be found under TD. Some companies, like Montreal-based aerospace company

Bombardier, have a .B after their symbol (BBD.B), which means investors can purchase only non-voting class B shares.

TECHNICAL STUFF

Companies have to meet a number of requirements to list, and the requirements vary depending on the industry. You can find out all about the wonderful world of listing at www.tmx.com, but here are the basics: Company execs have to show they're successful, or, if it's a new venture, that the management has a record of experience. Companies must also have a certain amount of assets, though it varies per sector — tech businesses, for example, require a minimum of $10 million in their treasury.

TSX Venture Exchange (TSXV)

The Calgary-based TSX Venture Exchange operates like the TSX, but it's for junior companies or new businesses looking for startup capital. More than 1,600 companies are listed on the exchange, with a total market cap of $61 billion. The mining industry makes most use of the TSXV — 47 percent of the world's mining companies are listed on the exchange — with oil and gas companies come in second. Some of these companies will eventually move to the TSX, and others will close shop and delist. Because it's mostly for smaller operations it can be a more volatile place to invest.

TIP

The TSXV is a good place for traders to play resource-based companies, because that's what makes up most of the index.

BRINGING THE TSX INTO THE 21ST CENTURY

The TSX is 159 years old. In 1861, 24 men got together at Toronto's Masonic Hall and started the exchange. Membership cost $5, there were only 18 listed securities, and trading was limited to one 30-minute session a day. In 1997, TSX closed its trading floor and went virtual — becoming, at that time, the largest floorless exchange in North America.

In 1999, Canada's trading landscape underwent a major change. At the time there were stock exchanges in most big Canadian cities, but that year it was decided the TSX would become the sole place to trade senior equities. The Montreal Exchange stuck to derivatives, and the rest of the exchanges formed the Canadian Venture Exchange (CDNX). Two years later, the TSX Group (the company that owns and operates the TSX) bought the CDNX, and in 2002 renamed it the TSX Venture Exchange (TSXV). Since then the TSX Group has become a public company itself, attracted international listings, merged with the Montreal Exchange, and changed its name to the TMX Group.

Aequitas NEO Exchange (NEO)

In 2015, Aequitas Innovations, a company backed by a number of larger businesses, such as Mackenzie Investments and the Royal Bank of Canada, launched the NEO Exchange. It's been marketed as an alternative to the TSX and says it puts "the interest of capital-raising companies, investors and dealers first." It only has 97 listings so far — mostly ETFs and Cannabis companies — but it says it represents close to 10 percent of all volume traded in Canadian-listed securities. Traders can buy and sell stock on the exchange, just like they can on any others.

Canadian Securities Exchange (CSE)

The CSE, originally called the Canadian National Stock Exchange, competes with the TSXV for micro-cap and emerging groth company listings. It launched in 2004 and claims to have a more streamlined reporting process for companies. As of the July 2020, it has 591 listings.

Alternative trading systems (ATS) and electronic communication networks (ECN)

Alternative trading systems (ATS), also called electronic communication networks (ECN), are like stock exchanges in that they facilitate the buying an selling of securities, though they're not stock exchanges themselves. These are groups of brokerage firms and investing companies that agree to trade among each other before putting the order out to another exchange, but they've grown enough to become something else. They have created new trading opportunities and reduced costs, but they've also added to the volatility in the market.

As a result, you may see that your trade has been executed through Alpha, Omega, Chi-X, CX2, or any of the other exchanges that have cropped up over the years. Many of these exchanges are designed to match one order with another automatically. If you have 100 shares of something to sell and someone else wants to buy 100 shares, your orders are matched and cleared. Trades that take place on these exchanges generally do so at smaller spreads and lower fees than trades on traditional exchanges, but fewer trades take place on them.

In any event, a broker that works closely with ECNs and alternative exchanges may be able to get you a better deal, which is important because in trading, very small price differences add up.

When we first wrote this book a decade ago, there were a number of independent ATSs in Canada. Some have since been purchased by larger companies. For instance, Chi-X Canada is now owned by Nasdaq, while Alpha ATS is now the TSX Alpha Exchange. Other ATSs include Instinet Canada Cross and MATCH Now. Generally, these systems list the exact same securities as the TSX but at different prices, though they don't vary too much in cost. At the time of writing, Shopify was trading at $1,416.97, and TSX Alpha listed it at $1,416.28. Luckily, traders don't have to worry about the different exchanges because the broker will automatically sort through every exchange and buy the stock at the best price.

TIP

Some traders swear like sailors as they rapidly buy and sell, but one F-word is worse than anything you'd hear a few minutes to close: *fees*. Brokers have to pay them every time they trade, and those costs are often passed down to the trader. When the TSX had a monopoly it could charge whatever it wanted; alternative trading systems were created in part to bring those fees down. Fortunately, fees have fallen. That's good news for traders who will hopefully see commission costs tumble as brokers pass on their savings to their customers.

Where U.S. stocks trade

Canadian traders don't just stick to homegrown stocks. There's a big world beyond our borders, with plenty of opportunities. Most also trade U.S. securities, which is why we spend a lot of time talking about American-based companies, exchanges, and products in this book. Here are some of the exchanges south of the border that you'll come across in your trading activities.

The New York Stock Exchange (NYSE)

The New York Stock Exchange (NYSE) is the most famous of all stock exchanges. Most of the largest U.S. corporations trade on it, and they pay a fee for that privilege.

To be listed on the NYSE, a company generally needs to have at least 2,200 shareholders excluding insiders, trade at least 100,000 shares a month for the last six months, carry a *market capitalization* (number of shares outstanding multiplied by price per share) of at least $100 million, and post total pre-tax earnings of $10 million over the previous three years.

The NYSE is more than 200 years old, but it has been going through some big corporate changes in order to stay relevant. It's a *floor-based exchange*. The trading area is a big open space in the building, known as the *floor*. The floor broker, who works for the member firm, receives the order electronically and then takes it over to the trading post, which is the area on the floor where the stock in question trades. At the trading post, the floor broker executes the order at the best available price.

Of course, the percentage of trading that has been done by actual people standing on the floor of an actual building has fallen steadily over the years. Most trading is done electronically by small day traders and big institutions alike, with computer algorithms representing a growing share of the trading activity.

To give you a clue about the importance of computerized trading, the NYSE allows brokerage firms to place their servers on the floor of the exchange — for a fee, of course. For some, the millisecond advantage is worth it.

Nasdaq

Nasdaq used to stand for the National Association of Securities Dealers Automated Quotation System, but now it's just a name, not an acronym, pronounced just like it's spelled. When Nasdaq was founded, it was an electronic communication network (more on those shortly) that handled companies that were too small or too speculative to meet NYSE listing requirements. What happened was that brokers liked using the Nasdaq network, and technology companies on the exchange (Microsoft, Intel, Apple) that were once small and speculative became huge international behemoths.

When a customer places an order, the brokerage firm's computer looks to see whether a matching order is on the network. Sometimes, the order can be executed electronically; in other cases, the brokerage firm's trader needs to call other traders at other firms to see whether the price is still good. A key feature of Nasdaq is its *market makers*, who are employees of member brokerage firms who agree to buy and sell minimum levels of specific stocks in order to ensure that some basic level of trading is taking place.

Nasdaq divides its listed companies into three categories:

» **The Nasdaq Global Select Market** includes the 1,000 largest companies on the exchange. Companies that make the list have a minimum average market capitalization of $550 million and total earnings of at least $11 million in the prior three fiscal years.

» **The Nasdaq Global Market** includes companies that are too small for the Global Select Market but that aren't exactly small. To make the Global Market, companies generally need to have a market capitalization of at least $75 million, at least 1.1 million shares outstanding, at least 400 shareholders, and a minimum price per share of $4.

» **The Nasdaq Capital Market** is for companies that do not qualify for the Nasdaq Global Market. To qualify here, companies need a market capitalization of at least $50 million, at least 1 million shares outstanding, about 300 shareholders, and a minimum price per share of $4.

TIP

As a day trader, you'll find that Nasdaq Global Select Market companies are the most liquid. You may also notice changes in trading patterns when a company is close to being moved between categories. An upgrade is a sign of good news to come and increased market interest. A downgrade means that the company most likely isn't doing well and will be of less interest to investors.

The high-risk over-the-counter exchanges

When the traditional floor-based exchanges were the primary game, a few companies emerged to trade stocks that were not eligible for exchange listing. These businesses are still around, and many traders like them because they can find stocks that have good volatility that are too small to attract the attention of the big guys with their big computers. However, the risk level is a lot higher: Some of these stocks don't trade enough for a day trader, and a few of these stocks aren't issued by legitimate companies.

Over-the-Counter Bulletin Board (OTC BB) and penny stocks

You've likely hear of penny stocks, which are companies that you can buy with the money in your piggy bank. These stocks trade on an Over-the-Counter Bulletin Board. Usually, these companies are too small to trade on a traditional exchange, and they're barely regulated, so buyer beware. While not all OTC BB stocks are considered penny stocks, which are stocks that trade below $1.00 per share, many of these kinds of companies can be purchased there.

Be careful of penny stocks: The market is so easy to manipulate that people can get ripped off. The most common type of penny stock fraud is the so-called *pump and dump*: A promoter buys shares of a penny stock at a low price and then gets on a message board and talks the company up. Other people jump in and bid up the price. The original promoter then sells to them, so they're left holding the bag when it turns out the stock is grossly overvalued.

If you do want to take the risk of day trading OTC BB stocks, then you'll need to use a broker that can facilitate this kind of transaction — but not all can.

TIP

In many cases, OTC BB are U.S. companies that used to be on Nasdaq, but the stock prices have lost too much of their value to maintain their listing. A Bulletin Board listing is often a last hurrah before oblivion.

OTC Link

Once upon a time, few electronic networks existed, and they didn't have enough room for many companies to trade on them. Smaller companies did not trade daily. To find current prices, brokerage firms subscribed to a price service that sent out a weekly newsletter listing the prices for those companies. The newsletter was printed on pink paper, so it became known as the *Pink Sheets*. In the more modern era, the newsletter has moved online and changed its name to OTC Link (www.otcmarkets.com).

OTC Link does not have listing requirements for companies. Most of the companies don't qualify for listing on the Nasdaq or OTC BB, usually because they aren't current on their filings with the Securities and Exchange Commission. These companies have four- or five-letter ticker symbols and are sometimes shown with the suffix *.PK* after the ticker. Orders for OTC Link companies are placed through brokerage firms who use the service to find prices and match buyers and sellers.

WARNING

Not all OTC Link companies are legitimate. Because of the minimal listing requirements, it tends to be the hangout for penny stocks (those trading at less than $1.00 per share), fraudulent companies, and securities that are easily manipulated by boiler-room operators. It can be a tough crowd, and a lot of people get burned.

Dark pools

Don't be put off by the word *dark*. Dark pools, also known as *dark liquidity,* are good for traders. These exchanges allow people to place buy and sell orders that will be executed only if someone takes the other side. Of course, that's how most markets operate, but dark pools don't publish the prices or the sizes of the orders. Traders use them for low-cost execution, not price discovery. The downside is that price listings carry information about where the market is headed. If you're interested in reading more, check out *Dark Pools & High Frequency Trading For Dummies* by Jay Vaananen (John Wiley & Sons, Inc.) for more information.

Examining Bonds

Bonds are almost impossible to day trade, but there are two good reasons to know about them:

>> Day traders often use options, futures, and ETFs based on bonds.

>> The bond market has a huge effect on the rest of the financial markets.

A *bond* is a loan. The bond buyer gives the bond issuer money. The bond issuer promises to pay interest on a regular basis. The regular coupon payments are why bonds are often called *fixed income investments.* Bond issuers repay the money borrowed — the principal — on a predetermined date, known as the *maturity.* Bonds generally have a maturity of more than ten years; shorter-term bonds are usually referred to as *notes,* and bonds that mature within a year of issuance are usually referred to as *bills.* Most bonds in Canada and the United States are issued by corporations (corporate bonds) or by the Federal government (Government of Canada bonds here and Treasury bonds in the U.S.). Provinces and some cities issue bonds (provincial and municipal) as well.

Over the years, enterprising financiers realized that some investors needed regular payments but others wanted to receive a single sum at a future date. So they separated the *coupons*, the interest payments on a bond, from the principal. The principal payment, known as a *zero-coupon bond*, is sold to one investor, while the coupons, called *strips*, are sold to another investor. The borrower makes the payments just like with a regular bond. (Regular bonds, by the way, are sometimes called *plain vanilla*.)

The borrower who wants to make a series of payments with no lump-sum principal repayment would issue an *amortizing* bond to return principal and interest on a regular basis. If you think about a typical mortgage, the borrower makes a regular payment of both principal and interest. This way, the amount owed gets smaller over time so that the borrower doesn't have to come up with a large principal repayment at maturity.

Other borrowers prefer to make a single payment at maturity, so they issue *discount bonds*. The purchase price is the principal reduced by the amount of interest that otherwise would be paid.

REMEMBER

If a company goes bankrupt, the bondholders get paid before the shareholders do. In some bankruptcies, the bondholders take over the business, leaving the current shareholders with nothing.

How bonds trade

Bonds often trade as single bonds, with a face value of $1,000, although some brokers take on only minimum orders of ten bonds. Bonds do not trade as frequently as stocks do because most bond investors are looking for steady income, so they hold their bonds until maturity. Bonds have less risk than stocks, so they show less price volatility. The value of a bond is mostly determined by the level of interest rates in the economy. As rates go up, bond prices go down; when rates go down, bond prices go up. Bond prices are also affected by how likely the loan is to be repaid. If traders don't think that the bond issuer will pay up, then the bond price will fall.

REMEMBER

Generally speaking, only corporate, provincial and municipal bonds have repayment risk. The Canadian government could default, but that scenario is unlikely as long as the government can print money. Most international government bonds have similarly low default risk, but some countries *have* defaulted. The most notable was Russia, which refused to print money to repay its debts in the summer of 1998 — a decision that caused huge turmoil in the world's financial markets, including the collapse of a major hedge fund, Long-Term Capital Management.

Investment banks and the federal government sell new bonds directly to investors. After they are issued, bonds are said to trade in the secondary market; some are listed, and some trade over-the-counter, meaning dealers trade them among themselves rather than over an organized exchange.

A bond price quote looks like this:

2.250 4/30/2021 n 98:6016 98:6125

Translation: This hypothetical bond is a Government of Canada note maturing in on April 30, 2021 and carrying an interest rate of 2.250 percent. Similar to stocks, the numbers right after the *n* (for *note*) list the bid and ask. The first number is the bid, the price that the dealer pays to buy the bond from you if you are selling. The second number is the ask, the price that the dealer charges you if you're buying. The difference is the spread, and that's the dealer's profit.

Listed bonds

Some larger corporate bonds are traded on the TSX and the New York Stock Exchange. Those wanting to buy or sell them place an order through their brokerage firm, which sends an order to the floor broker. The process is almost identical to the trading of listed stocks.

Over-the-counter trading

Most corporate and municipal bonds trade over-the-counter, meaning no organized exchange exists. Instead, brokerage firms use electronic price services to find out where the buyers and sellers are for different issues. Over-the-counter bonds don't trade much. Buyers often give their quality, interest rate, and maturity requirements to their broker, and the broker waits until a suitable bond comes to market. In Canada, Questrade publishes a daily Bonds Bulletin, which lists all sorts of bonds — from guaranteed investment certificates to corporates — that can be purchased through its platform.

Treasury dealers

Unlike the corporate and municipal bond market, the U.S. Treasury market is one of the most liquid in the world. The best way to buy a new Treasury bond is directly from the government because no commission is involved. You can get more information from the Treasury Department's website, www.treasurydirect.gov; it has information on all kinds of government bonds for all kinds of purchasers.

After the bonds are issued, they trade on a secondary market of Treasury dealers. These are large brokerage firms registered with the government who agree to buy and sell bonds and maintain a stable market for the bonds. If your brokerage firm is not a Treasury dealer, it has a relationship with one that it can send your order to.

Treasury dealers do quite a bit of day trading in Treasury bonds for the firm's own account. After all, the market is liquid enough that day trading is possible. Few individual day traders work the Treasury market, though, because it requires a great deal of capital and leverage to make a high return.

Cashing In with Currency

Cash is king, as they say. It's money that's readily available in your day trading account to buy more securities. For the most part, the interest rate on cash is very low, but if you close out your positions every night, you'll always have a cash balance in your brokerage account. The firm will probably pay you a little interest on it, so it will contribute to your total return, but not by much.

But one type of cash investment can be really exciting for a day trader, and that's currency. Every day, trillions (yes, that's trillions with a *t*) of dollars of currency are exchanged between governments, banks, travelers, businesses, and speculators. With every trade and every blip in exchange rates, you have new opportunities to make money. Currency is a bigger, more liquid market than the U.S. stock and bond markets combined. It's often referred to as the *forex* market, short for *foreign exchange*. Foreign currency may be an attractive place to store some of your trading cash, and it can be a great asset to day trade.

How currency trades

The exchange rate is the price of money. It tells you how many dollars it takes to buy yen, pounds, or euros. The price that people are willing to pay for a currency depends on the investment opportunities, business opportunities, and perceived safety in each nation. If Canadian businesses see great opportunities in Thailand, for example, they have to trade their dollars for baht in order to pay rent, buy supplies, and hire workers there. This situation increases the demand for baht relative to the dollar and causes the baht to go up in price relative to the dollar.

Exchange rates are quoted on a bid-ask basis, just as bonds and stocks are. A quote may look like this:

CDNJPY= 111.98 111.99

This is the exchange rate for converting the U.S. dollar into Japanese yen. The bid price of 11.98 is the amount of yen that a dealer would give you if you wanted to sell a dollar and buy yen. The ask price of 111.99 is the amount of yen the dealer would charge you if you wanted to buy a dollar and sell yen. The difference is the dealer's profit, and naturally, you'll be charged a commission too.

How the Canadian dollar is traded

The most common currency transaction is the euro against the U.S. dollar, mainly because Europe is one of the largest trading blocs in the world and a lot of business is done between those two countries. But Canadians often trade the loonie against the greenback for two reasons: The U.S. is our biggest trading partner, and it's just what we know. You can, of course, trade the Canadian dollar against any other currency too.

TIP

Beginners may want to stick to the Canada–U.S. relationship, simply because most news outlets in the Great White North report on currency fluctuations relative to the American buck. Understanding how to trade the loonie against the yen takes a bit more work.

REMEMBER

Note that with currency, you're a buyer and a seller at the same time, which can increase the profit opportunities, but it can also increase your risk.

Day traders can trade currencies directly at current exchange rates, which is known as *trading in the spot market.* When you exchange money to go on vacation in a foreign land, you are exchanging on the spot, and you are allowed to do it as a trader or as an investor. Day traders can also use currency exchange-traded funds (discussed earlier in this chapter) or currency futures (discussed later in this chapter) to profit from the changing prices of money.

Where currency trades

Spot currency — the real-time value of money — does not trade on an organized exchange. Instead, banks, brokerage firms, hedge funds, and currency dealers buy and sell amongst themselves all day, every day.

TIP

Day traders can open dedicated forex accounts through their brokers or currency dealers and then trade as they see opportunities during the day.

If you are interested in trading currencies, be sure to check out the fees involved. Some banks and brokerages are really set up to do forex trades for businesses and travellers, so the fees will be too high for you to have a decent profit potential.

Considering Commodities and How They Trade

Commodities are basic, interchangeable goods sold in bulk and used to make other goods. Examples include oil, gold, wheat, and lumber. Commodities are popular with investors as a hedge against inflation and uncertainty. Stock prices can go to zero, but people still need to eat! Although commodity prices usually tend to increase at the same rate as in the overall economy, meaning they maintain their real (inflation-adjusted) value, they can also be susceptible to short-term changes in supply and demand. A cold winter increases demand for oil, a dry summer reduces production of wheat, and a civil war could disrupt access to platinum mines.

Day traders aren't going to buy commodities outright. If you really want to haul bushels of grain around all day, you can do that without taking on the risks of day trading (you'd get more exercise, too). Instead, day traders who want to play with commodities can look to other investments. The most popular way is to buy futures contracts, which change in price with the underlying commodity. Increasingly, many people trade commodities through exchange-traded funds that are based on the value of an underlying basket of commodities.

So why do we mention commodities in this chapter? Because this chapter covers the basic stuff, and Chapter 5 gets into the derivatives and derivations.

REMEMBER

Commodity prices affect the broad economy, not just the prices of commodities contracts on the futures exchanges. If you day trade stocks in particular, you may find that changes in the price of oil or agricultural commodities affect many of the companies that you are involved with as well as the broader stock market indexes.

IN THIS CHAPTER

» **Expanding the pool of trading tools**

» **Trading sector trends with ETFs**

» **Inventing opportunities from invented money**

» **Deriving profits from derivatives**

» **Arbitraging your way to new opportunities**

Chapter **5**

Assets 102: ETFs, Cryptocurrency, Options, and Derivatives

The basic financial assets — stocks, bonds, cash, and commodities — do a pretty good job of creating opportunities for people to hedge and speculate, but they have some limitations. The basic assets are just that: They're securities that represent ownership in a business, a loan to a government or corporation, raw materials, or cold hard cash. They are nice, concrete, easy.

But they aren't perfect. Nothing is, right? Some people wanted other ways to trade these assets, or parts of these assets, or hedge themselves against the financial risks that come with owning the underlying asset. The result of research, market demand, and more than a little financial engineering come the alternatives that we cover in this chapter.

These asset classes are particularly important for day traders. For example, although bonds play a huge role in the financial markets, they're difficult for day traders to use. By trading interest rate futures or T-bill options, a trader can get exposure to the bond markets with smaller capital commitment and easier trading.

Others of these assets, like cryptocurrencies, now exist mostly for the pleasure of traders but may become used like dollars and yen at some point in the future.

Some of these alternatives have greater liquidity than their counterpart in the traditional market, which is important for day traders. Others allow you to trade such narrow financial concepts as volatility or the future nature of money. As you get into them, you'll find ideas for trading and a deeper understanding of the financial markets.

Explaining Exchange-Traded Funds (ETFs) in Plain English

An *exchange-traded fund* (ETF) is a tradable security that represents a share in a collection of stocks, bonds, or other underlying securities.

In essence, ETFs are a cross between mutual funds and stocks, and they offer a great way for day traders to get exposure to market segments that may otherwise be difficult to trade. The category is sometimes called *exchange-traded products* because some of the funds are structured more as a trading strategy than as mutual funds.

To set up an ETF, a money-management firm buys a group of assets — stocks, bonds, or others — and then lists shares that trade on the market. In most cases, the purchased assets are designed to mimic the performance of an index, and investors know what those assets are before they purchase shares in the fund. The big advantage for day traders is that an ETF can be bought or sold at any time during the trading day, long or short, with cash or on margin, through a regular brokerage account. This flexibility is great for day traders.

Although an ETF looks a little bit like an index mutual fund or a market index futures contract, it has a very different structure. ETFs have two types of shares:

» **Creation units:** These shares are held by authorized participants, which are different trading and brokerage firms that agree to commit cash to the fund. Creation unit holders can exchange their shares for the actual securities held in the fund, or they can add the appropriate securities to the fund in order to make new creation units. They do this to keep the value of the ETF in line with the underlying market index. So if the price of an ETF falls below the value of the securities in it, the authorized participants will trade in their creation units for the securities and then sell them on the open market. If the price of an ETF rises above the value of the securities, then the authorized participants will buy up the securities and exchange them for more creation units that they can sell at a nice profit.

» **Retail shares:** These ETF shares are listed on the exchange to be bought and sold by regular investors and traders. If you day trade ETFs, you'll be working with the retail shares.

Most of the time, the price of both the creation units and the retail shares are right in-line with the price of the securities. On occasion, though, the value of the ETF and its investments will diverge. This usually happens at times of extreme market stress, so you may never see it. If you do, though, you may have an opportunity to make money.

REMEMBER

Some funds that look like ETFs are actually *exchange-traded notes* (ETN). These funds are organized under a different section of federal securities laws. From the perspective of a day trader, there is no difference between an ETF, and ETN, and other exchange-traded products.

ETFs have different investment styles that affect how they trade, and the next sections discuss how these work. Understanding the differences among ETFs can help you better target changing markets — and avoid making costly mistakes. You can find out more about the thousands of different ETFs on the market at `www.morningstar.com/ETFs.html` and for Canada at `www.morningstar.ca/ca/collection/27104/27205/etf-insight.aspx`.

Traditional ETFs

Traditional ETFs are available on the big market indexes, like the S&P/TSX Composite Index (the first ETF was created in Canada to mimic the Toronto 35 Index), Standard & Poor's 500, and the Dow Jones Industrial Average. They are also available in a variety of domestic bond indexes, international stock indexes, foreign currencies, and commodities. Because traders are often interested in a market segment that doesn't have an index on it, some ETF companies develop their own niche indexes and issue ETFs based on them. Hence, you can find ETFs for such markets as green energy and Islamic investing. The liquidity in the securities in the underlying index may be low, though, so these funds may be more volatile in trading — and may even have arbitrage opportunities.

Traditional ETFs can be used as long-term investments, and traders can use them. The retail shares can be sold long or short, or traded on margin, so they're a useful way to place trades on broad market trends or to take advantage of short-term technical opportunities.

Strategy ETFs

Not all ETFs trade on stock indexes. Many are what are known as *strategy ETFs*, funds that are based on a hedge fund–investing strategy rather than an underlying index. They can be dangerous for long-term investors who don't know what they're buying, but hey, this book is for traders! As with traditional ETFs, a strategy ETF can be held for the long term, or the shares can be traded long, short, or on margin.

Instead of setting up a portfolio of stocks and bonds to match an index, a strategy ETF may have a portfolio manager who chooses the investments. It may use options, futures, leverage, or short selling to generate an investment result that matches an index — or that deviates from it in more or less predictable ways. Its risk and return structure is different, and recognizing that information upfront can reduce heartache and improve profits.

Traders often find great opportunities in strategy ETFs. They give you a bigger toolbox to use to take on the markets, especially in times when the market is under stress. Just keep in mind that a strategy ETF may move in strange ways, especially if you're looking at it for more than a few minutes of trading.

Inverse ETFs

An *inverse ETF* is designed to move the opposite of the underlying index. If the index is up, the inverse ETF should be down, and vice versa. An inverse ETF is useful as a way to speculate on a decline in the stock market or to remove the risk of the market from a portfolio (something that some hedge funds try to do).

Leveraged ETFs

A *leveraged ETF* is designed to return a multiple of the return on an index. A 5x ETF will return five times what the underlying index does, a groovy thing if the market is up 10 percent — and devastating if the market is down. A leveraged ETF is used to add risk to investment portfolios.

Option and Managed Futures ETFs

Some ETFs are designed to give stock traders a way to get exposure to commodities markets. These types of ETFs do this by investing in options and futures rather than stocks or bonds, which creates good trading opportunities, but it can also make for unusual trading trends.

How ETFs trade

For day traders, the advantage of ETFs is that they can be bought and sold just like stocks. Customers place orders, usually in round lots, through their brokerage firms. The price quotes come in decimals and include a spread for the dealer.

The fact that ETFs trade the same way that stocks do makes them relatively easy for you to get started. You need a brokerage account with a margin agreement.

TIP

Some brokers waive commission for trades in certain ETFs, but this benefit is designed for long–term investors. Because commission is rarely waived for day traders, you'll want to compare total costs including execution rather than simply looking at the commission rate.

Traders can use ETFs to trade on trends in a relevant sector. For example, a trader who sees that a broad market index is headed for a breakout in the next hour or so may look to make a profit on that by taking a long position in an ETF that is tied to that index. Other traders may look at the trading patterns and indicators for a particular ETF and make a trade based on the performance of the ETF rather than that of the underlying index.

ETF risks

ETFs have changed the trading game over the years, and new products are being introduced all the time to expand the range of ways that investors and traders can manage their market exposure. But for all their popularity, two big risks remain:

» The first risk is *tracking error*, or the difference between the value of an ETF and the value of the index or strategy that it's supposed to track. The creation units are designed to manage the tracking error; the idea is that the big trading firms that make up the authorized participants engage in arbitrage (refer to the later section, "Comprehending Arbitrage and the Law of One Price") to force the values into alignment. Most of the time, the process works like a charm, but every now and again, ETF values get way out of whack. This usually happens when the markets are having a wild day and traders are using ETFs to make a profit the volatility.

» The second risk is *choosing the wrong ETF*. The increase in strategy ETFs increases this risk. A trader who isn't paying attention may take a position in an ETF that won't behave in a predictable way or at least not one that follows the same logic as an ordinary stock or bond. At an extreme, the annals of finance are full of sad stories of investors who took large positions in inverse ETFs after a down market year because these funds seemed to perform so well, without realizing that an inverse ETF would be down in a year that the market goes up. Ouch!

Getting Familiar with Cryptocurrency

A currency — whether it be a U.S. dollar, a Canadian dollar, or a Mexican peso — is simply a tool that helps people make buy and sell goods and services. Governments (or groups of governments, in the case of the euro or the Central African CFA franc) issue currencies. As with any other asset, the value of a currency is determined by supply and demand.

The world's currencies mostly work quite well, but the supply and demand can be, and often is, influenced by the political and economic decisions of a country's leaders. For example, a country's leaders may decide to pay off government debt by printing more money. This easy solution to one problem increases supply of the currency relative to demand, and so each unit of currency becomes worth less. At an extreme, you get extreme hyperinflation that destroys a currency and destabilizes a country, as has been experienced in Argentina, Venezuela, and Zimbabwe.

The problem of government officials undermining currency has led to all sorts of creative ideas for how to separate wealth and currency from any one country. The latest development, made in 2009, is Bitcoin, a digital currency that has been followed by many other digital currencies, also known as *cryptocurrencies*. These digital currencies have had wild price gyrations as people try to figure out what each cryptocurrency should be worth, and those price gyrations have attracted traders.

WARNING

Cryptocurrency could be a revolution in finance, or it could be a massive bubble. When the Beanie Baby bubble of the late 1990s blew up, at least people were left with cute toys. A one hundred trillion dollar Zimbabwean bank notes is a novelty item popular with financial types. With a Bitcoin, you could be left with nothing but a few lines of computer code, so proceed with caution.

Here we discuss how cryptocurrencies work. After you have a better understanding of cryptocurrencies, you can determine if they are right for your trading strategies.

Bitcoin and blockchain

Bitcoin emerged in 2009 in an academic paper written by an author or group of authors using the name Satoshi Nakamoto. (You can find the original paper at `https://bitcoin.org/bitcoin.pdf`.) Nakamoto set up the idea of an electronic coin that was actually a chain of digital signatures — a *blockchain*. When a coin is transferred from one owner to another, a code is added to the blockchain known as a *hash*. The hash includes data about the previous transaction and the public key of the next owner. Someone can go through to verify these hashes to show the chain of ownership.

Bitcoin was designed specifically as a reward for solving a series of increasingly difficult equations (which requires a lot of computer power and electricity.) The total number of Bitcoin that can be found is limited. The idea is to be a new currency that operates independently of the banking system, that can't have its supply manipulated by government planners and that carries built-in protection against fraud and theft.

Note: Blockchain isn't the same as cryptocurrency. Blockchain itself has a lot of applications for tracking the movement of goods from one place to another, documents from reader to reader, or securities from one trader to another. It's a great innovation, but it isn't a tradable asset. You don't need to use Bitcoin to use a blockchain.

In theory, Bitcoin could replace all the money in the world. In that case, each Bitcoin could be really valuable. Or, it could become completely worthless because people come to see it as a game developed by a few programmers. It's too soon to know. If we had to take a guess, we'd say that traditional currencies mostly work quite well and aren't going away soon — although bank accounts could well be managed by blockchain someday.

Other cryptocurrencies

As Bitcoin caught on, other cryptocurrencies were developed to capitalize on the demand or to make refinements on the concept of digital money. Some of them address the function of the blockchain, whereas others have different approaches to currency creation. And some even started out as jokes, such as the case with Dogecoin. They all have the same underlying problem as Bitcoin — they aren't used in commerce. They all have the same potential payoff, if there is a fundamental change in the way money is created and used in the world.

Units of cryptocurrency are often referred to as *coins* or *tokens.* The following sections examine the two main ways that new cryptocurrencies are created.

Forks

A *fork* is a change in the blockchain that starts a new series of blocks to record the transfer of a new set of coins. Programmers who hold the underlying coins develop forks, often to improve the way that the blockchain works. For example, Litecoin was forked from Bitcoin in order to set up a faster blockchain.

REMEMBER

As a day trader, forks probably won't affect you, but they can create some short-term deviations in value. If you see that a particular coin's price is radically lower from where it was before, make sure that a fork didn't cause a reconfiguration of the trading value.

Initial coin offerings (ICOs)

An *initial coin offering (ICO)* is a way that companies can raise money without issuing stock. Instead, they establish a blockchain and sell the coins that run on it. The idea is that the coins will become more valuable as the business takes off. In other cases, the coins being offered are designed to be used to buy the company's goods or services once they come to market.

WARNING

This process has created a lot of new cryptocurrencies, but it's unclear if the businesses that offer them are going to be successful. The SEC and the OSC have been concerned that some of these offerings should actually be handled as registered offerings of securities and that others are outright frauds. Tread carefully if you want to participate in an ICO, and pay attention to a token that seems to be trading strangely.

Understanding how cryptocurrencies trade

The market for cryptocurrencies is wild. It's based on supply and demand, of course, but the supply and demand is mostly driven by the interest of traders. Unlike with regular currencies, people aren't supplying or demanding cryptocurrency to import machine parts, pay for a hotel room in another country, or buy stocks trading in emerging markets. Many people who are active in the crypto world believe that the replacement of regular money with cryptocurrency will happen sooner rather than later, so they tend to buy and hold their coins – or *hodl* them, a slang term based on the misspelling of hold.

REMEMBER

Some merchants accept cryptocurrency, although most of them immediately exchange it for traditional currencies. Some folks engaging in illegal activities prefer cryptocurrency because the blockchains create anonymous receipts, which is why crypto is often used for ransom in data thefts or as a form of exchange for online drug deals. Some people experiment with cryptocurrencies in countries without a stable currency, such as Argentina or Venezuela, but they represent extremely small parts of the global economy.

In the next sections, we cover some of the unique aspects of cryptocurrencies that day traders need to consider. Crypto is almost, but not quite, like other assets that you may want to trade.

Unlocking valuation with technical analysis

If most trade in cryptocurrency is due to the supply and demand of traders, then that's the relevant factor in trading. The changes in supply and demand from all of the market's traders show up in the charts. You don't necessarily need to know the reason for the change to make a short-term profit from it.

Ultimately, then, cryptocurrencies trade based on technical analysis — and they will until it's known for sure if there is any value to them in the rest of the economy.

Watching out for pump and dump

The *pump and dump* is common in the crypto world just as it is in the world of penny stocks (refer to Chapter 4 for more information). This is the process of buying an asset, promoting it to others, and then selling it as the other buyers bid up the price. Pump and dump is illegal, but it isn't always caught. People buy up a currency and then start to promote it on Reddit, YouTube, or other social media channels. When others start to buy the token, they turn around and sell it. Some scammers charge subscriptions to participate. With so many different types of cryptocurrency floating around and so little regulation around those who trade it, it's no wonder that these things happen. We suggest that you don't get involved with it because you may lose your money or even your freedom.

THE PRICE DISCOVERY FUNCTION OF TRADING

Supply and demand determines the price of an asset. That's easy, right? By bringing supply and demand together, the financial markets provide *price discovery*, meaning that the price in the market reflects all of the different sources of information and need in the world, which is one of the most important functions of the markets. In a sector like cryptocurrency, determining the long-run value is critical, at least unless or until crypto is accepted in the same way as traditional currencies.

Opening up your wallet

If you do decide to get cryptocurrency, follow these steps:

1. **Get an account called a wallet.**

   A *wallet* is an account for holding and trading cryptocurrency. It gives you a number to use to record your transactions on the blockchain called an *address*. Bitcoin.org, the website of a consortium of Bitcoin users, has a list of wallets at https://bitcoin.org/en/choose-your-wallet. Different wallets have different security and transaction policies, so compare carefully. Some are free whereas others come with fees to download or to make transactions.

   WARNING

   Although the blockchain can't be hacked, wallets can be. Over the years, some wallet operators have lost clients' coins due to mismanagement, and others have had customer accounts be stolen.

2. **After you select your wallet, transfer cash from your bank account and use it to buy whatever cryptocurrency you want to own.**

   This process is known as a *fiat exchange*.

   Cryptocurrencies, like all currencies, are traded over the counter rather than on an exchange. However, the brokers that handle cryptocurrency refer to themselves as *cryptocurrency to cryptocurrency exchanges*. They are software platforms that help you find others who are buying and selling the tokens in which you're interested. They generally charge a percentage of the transaction as a fee.

Knowing where to trade crypto derivatives

You can trade cryptocurrency on traditional exchanges in different ways. Here are a few ways, with the easiest listed first:

>> Through Bitcoin futures offered by the Chicago Board Options Exchange.

>> Through a unit investment trust (a type of investment fund related to mutual funds) called the Bitcoin Investment Trust, ticker symbol GBTC.

>> Through publicly traded companies with large exposure to cryptocurrency and blockchain, ranging from IBM to a penny stock called Long Blockchain Corp., which actually makes bottled iced tea but had a pop in its stock price when it changed its name. (We wish we were making this up, but we're not.)

>> Through ETFs that hold cryptocurrency. As we write this, securities regulators have rejected the applications from investor groups that have proposed crypto ETFs, but crypto ETFs may be on the market some time in the near future.

Avoiding the risks of cryptocurrencies

Day trading is risky. Right now, trading in cryptocurrencies is even riskier than day trading. Of course, that risk creates opportunities if you know what the biggest risks are ahead of time. Here are some risks:

>> Cryptocurrencies may have absolutely no value whatsoever. We can't emphasize this point enough. No one knows if cryptocurrency in general will catch on, let alone any particular coin.

>> The security of the wallet is another risk. Because blockchain is anonymous, whoever "finds" a coin can keep it. There haven't been many crypto thefts, but there have been enough that you should be pay attention to security when looking at wallets and exchanges.

TIP

A lot of people become interested in cryptocurrency because of their political leanings. They think that the government shouldn't be in the business of issuing currency for all sorts of reasons. However, the number of people holding these political beliefs doesn't mean that the market for cryptocurrency is going to take off anytime soon. You have to trade what you see, not what you want to see happen. A sincerely held political belief is nothing more than a wish, and the market doesn't trade on wishes. Make political change by voting, not by trading cryptocurrency.

Dealing in Derivatives

Derivatives are financial contracts that draw their value from the value of an underlying asset, security, or index. For example, an S&P/TSX 60 futures contract gives the buyer a cash payment based on the price of the S&P/TSX 60 index on the day that the contract expires. The contract's value thus depends on where the index is trading. You're not trading the index itself; instead, you're trading a contract with a value derived from the price of the index. The index value changes all the time, so day traders have lots of opportunities to buy and sell.

Many day traders choose derivatives because these products give traders access to much of the economic universe, including stocks, bonds, commodities, and currencies. Furthermore, derivatives may have more favorable tax treatment for day traders than many other assets; more than one new day trader playing the stock market has been burned by the so-called *wash-sale rule,* which limits the deductibility of short-term losses. (We discuss this rule later in the book.) Futures aren't subject to wash-sale rules. Read on to find out more and see if they are right for you!

Getting to know types of derivatives

Day traders are likely to come across three types of derivatives: options, futures, and warrants. Options and futures trade on dedicated derivatives exchanges, whereas warrants trade on stock exchanges.

Options

An *option* is a contract that gives the holder the right, but not the obligation, to buy or sell the underlying asset at an agreed-upon price at an agreed-upon date in the future. An option that gives you the right to buy is a *call,* and one that gives you the right to sell is a *put.* A call is most valuable if the stock price is going up, whereas a put has more value if the stock price is going down.

TIP

Here's one way to remember the difference: You *call up* your friend to *put down* your enemy.

For example, a MSFT 2020 June 105 call gives you the right to buy Microsoft at $105.00 per share on the third Friday in June of 2020. If Microsoft is trading above $105.00, the option would be *in the money.* You could exercise the option and make a quick profit. If it is selling below $105.00, you could buy the stock cheaper in the open market, so the option would be worthless.

You can find great information on options, including online tutorials, on the Montreal Exchange's website, www.m-x.ca. For an American perspective visit the Chicago Board Options Exchange's website, www.cboe.com.

Very few people who buy and sell options plan to hold them until expiration. They buy them either to speculate on price changes or to protect themselves against them. The price of an option depends on four things:

- » **The price of the underlying stock:** The opportunity to buy a stock at a predetermined price (a *call option*) is more valuable if the price goes up. If June 2020 rolls around with Microsoft at $180 per share, wouldn't you love the opportunity to buy a share for only $105? Likewise, a *put option*, which gives you the right to sell an asset, is more valuable if the underlying falls in price.

- » **The volatility of the underlying:** The more the stock jumps around in price, the more likely it is to be in the money on the expiration date — and the more likely another trader will want protection against price fluctuations.

- » **The amount of time until expiration:** The longer the time period, the more likely that something — anything — could happen to place the option in the money.

- » **Interest rates:** When interest rates are higher, a stock trader would get more value from buying a call option and putting the rest of the account into cash instead of using all the cash to buy the underlying stock. This increase in interest rates makes the option more valuable.

Traders are looking at these factors and buying puts and calls based on what they see in the short term. The relatively active trading and the leveraged exposure to the underlying asset make derivatives popular with day traders.

Futures

A *futures* contract gives you the obligation to buy a set quantity of the underlying asset at a set price and a set future date. Futures started in the agricultural industry because they allowed farmers and food processors to lock in their prices early in the growing season, reducing the amount of uncertainty in their businesses. Futures have now been applied to many different assets, ranging from pork bellies (which really do trade — they are used to make bacon) to currency values. A simple example is a lock in a home mortgage rate; the borrower knows the rate that will be applied before the sale is closed and the loan is finalized. Day traders use futures to trade commodities without having to handle the actual assets.

Most futures contracts are closed out with cash before the settlement date. Financial contracts — futures on currencies, interest rates, or market index values — can only be closed out with cash. Commodity contracts may be settled with the physical items, but almost all are settled with cash. No one hauls a side of beef onto the floor of the Chicago Board of Trade!

As with options, futures contracts have value to both hedgers and speculators. Most futures are closed out with an offsetting contract before the expiration date, and the value can fluctuate quite a bit between the time that a contract is launched and its expiration, which creates a lot of opportunities for day traders.

Warrants

A *warrant* is similar to an option, but it's issued by the company rather than sold on an organized exchange. (After they are issued, warrants trade similarly to stocks.) A warrant gives the holder the right to buy more stock in the company at an agreed-upon price in the future.

A cousin of the warrant is the *convertible bond*, which is debt issued by the company. The company pays interest on the bond, and the bondholder has the right to exchange it for stock, depending on where interest rates and the stock price are. Convertibles trade on the stock exchanges.

Contract for difference (CFD)

A *contract for difference* allows traders to get exposure to an underlying asset, such as a share, index, currency, or commodity, without actually owning the asset itself.

CFDs are similar to futures contracts, but they have no fixed expiry date or contract size. A trader makes money depending on what the difference is between the initial contract price and the time the CFD is sold.

Buying and selling derivatives

Derivatives trade a little differently than other types of securities because they are based on promises. When someone buys an option on a stock, they aren't trading the stock with someone right now; they're buying the right to buy or sell it in the future. That means that the option buyer needs to know that the person on the other side is going to pay up. Because of that, the derivatives exchanges have systems in place to make sure that those who buy and sell the contracts will be able to perform when they have to. Requirements for trading derivatives are different than in other markets.

The different exchanges, not the companies or industries covered by the contracts, issue options and futures. You can buy and sell them through any brokerage firm that is registered with the exchanges. Most brokers handle options, but not all handle futures. (To be precise, a broker that handles futures is known as a *futures commission merchant*, or FCM). Your broker will require you to sign a form called an *options agreement* to show that you understand the risks involved in trading them.

TIP

The options and futures exchanges have an interest in getting more people to trade their products, so they offer great educational resources. The CME Institute has a lot of information that can help get you started at https://institute.cmegroup.com/.

How derivatives trade

The word *margin* is used differently than our discussion on Chapter 4 when discussing derivatives in part because derivatives are already leveraged. You aren't buying the asset, just exposure to the price change, so you can get a lot of bang for your buck. Margin increases your potential return as well as your potential risk, which is why they're popular with day traders.

REMEMBER

Margin in the derivatives market is the money you have to put up to ensure that you'll perform on the contract when it comes time to execute it. In the stock market, margin is collateral against a loan from the brokerage firm. In the derivatives markets, margin is collateral against the amount you may have to pay up on the contract. The more likely it is that you will have to pay the party who bought or sold the contract, the more margin money you have to put up. Some exchanges prefer to use the term *performance bond* instead of *margin*.

To buy a derivative, you put up the margin with the exchange's clearing house. That way, the exchange knows that you have the money to make good on your side of the deal — if, say, a call option that you sell is executed or you lose money on a currency forward that you buy. Your brokerage firm arranges for the deposit.

At the end of each day, derivatives contracts are *marked-to-market*, meaning that they are revalued. Profits are credited to the trader's margin account, and losses are deducted. If the margin falls below the necessary amount, the trader gets a call and has to deposit more money.

By definition, day traders close out at the end of every day, so their options aren't marked-to-market. The contracts are someone else's problem, and the profits or losses on the trade go straight to the margin account, ready for the next day's trading.

Where derivatives trade

In the olden days, derivative trading involved *open outcry* on physical exchanges. Traders on the floor received orders and executed them among themselves, shouting and using hand signals to indicate what they wanted to do. As we write this, vestiges of floor trading remain on some derivatives exchanges, but there are fewer and fewer of them.

The old-line exchanges, like the Chicago Board Options Exchange or the Montreal Exchange, still exist, although almost all of their operations are online. As electronic trading has become more popular, it has chased many experienced floor traders into retirement because they can't all make the transition, and it has caused much restructuring and consolidation among the exchanges.

Comprehending Arbitrage and the Law of One Price

Arbitrage literally means risk-free profit. It is possible to achieve this, sort of. Here's how it works:

In the financial markets, the general assumption is that, at least in the short run, the market price is the right price. Only investors, those patient, long-suffering accounting nerds willing to hold investments for years, see deviations between the market price and the true worth of an investment. For everyone else, especially day traders, what you see is what you get.

Under *the law of one price,* the same asset has the same value everywhere. If markets allow for easy trading — and the financial markets certainly do — then any price discrepancies are short-lived because traders immediately step in to buy at the low price and sell at the high price. In the following sections we explore how market efficiency limits arbitrage opportunities and how you can step in when the moment is right.

Understanding how arbitrage and market efficiency interact

The law of one price holds as long as markets are efficient, although market efficiency is a controversial topic in finance. In academic theory, markets are perfectly efficient, and arbitrage simply isn't possible. That makes a lot of sense if you're testing different assumptions about how the markets would work in a perfect world. Long-term investors would say that markets are inefficient in the short run but perfectly efficient in the long run, so they believe that if they do their research now, the rest of the world will eventually come around, allowing them to make good money.

Traders are somewhere in the middle in their perspective of market efficiency. The market price and volume are pretty much all the information they have to go on. The price may be irrational, but that doesn't matter today. The only thing a trader wants to know is whether an opportunity exists to make money given what's going on right now.

In the academic world, market efficiency comes in three flavours, with no form allowing for arbitrage:

>> **Strong form:** Everything, even inside information known only to company executives, is reflected in the security's price.

>> **Semi-strong form:** Prices include all public information, so profiting from insider trading may be possible.

>> **Weak-form:** Prices reflect all historical information, so research that uncovers new trends may be beneficial.

Those efficient-market true believers are convinced that arbitrage is imaginary because someone would've noticed a price difference between markets already and immediately acted to close it off. But who are those mysterious someones? They are day traders! Even the most devout efficient-markets adherent would, if pressed, admit that day traders perform a valuable service in the name of market efficiency. The 2008 financial crisis and the 2010 flash crash thinned the ranks of the efficient-market true believers.

Those with a less rigid view of market activity admit that arbitrage opportunities exist but that they are few and far between. A trader who expects to make money from arbitrage had better pay close attention to the markets to act quickly when a moment happens.

Finally, people who don't believe in market efficiency believe that market prices are usually out of sync with asset values. They do research in hopes of learning things that other people don't know. This mindset favours investors more than traders because it can take time for these price discrepancies to work themselves out.

TIP

Because arbitrage requires traders to work fast, it tends to work best for traders who are willing and able to automate their trading. If you're comfortable with programming and relying on software to do your work, arbitrage may be a great strategy for you. Remember that the big players have an advantage.

Creating synthetic securities

If you're feeling creative, then consider creating synthetic securities when looking for arbitrage opportunities. A *synthetic security* is a combination of assets that have the same profit-and-loss profile as another asset or group of assets. For example, a stock is a combination of a short *put option*, which has value if the stock goes down in price, and a long *call option*, which has value if the stock goes up in price. By thinking of ways to mimic the behaviour of an asset through a synthetic security, you can find more ways for an asset to be cheaper in one market than in another, leading to more potential arbitrage opportunities.

A typical arbitrage transaction involving a synthetic security, for example, involves shorting the real security and then buying a package of derivatives that match its risk and return. Many of the risk-arbitrage techniques involve the creation of synthetic securities.

One of the reasons that the different securities in this chapter were created was to help traders construct synthetic securities for both risk management and for trading opportunities. And, their very existence creates arbitrage opportunities where you may be able to profit.

REMEMBER

Complex arbitrage trading strategies require more testing and simulation trading (refer to Chapter 14 for more information) and may possibly involve losses while you fine-tune your methods. Be sure you feel comfortable with your trading method before you commit big time and big dollars to it.

Taking advantage of price discrepancies

So how can you as a day trader take advantage of what you know about the one-price rule? Suppose that what you see in New York isn't what you see in London, or that you notice that futures prices aren't tracking movements in the underlying asset. How about if you see that the stock of every company except one in an industry has reacted to a news event?

Well, then, you have an opportunity to make money, but you'd better act fast because other people will also probably see the discrepancy. What you do is simple: You sell as much of the high-priced asset in the high-priced market as you can, borrowing shares if you need to, and then you immediately turn around and buy the low-priced asset in the low-priced market.

TIP

Think of the markets as a scale, and you, the arbitrageur, must bring fairness to them. When the markets are out of balance, you take from the high-priced market (the heavier side of the scale) and return it to the low-priced market (the lighter side) until both even out at a price in between.

If you start with a high price of $8 and a low price of $6 and then buy at $6 and sell at $8, your maximum profit is $2 — with no risk. Until the point where the two assets balance at $7, you can make a profit on the difference between them.

Of course, most price differences are on the order of pennies, not dollars, but if you can find enough of these little pricing errors and trade them in size, you can make good money.

TIP

Sometimes, the price differences are less than a penny, a situation the traders call *subpennying*. A day trader really can't work with that amount. To see if subpennying is going on with an asset that you trade, set your price screens to display four decimal places rather than only two.

Reducing arbitrage opportunities: High-frequency trading

Most of the large brokerage firms and many large hedge funds have invested crazy amounts of time and money to develop *high-frequency* and *algorithmic* trading strategies. These strategies use computer programs that control billions of dollars and make extremely short-term trades — sometimes holding only for seconds — whenever the programs spot short-term discrepancies in the market. In some ways, this practice has made the market more efficient, because these program traders fix prices that are out of whack in no time. But they have also added to volatility, sometimes due to program glitches and sometimes because the trades go on even when they shouldn't, because no human is there to stop them.

In fact, many observers of the *market microstructure,* which is the underlying trading environment, think that the amount of high-frequency and algorithmic trading has reduced efficiency. They see evidence that the larger number of market participants have led to knee-jerk reactions when different programs malfunction or entire systems fail. The downside for the day trader is that these programs have eliminated many arbitrage opportunities that once made up the bread and butter of many a trader's earnings.

Chapter **6**

Increasing Risk and Potential Return with Short Selling and Leverage

In a certain sense, day trading isn't risky at all. Day traders close out their positions overnight to minimize the possibility of something going wrong while the trader isn't paying attention. Each trade is based on finding a small price change in the market over a short period of time, so nothing is likely to change dramatically. But here's the thing: Trading this way leads to small returns. Trading full time is hard to justify if you aren't making a lot of money when you do it, no matter how low your risk is.

And some days, there aren't many good trades to make. You may be looking for securities to go up, but they don't. Zero trades lead to zero risk — and zero return. For this reason, savvy traders think about other ways to make money on their trades, even when doing so involves taking on more risk. That risk is what generates the return that many traders crave.

In this chapter, we cover two techniques for finding trades and increasing returns: *short selling* and *leverage.* Both involve borrowing, and both increase risk. They're common to day trading, and other market participants as well use them, so the rules and procedures are set.

Understanding the Magic of Margin

The dollars you make from trading depend on two things: your percentage return on your trades and the dollars you have to start out with. If you double your money but have only a $1,000 account, you're left with $2,000. If you get a 10 percent return but have a $1,000,000 account, you make $100,000. Which would you rather have? (Yes, we know, you'd rather double your money with the $1,000,000 account. But we didn't give you that choice, alas.)

The point is that the more money you have to trade, the more dollars you can generate, even if the return on the trade itself is small. If you have $500,000 and borrow $500,000 more, then your 10 percent return gives you $100,000 to take home, not $50,000. You've doubled the dollars returned to you by doubling the money you used to place the trades, *not* by doubling the performance of the trade itself. Clever, huh?

REMEMBER

Here are two important things to remember about borrowing, which is known in trading as *leverage:*

>> Leverage gives you more money to trade, which helps you generate more dollars for your account — or lose more dollars, if you aren't careful or have a string of reversals.

>> When you borrow money or shares of stock, you have to pay it back, no matter what happens. That's why borrowing can be risky.

Day traders and other short-term traders aren't looking to make big money on any single trade. Instead, the goal is to make small money on a whole bunch of trades. Unfortunately, all those little trades don't easily add up to something big. That's why many day traders turn to leverage. They either borrow money or stock from their brokerage firm or they trade securities that have built-in leverage, such as futures and foreign exchange.

Making margin agreements

Leverage not only adds risk to your own account but also adds risk to the entire financial system. If everyone borrowed money and then some big market catastrophe happened, no one would be able to repay their loans, and the people who lent the money would go bust, too.

As a result, an incredible amount of oversight goes with leverage strategies. In Canada, IIROC and the Ontario Securities Commission regulate how much money a trader can borrow. In the U.S., that falls to the Securities and Exchange Commission, the Commodity Futures Trading Commission, the different exchanges, and even the U.S. Treasury Department. Many brokerage firms have even stricter rules in place as part of their risk management.

This extensive oversight means that you have about as much flexibility when you borrow from your broker to buy and sell securities as you would have if you borrowed from your friendly neighbourhood loan shark to play a high-stakes poker game. In other words, not much.

Margin loans, which are loans from your broker that increase your buying power, are highly regulated, and you must meet the broker's terms. If you fail to repay the loan, your positions will be sold from underneath you. If you try to borrow too much, you will be cut off. No amount of begging and pleading will help you.

Your brokerage firm makes you sign a margin agreement, which says that you understand the risks and limits of your activities. You probably can't have a margin account unless you meet a minimum account size, maybe $10,000 or more, and the amount you can borrow depends on the size of your account. Generally, a stock or bond account must hold 50 percent of the purchase price of securities when you borrow the money. The price of those securities can go down, but if they go down so much that the account ends up holding only 25 percent of the value of the loan, you get a margin call. (Some brokers call in loans faster than others; their policies are disclosed in their margin agreements.)

TIP

Brokerage firms handle margin trades all the time. You do the paperwork once, when you sign a margin agreement. Then each time you place an order, you're asked whether you're making the trade with cash or on margin. Click the box marked "Margin," and you've just borrowed money. It's that easy. The loan is automatically repaid when you close the position or when you deposit more money in your account.

Understanding the costs and fees of margin

Every brokerage firm charges interest on margin. The stated number is usually an annualized rate; if the rate given is 8 percent, for example, then you'd owe that much if your loan was outstanding for the entire year. (Some investors have margin loans in place that long.) A day trader, whose loan may only be outstanding for a few hours, probably has to pay interest, too. Some brokerage firms charge by the day; others may charge interest over three days because it takes three days for a trade to settle.

Determining margin rates

The interest rate that a brokerage firm charges varies over time. Many firms tie their margin rate to an underlying rate of interest in the broader market, such as *Libor* (the London Interbank Offering Rate, or what international banks charge each other for loans), the *prime rate* (the rate that Canadian and U.S. banks charge their best customers for loans), or another rate that is quoted in the financial markets. In fact, these rates are often used as the margin rates that the major banks charge their best and largest trading customers.

If you're a day trader with a few thousand dollars on account instead of a global bank's proprietary trading desk with a few billion, you'll pay a markup to the basic margin rate. These rates will fluctuate with the market rate of interest, so if interest rates go up in the economy as a whole, they'll increase for day traders, too.

REMEMBER

Some brokerage firms don't charge day traders commissions per trade, but they often have higher margin rates. Because most day trading is done on margin, be sure to compare the total cost of trading when comparing brokerage firms.

In addition to margin interest, some firms charge a higher commission on margin trades than for cash trades. They justify this policy with the higher levels of paperwork and risk management required on margin accounts. Some firms go with the higher commission rather than charge interest on intraday loans. Your trading life will be easier if you find out your firm's policies and fees before you open a margin account.

Margin in the derivatives markets

If you trade derivatives, margin works differently. Futures and options contracts themselves are leveraged, so you aren't charged interest. You have to settle your profits and losses at the end of the day, however (don't worry; the exchange's clearing house does it for you). You can't use the money held as margin for other trades. At some exchanges, margin is known as a performance bond.

Derivatives traders neither pay nor receive interest on the amount in their margin accounts because the market interest rate is included in the value of the option or the future.

Managing margin calls

If the value of your account starts falling and it looks like it's falling below the 25 percent maintenance margin limit, you get a *margin call,* in which your broker calls you and asks you to deposit more money in your account. If you can't make the necessary deposit, the broker starts selling your securities to close out the loan. And if you don't have enough to pay off the loan, the broker closes your account and puts a *lien,* which is a claim on your assets, against you.

TIP

Most brokerage firms have risk-management limits in place, so you'll probably get plenty of warning before you get a margin call or see your account closed out. After all, neither you nor your brokerage firm wants to lose money. Just keep in mind that a margin call is a possibility. If your account falls to the maintenance level, ask yourself, as objectively as you can, whether your idea is still good or whether you're just wishing and hoping that it is.

At least one brokerage firm advertises that, as a service to you, it will close out your account as soon as you lose the amount in it in order to keep you from losing more money. This service helps the brokerage firm as much as it helps you, because it keeps the firm from dealing with the hassles of chasing down additional margin. This is one example of the built-in risk management policies that firms use to limit risks to everyone.

Enjoying margin bargains for day traders

Day traders are often able to avoid margin calls because they borrow money for such short periods of time. Good day traders look for small market moves and cut their losses early, which minimizes the risk of using other people's money. And by definition, day traders close out their positions every night.

The Switch-Up of Short Selling

Traditionally, investors and traders want to buy low and sell high. They buy a position in a security and then wait for the price to go up. This strategy isn't a bad way to make money, especially because, if the country's economy continues to grow even a little bit, businesses are going to grow and so are their stocks.

But even in a good economy, some securities go down. The company may be mismanaged, it may sell a product that's out of favour, or maybe it's just having a string of bad days. For that matter, maybe it went up a little too much in price, and investors are now coming to their senses. In these situations, you can't make money buying low and selling high. Instead, you need a way to reverse the situation.

The solution? Selling short. In short — ha! — *selling short* means that you borrow a security and sell it in hopes of repaying the loan of the shares by buying back cheaper shares later on.

REMEMBER

In trading lingo, when you own something, you are considered to be *long*. When you sell it, especially if you do not already own it, you are considered to be *short*. You don't have to be long before you go short.

Selling short

Most brokerage firms make selling short easy. You simply place an order to sell the stock, and the broker asks whether you're selling shares that you own or selling short. After you place the order, the brokerage firm goes about borrowing shares for you to sell. It loans the shares to your account and executes the sell order.

REMEMBER

You can't sell short unless the brokerage firm is able to borrow the shares. Sometimes so many people have sold a stock short that no shares are left to borrow. In that case, you have to find another stock or another strategy.

When the shares are sold, you wait until the security goes down in price, and then you buy the shares in the market at a bargain. You then return these purchased shares to the broker to pay the loan, and you keep the difference between where you sold and where you bought — less interest, of course.

You can earn interest on the money you receive for selling the stock, and investors who are active on the short side of the market figure this into their returns. However, day traders don't hold on to their positions long enough to earn interest.

REMEMBER

The stock exchanges are in the business of helping companies raise money, so they have rules in place to help maintain an upward bias in the stock market. These rules can work against the short seller. The key regulation is what's called the *uptick rule,* which means you can only sell a stock short when the last trade was a move up. You can't short a stock that's moving down.

Figure 6-1 shows how short selling works. The trader borrows 400 shares selling at $25 each and then sells them. If the stock goes down, she can buy back the shares at the lower price, making a tidy profit. If the stock stays flat, she loses money because the broker will charge her interest based on the value of the shares she borrowed. And if the stock price goes up, she not only loses money on the interest expense but also is out on her investment.

The trader borrows 400 shares of SuperCorp shares to sell. The shares are trading at $25 each. She sells them for $10,000. The brokerage firm charges 10% interest

FIGURE 6-1:
Looking at short
selling in the
equities market.

Beginning Price	Shares Borrowed	Proceeds from Sale	Repurchase Price	Repurchase Cost	Loan Value	Net Profit	Interest Expense	Rate of Return	% Change in Stock Price
$ 25	400	$ 10,000	$ 40	$ (16,000)	10,000	$ (6,000)	$ 1,000	-70%	60%
$ 25	400	$ 10,000	$ 25	$ (10,000)	10,000	$ -	$ 1,000	-10%	0%
$ 25	400	$ 10,000	$ 15	$ (6,000)	10,000	$ 4,000	$ 1,000	30%	-40%

© John Wiley & Sons, Inc.

**TECHNICAL
STUFF**

The interest and fees that the broker charges traders who borrow stock accrue to the broker, not to the person who actually owns the stock. In fact, the stock's owner will probably never know that his shares were loaned out.

Short selling in Canada

Short selling is essentially the same no matter where you trade, but Canada has more relaxed rules around it than the U.S. For instance, unlike in the U.S., naked short selling is permitted. That's when a short seller sells shares that it doesn't own, and has made no prior arrangement to borrow or buy, but hopes to buy those shares before it has to settle the trade.

Naked short selling is particularly risky, because it increases the risk of a failed trade. It can also distort share prices and lead to what's called a *short and distort campaign.* That's when an investor shorts a stock and then spreads negative rumours about the company to drive down the stock price. It works best for naked short selling because traders can do their dirty work without having to borrow the security. It's only after the stock price declines that the traders buy the stock, which they then use to fulfill their short-selling contract. Profit is made off the spread of the borrowing price and the lower price at which the shares were delivered.

As well, unlike in the U.S., Canada doesn't have an uptick rule, which stops a short sale when a price declines rapidly over a specific period of time.

Choosing shorts

Investors — those people who do careful research and expect to be in their positions for months or even years — look for companies that have inflated expectations and are possibly fraudulent. Investors who work the short side of the market spend hours doing careful accounting research, looking for companies that are likely to go down in price some day.

Day traders don't care about accounting. They don't have the time to wait for a short to work out. Instead, they look for stocks that go down in price for more mundane reasons, like more sellers than buyers in the next ten minutes. Most day traders who sell short simply reverse their long strategy. For example, some day traders like to buy stocks that have gone down for three days in a row, figuring that they'll go up on the fourth day. They'll also short stocks that have gone up three days in a row, figuring that they'll go down on the fourth day. You don't need a CPA to do that!

Trading strategies are covered in more detail in Chapters 10 and 11, if you are looking for some ideas.

Losing your shorts?

Shorting stocks carries certain risks because a short sale is a bet on things going wrong. Because, in theory, there's no limit on how much a stock can go up, there's no limit on how much money a short seller can lose. Two traps in particular can get a short seller. The first is a short squeeze due to good news; the second is a concerted effort to hurt traders who are short.

Squeeze my shorts

With a *short squeeze,* a company that has been popular with a lot of short sellers has some good news that drives the stock price up. Or, maybe some other buyers simply drive up the price in order to force the shorts to sell, which is a common form of market manipulation. When the price goes up, short sellers lose money, and some may even have margin problems. And the original reason for going short may be proven to be wrong. Those who are short start buying the stock back to reduce their losses, but their increased demand drives the stock price even higher, causing even bigger losses for people who are still short. Ouch!

Calling back the stock

All is not sweetness and light in the world of short selling. Many market participants distrust those folks who are doing all the careful research, in part because they are often right. Company executives are often optimists who don't like to hear bad news, and they blame short sellers for all that is wrong with their stock price. Meanwhile, some short sellers have been known to get impatient and start spreading ugly rumours if their sale isn't making money.

Many companies, brokers, and investors hate short sellers and try tactics to bust them. Sometimes they issue good news or spread rumours of good news to create a squeeze. Other times, they collectively ask holders of the stock to request that their brokerage firm not loan out their shares, which means that those who shorted the stock have to buy back and return the shares even if doing so makes no sense.

Leveraging All Kinds of Accounts

Leverage is the use of borrowed money to increase returns. Day traders use leverage a lot to get bigger returns from relatively small price changes in the underlying securities. And as long as they consistently close their positions out at the end of the day, day traders can borrow more money and pay less interest than people who hold securities for a longer term.

The process of borrowing works differently in different markets. In the stock and bond markets, it's straightforward: When you place the order, you just tell your broker you're borrowing. In the options and futures markets, the contracts you buy and sell have leverage built in to them. Although you don't borrow money outright, you can control a lot of value in your account for relatively little money down. The following sections go into more detail on these points.

In stock and bond markets

Leverage is straightforward for buyers of stocks and bonds: You simply click the box marked "Margin" when you place your order, and the brokerage firm loans you money. Then when the security goes up in price, you get a greater percentage return because you've been able to buy more for your money. Of course, that also increases your potential losses. (For more detail on the margin process, head to the earlier section "Understanding the Magic of Margin.")

Figure 6-2 shows how leverage works. The trader borrows money to buy 400 shares of SuperCorp. If the stock goes up 4 percent, she makes 8 percent. Whoohooo! But if the stock goes down 4 percent, she still has to repay the loan at full dollar value, so she ends up losing 8 percent. That's not so good.

A trader buys $10,000 of SuperCorp with $5,000 of her own cash and a $5,000 loan
SuperCorp trades at $25/share, so the trader purchases a total of 400 shares.
The trader closes out at the end of the day, so no interest is charged.
What happens as the stock price changes?

Ending Price	Ending Value	Loan Value	Net Equity	Trader's Rate of Return	% Change in Stock Price
$ 26.00	$ 10,400	$ 5,000	$ 5,400	8%	4%
$ 25.50	$ 10,200	$ 5,000	$ 5,200	4%	2%
$ 25.00	$ 10,000	$ 5,000	$ 5,000	0%	0%
$ 24.50	$ 9,800	$ 5,000	$ 4,800	-4%	-2%
$ 24.00	$ 9,600	$ 5,000	$ 4,600	-8%	-4%

FIGURE 6-2:
An example of
trading stocks on
margin.

© John Wiley & Sons, Inc.

REMEMBER

If you hold your margin position overnight or longer, you have to start paying interest, which cuts into your returns or increases your losses.

In options markets

An *option* gives you the right, but not the obligation, to buy or sell a stock or other item at a set price when the contract expires. A *call option* gives you the right to buy, so you would buy a call if you think the underlying asset is going up. A *put option* gives you the right to sell, so you would buy a put if you think the underlying asset is going down. (You can read more about options in Chapter 4.) By trading an option, you get exposure to changes in the price of the underlying security without actually buying the security itself. That's the source of the leverage in the market.

A day trader can use options to get an exposure to price changes in a stock for a lot less money than buying the stock itself would cost. Suppose a call option is *deeply in the money,* meaning that its *strike price* (the price at which you would buy the stock if you exercised the option) is far below the current stock price. In this event, the obvious thing to do is to set option price at the difference between the current stock price and the strike price, which is more or less what happens — more in theory, less in practice. When the stock price changes, the option price changes by almost exactly the same amount, enabling you to buy the price performance of the stock at a discount, with the discount being the strike price of the option.

Figure 6-3 shows the performance-boosting leverage from this strategy. The trader buys call options with an exercise price of $10 on a stock trading at $25. The option price changes the same amount that the stock price does, but the call holder gets a greater percentage return than the stockholder.

A trader buys deep in-the-money call options on SuperCorp. The exercise price is $10, and the stock is trading at $25.

FIGURE 6-3:
How the option value changes with the stock price.

Stock Price	Initial Option Price	Exercise (Strike) Price	New Option Price	Stock Price Change	Option Price Change
$ 26.00	$ 15.00	$ 10.00	$ 16.00	4%	7%
$ 25.50	$ 15.00	$ 10.00	$ 15.50	2%	3%
$ 25.00	$ 15.00	$ 10.00	$ 15.00	0%	0%
$ 24.50	$ 15.00	$ 10.00	$ 14.50	-2%	-3%
$ 24.00	$ 15.00	$ 10.00	$ 14.00	-4%	-7%

© John Wiley & Sons, Inc.

Day traders can use many other options strategies, but a discussion of them goes beyond the scope of this book. The appendix has some resources to help you in your research.

In futures trading

A *futures* contract gives you the obligation to buy or sell an underlying financial or agricultural commodity, assuming you still hold the contract at the expiration date. That underlying product ranges from the value of treasury bonds to barrels of oil and heads of cattle, and you're only putting money down now when you purchase the contract. You don't have to come up with the full amount until the contract comes due — and almost all options and futures traders close out their trades long before the contract expiration date. Futures are discussed in Chapter 4, but here we talk about how leverage works in the futures market.

TECHNICAL STUFF

Although most options and futures contracts settle with cash long before the due date, contract holders have the right to hold them until the due date and, in the case of options on common stock and agricultural derivatives, demand physical delivery. It's rare, but the commodity exchanges have systems in place for determining the transport, specifications, and delivery of grain, cattle, or ethanol. One advantage of day trading is that you close out the same day, without ever even thinking about the fine print of physical delivery.

Because *derivatives* have built-in leverage that allows a trader to have big market exposure for relatively few dollars up front, they've become popular with day traders. Figure 6-4 shows how derivative leverage works. Here, a trader is buying the Chicago Mercantile Exchange's E-mini S&P 500 futures contract, which gives her exposure to the performance of the Standard and Poor's 500 Index, a standard measure of the stock performance of a diversified list of 500 large American companies. The futures contract trades at 50 times the value of the index, rounded to the nearest $0.25. The minimum margin that this trader must put down on the contract is $3,500. Each $0.25 change in the index leads to a $12.50 ($0.25 × 50) change in the value of the contract, and that $12.50 is added to or subtracted from the $3,500 margin.

A day trader buys a Chicago Mercantile Exchange E-Mini S&P 500 futures contract.
The contract price is $50 x the index level. To buy it, the trader must post margin of $3,500

Initial Index Value	Ending Index Value	Multiplier	Initial Contract Value	Contract Value	Value Change in Dollars	Value Change in Percent	Initial Margin	Ending Margin	Percent Change in Margin
1,457.50	1,458.50	$ 50.00	$ 72,875.00	$ 72,925.00	$ 50.00	0.07%	$ 3,500.00	$ 3,550.00	1.43%
1,457.50	1,458.00	$ 50.00	$ 72,875.00	$ 72,900.00	$ 25.00	0.03%	$ 3,500.00	$ 3,525.00	0.71%
1,457.50	1,457.50	$ 50.00	$ 72,875.00	$ 72,875.00	$ -	0.00%	$ 3,500.00	$ 3,500.00	0.00%
1,457.50	1,457.00	$ 50.00	$ 72,875.00	$ 72,850.00	$ (25.00)	-0.03%	$ 3,500.00	$ 3,475.00	-0.71%
1,457.50	1,456.50	$ 50.00	$ 72,875.00	$ 72,825.00	$ (50.00)	-0.07%	$ 3,500.00	$ 3,450.00	-1.43%

FIGURE 6-4: Margin and the derivatives trade with built-in leverage.

© John Wiley & Sons, Inc.

REMEMBER

Some exchanges use the term *margin,* and others prefer to use *performance bond.* Either term refers to the same thing: money you put in up front to ensure that you can meet the contract terms when it comes due. If you hold the contract overnight, your account is adjusted up or down to reflect the day's profits. If it gets too low, you're asked to add more money.

In foreign exchange

The *foreign exchange,* or *forex,* market is driven by leverage. Despite the nervous reports you may hear in the financial news, exchange rates tend to move slowly, by as little as a tenth or even a hundredth of a penny a day. And the markets are so huge that hedging risk is easier in the currency markets than in other financial markets. You may have trouble borrowing shares of stock that you want to short, but you should have no trouble ever borrowing yen. To get a big return, forex traders almost always borrow huge amounts of money.

In the stock market, day traders can generally borrow up to three times the amount of cash and securities held in their accounts. Forex trading is also regulated by IIROC. Although some offshore brokers will allow traders to borrow 400 times the amount in their accounts, legitimate Canadian firms will only let people borrow about 20 times. (You'll need to put up between 3 percent and 5 percent of a trade.)

Forex firms allow such huge borrowing because they can hedge their risks so that if you lose money, they make money. If you sell dollars to buy euros, for example, the firm can easily go in and sell euros to buy dollars. This capability makes its position net neutral. If the euro goes down relative to the dollar, you lose money, but the firm can offset its risk because its counter-trade went up. And, of course, the firm is receiving interest for the margin that you're using.

WARNING

The reason that a forex firm hedges its risks against its day trading customers is that most day traders lose money. The firm knows that if it bets against the aggregate trades held by its customers, it'll probably come out ahead. Don't trade in forex or any other market until you've worked out a strategy and practised it so that you can avoid becoming a statistic. Chapter 14 has information on testing and evaluating trading strategies.

Figure 6-5 shows how leverage in foreign exchange makes good returns possible. Here, the trader starts with a $1,000 account and borrows the maximum amount the forex firms allow, $400 for each dollar in the account. All $401,000 is put to work buying euros. Note that the euro value stays constant, but the dollar value of those euros changes by hundredths of a penny. Thanks to leverage, the return is 11 percent — not bad for a day's trading! Of course, you could lose 11 percent, which wouldn't be so good.

A trader has a $1,000 forex account. He borrows 400 times that amount — $400,000 — to buy euros.

FIGURE 6-5: Trading foreign exchange on margin.

Initial Dollar/Euro Rate	Ending Dollar/Euro Rate	Initial Account Value	Amount Purchased ($)	Amount Purchased (€)	Ending Value (€)	Ending Value ($)	Loan Value	Ending Account Value	Trader's Rate of Return	% Change in Exchange Rate
0.7477	0.7475	$ 1,000	$ 401,000	€ 299,828	€ 299,828	$ 401,107	$ 400,000	$ 1,107	11%	-0.03%
0.7477	0.7476	$ 1,000	$ 401,000	€ 299,828	€ 299,828	$ 401,054	$ 400,000	$ 1,054	5%	-0.01%
0.7477	0.7477	$ 1,000	$ 401,000	€ 299,828	€ 299,828	$ 401,000	$ 400,000	$ 1,000	0%	0.00%
0.7477	0.7478	$ 1,000	$ 401,000	€ 299,828	€ 299,828	$ 400,946	$ 400,000	$ 946	-5%	0.01%
0.7477	0.7479	$ 1,000	$ 401,000	€ 299,828	€ 299,828	$ 400,893	$ 400,000	$ 893	-11%	0.03%

© John Wiley & Sons, Inc.

An exchange rate is just the price of money. If the Canadian dollar–American dollar rate is 1.0121, that means one loonie will buy US$1.01.

Borrowing in Your Trading Business

Leverage is only part of the borrowing involved in your day trading business. Like any business owner, sometimes you need more cash than your business generates. Other times, you see expansion opportunities that require more money than you have on hand. In this section, we discuss why and how day traders can borrow money over and above leveraged trading.

Taking margin loans for cash flow

If day trading is your job, then you face a constant pressure: How do you cover the costs of living while keeping enough money in the market to trade? One way to do so is to have another source of income — from savings, a spouse, or a job that doesn't overlap with market hours. Other day traders take money out of their trading account.

If the market hasn't been cooperative, your account may not have enough in it to allow you to withdraw funds while still maintaining enough capital to trade. One option is to arrange a margin loan through a brokerage firm. With a margin loan, the firm lets you take out a loan against the cash in your account (or securities that you are holding, not trading). You can spend the money any way you like, but you're charged interest and you have to repay it. Still, a margin loan is a good option to know about because day-trade earnings tend to be erratic.

Borrowing for trading capital

Some day traders use a double layer of leverage: They borrow the money to set up their trading accounts and then they borrow money for their trading strategies. If the market cooperates, this type of borrowing can be a great way to make money, but if the market doesn't cooperate, you could end up owing a lot of people money that you don't have.

If you want to take the risk, though, you have a few resources to turn to other than your relatives: You can borrow against your house, use your credit cards, or find a trading firm that will give you some money to work with.

Borrowing against your house

Yes, you can use a mortgage or a home equity line of credit to get the money for your day trading activities. In general, this option carries low interest rates because your house is your collateral, plus the loan is tax deductible. Still, borrowing against your house can be a relatively low-cost way to pull value stored in your house for use in trading.

WARNING

The risk? If you can't pay back the loan, you can lose your residence. If you decide to pursue this strategy, just don't borrow against your car, too, because you'll need a place to live when the bank forecloses.

Putting it on the card

The business world is filled with people who started businesses using credit cards. And you can do that. If you have good credit, credit card companies are happy to lend to you.

WARNING

Naturally, credit card companies charge you a mighty high rate of interest, one that even the sharpest traders will have trouble covering from their returns. If the only way you can raise the capital for day trading is through your credit card, consider waiting a few years and saving your money before taking the plunge. Because day trading income can be erratic, you may end up using your credit cards to cover your living expenses some months. You may want to save your credit for that rather than dedicate it directly for your day trading.

Accepting risk capital from a prop trading firm

Some firms that are in the business of trading are willing to stake new traders. You may have to go through a training period or pay a fee to rent a desk at their office or to use their software remotely. The firm watches your trading patterns, including both your profits and your risk management. If the principals like what they see, they may offer you money to manage along with your own capital. You will receive a cut of the profits on the funds you trade for them.

WARNING

Borrowing money to expand your trading business may be a good idea. Borrowing money because you're and hoping that the next trade hits it big is a terrible, terrible idea.

Assessing Risks and Returns from Short Selling and Leverage

Leverage introduces risk to your day trading, and that can give you greatly increased returns. Most day traders use leverage, at least part of the time, to make their trading activities pay off in cold, hard cash. The challenge is to use leverage responsibly. Chapter 7 goes into money management in great detail, but here we cover the two issues most related to leverage: losing your money and losing your nerve. Understanding those risks can help you determine how much leverage you should take and how often you can take it.

Losing your money

Losing money is an obvious hazard. Leverage magnifies your returns, but it also magnifies your risks. Any borrowings have to be repaid regardless. If you buy or sell a futures or options contract, you are legally obligated to perform, even if you have lost money. That can be really hard.

REMEMBER

Day trading is risky in large part because of the amount of leverage used. If you don't feel comfortable with that, you may want to use little or no leverage, especially when you are new to day trading or when you are starting to work a new trading strategy.

Losing your nerve

The basic risk and return of your underlying strategy isn't affected by leverage. If you expect that your system will work about 60 percent of the time, that should hold no matter how much money is at stake or where that money came from. However, trading with borrowed money likely *does* make a difference to you on some subconscious level.

WARNING

Trading is very much a game of nerves. If you hesitate to make a trade, cut a loss, or otherwise follow your strategy, you're going to run into trouble.

Say you're trading futures and decide that you'll accept three downticks before selling and that you'll look for five upticks before selling. This strategy means you're willing to accept some loss, cut it if it gets out of hand, and then be disciplined about taking gains when you get them. It keeps a lid on your losses while forcing some discipline on your gains.

Now, suppose you're dealing with lots and lots of leverage. Suddenly, those downticks become too real to you — it's money you don't have. Next thing you know, you only accept two downticks before closing out. But doing so keeps you from getting winners. Then you decide to ride with your winners, and suddenly you aren't taking profits fast enough, and your positions move against you. Your fear of loss is making you sloppy. That's why many traders find it better to borrow less money and stick to their system rather than borrow the maximum allowed and let that knowledge cloud their judgment.

Chapter 7

Managing Your Money and Positions

You can't trade if you don't have money. Sure, your brokerage firm will loan you some funds, but only if you have some of your own funds to stake as margin. You have to keep some powder dry.

So how much of your money should you put on the line each time you trade? Risk too much, and you can be put out of business when you lose your capital. Risk too little, and you can be put out of business because you can't make enough money to cover your costs and time.

Over time, many academic theorists and experienced traders have developed different systems of money management designed to help traders, investors, and even gamblers manage their money in such a way as to maximize return while protecting capital. In this chapter, we explain how some of the better-known systems work so that you can figure out how to best apply them to your own trading. Doing so can help you protect your trading funds and figure out what size trades to enter so that you can stay trading as long as you like.

REMEMBER

Some of the material in this chapter is related to *leverage*, which is borrowing money to trade. Because leverage can dramatically increase the money that you have available to trade, as well as the risk and return profile of the trades that you make, it affects how you manage your money. Flip to Chapter 6 for more information on leverage and why you may want to use it.

Setting Your Earnings Expectations

Return is a function of risk. If you want a guaranteed return, go down to your bank and open a savings account. The returns will be almost comically low, but you'll have no risk. If you want anything higher than what your bank is quoting, well, you have to take on at least a little bit of risk. When you take on risk, you increase both your likelihood of return and your likelihood of loss.

Successful day traders lose money all the time, but they're able to keep trading. If you're looking at a trade with even a 0.5 percent chance of 100 percent loss, the odds indicate that you would lose everything over the course of 200 trades — but only if you put all your money into each trade. If you put only some of your money in that trade, then you'll never lose everything in it. Sure, you won't get all of the upside potential, but you'll be able to hit the potential high return more often because you can make that trade more often.

REMEMBER

The key term in investing is *diversification*: If your money is spread out among different assets, your long-return return will be higher for less total risk than if you commit to only one asset.

Trading isn't investing, but the power of diversification holds. If you divide your money among a few different trades or always keep some cash on hand in your account for the next trade, you'll almost definitely make more money in the long run than if you put all your money on one idea. Sure, risking everything on one idea may work a few times, but are you that lucky? If you're smart about your money management, you don't need luck.

Finding your expected return

Before you can figure out how to manage your money, you need to figure out how much money you can expect to make. This amount is your *expected return*, although some traders prefer the word *expectancy*. You start by laying out your trading system and testing it (refer to Chapter 14). You're looking for four numbers:

>> How many of your trades are losers?

>> What's the typical percentage loss on a losing trade?

>> How many of your trades are winners?

>> What's the typical percentage gain on a winning trade?

Say that you determine that a certain trade loses 40 percent of the time, and it loses 1 percent. Sixty percent of the time, the trade wins, and winning trades are up 1.5 percent. With these numbers, you can calculate your per-trade expected return, like this:

% of losing trades × loss on losing trades + % of winning trades × gain on winning trades = expected return

Which in this example works out to be

$0.40 \times -0.01 + 0.60 \times 0.015 = -0.004 + 0.009 = 0.005$, which is the same as 0.5%.

On average, then, you would expect to earn 0.5 percent on every trade you make. Make enough trades with enough money, and it adds up.

REMEMBER

You are more likely to make more money if you have a high expectation of winning trades and if those winners are expected to perform well. As long as probability of loss exists, you stand to lose money.

Determining your probability of ruin

Expected return is the happy number. It's how much money you can expect to make if you stay in the trading game. But it has a counterpart that, while not so happy, is at least as important: the *probability of ruin.*

Yes, ruin.

As long as some probability of loss exists, no matter how small, there is some probability that you can lose everything when you're trading. How much you can lose depends on how large each trade is relative to your account, the likelihood of each trade having a loss, and the size of the losses as they occur. (Don't think it can happen? That's what the top executives at AIG, Bear Stearns, Lehman Brothers, and Washington Mutual said.)

Many traders who have winning trading strategies find themselves shut down because a few bad trades ruined them. Every trader has some losses, but these losses don't have to end your trading career if you know the probability of ruin and how to use it. The equation you use to calculate the probability of ruin (R) is

$$R = \left[\frac{1-A}{1+A} \right]^{C}$$

In this equation, A is the advantage on each trade. That's the difference between the percentage of winning trades and the percentage of losing trades. In the expected return example discussed earlier, trades win 60 percent of the time and lose everything 40 percent of the time. In that case, the trader's advantage would be

60% – 40% = 20%

And c is the number of trades in an account. Assume that you're dividing the account into ten equal parts, with the plan of making ten trades today. The probability of ruin today is 1.7 percent, as shown in this equation:

$$1.7\% = \left[\frac{1-0.20}{1+0.20} \right]^{10}$$

Now 1.7 percent isn't a high likelihood of ruin, but it's not zero, either. It can happen. If your advantage is smaller, if the expected loss is larger, or if the number of trades is fewer, then the likelihood becomes even higher.

Figure 7-1 shows you the relationship between the trader's advantage, number of trades, and the corresponding probability of ruin, rounded to the nearest percentage.

Probability of Ruin

Trader's Advantage		Number of Trades									
		1	2	3	4	5	6	7	8	9	10
	2%	96%	92%	89%	85%	82%	79%	76%	73%	70%	67%
	4%	92%	85%	79%	73%	67%	62%	57%	53%	49%	45%
	6%	89%	79%	70%	62%	55%	49%	43%	38%	34%	30%
	8%	85%	73%	62%	53%	45%	38%	33%	28%	24%	20%
	10%	82%	67%	55%	45%	37%	30%	25%	20%	16%	13%
	12%	79%	62%	49%	38%	30%	24%	18%	15%	11%	9%
	14%	75%	57%	43%	32%	24%	18%	14%	10%	8%	6%
	16%	72%	52%	38%	27%	20%	14%	10%	8%	5%	4%
	18%	69%	48%	34%	23%	16%	11%	8%	5%	4%	3%
	20%	67%	44%	30%	20%	13%	9%	6%	4%	3%	2%

FIGURE 7-1:
Adding trader's advantage to the mix.

© John Wiley & Sons, Inc.

The bigger the edge and the more trades you can make, the lower your probability of ruin. Now, this model is a simplification in that it assumes that a losing trade goes to zero, and that's not always the case. In fact, if you use stops you should never have a 100 percent loss. But you can see steady erosion in your account that will make it harder for you to make money. Hence, probability of ruin is a useful calculation that shows whether you'll lose money in the long run.

REMEMBER

The more trades you can make with your account, the lower your probability of ruin. That's why money management is a key part of risk management.

Gaining Advantage with a Money-Management Plan

As long as there's some chance of losing all your money, you want to avoid betting it all on any one trade. But as long as there's a chance of making money, you want to have enough exposure to a winning trade so that you can post good profits. How do you figure out how much money to risk?

Later in this chapter, we describe some of the different money-management systems that traders use to figure out how much money to risk per trade. But first, we want to explain the logic behind a money-management system so that you understand why you need one. That way, you can better manage your funds and improve the dollar returns to your trading.

Minimizing damage while increasing opportunity

Expected return gives you an idea of how much you can get from a trade on average, but it doesn't tell you how much that return may vary from trade to trade. The average of 9, 10, and 11 is 10; the average of −90, 10, and 110 is also 10. The first number series is a lot narrower than the second. The wider the range of returns that a strategy has, the more *volatile* it is.

Day traders seek more volatile securities because they offer more opportunities to make money during any given day. For this reason, they need to have ways to minimize the damage that may occur while being able to capitalize on the upward swings. Money management can help with that.

MEASURING VOLATILITY

You can measure volatility in several ways. One common measurement is *standard deviation,* which tells you how much your actual return is likely to differ from what you expect to get. The higher the standard deviation, the more volatile, and riskier, the strategy.

In the derivatives markets, volatility is measured by a group of numbers known as the *Greeks:* delta, gamma, vega, and theta. These numbers are based on calculus, but don't worry if you forgot it or never took it!

- **Delta** is a ratio that tells you how much the option or future changes in price when the underlying security or market index changes in price. Delta changes over time.

- **Gamma** is the rate of change on delta. A derivative's delta will be higher when it is close to the expiration date, for example, than when the expiration date is further away.

- **Vega** is the amount that the derivative would change in price if the implied volatility of the underlying security shifted by 1 percent.

- **Theta** is the amount that a derivative's price declines as it gets closer to the day of expiration.

Staying in the market longer

You have only a limited amount of money to trade. Whether it's $1,000 or $1,000,000, once the money's gone, you're out. The problem is that you can have a long string of losing trades before the markets go in a direction that favours you and your system.

Say you trade 100 percent of your account. If you have one trade that goes down 100 percent, then you have nothing. If you divide your account into ten parts, then you can have ten total losers before you're out. If you start with ten equal parts and double each time you lose, you can be out after four losing trades.

On the other hand, if you divide your account into 100 portions, then you can endure 100 losing trades. If you trade fractions of your account, then you can keep going indefinitely, or at least until you get down to a level that's too low to place a minimum order. (That's the philosophy behind the Kelly criterion, described later in this chapter.) Money management can keep you in the game longer, and that gives you more opportunities to place winning trades.

REMEMBER

The riskier your trading strategy, the more thought you need to put into money management. Otherwise, you can find yourself out of the market in no time.

Getting out before you lose everything

A money-management system works best if the trader using it knows when to close out a position. You have to have a trading plan and know when you're willing to get out: at the recent high? A few ticks below the most recent high? A few ticks up from where you entered? A few ticks below where you entered, to limit your losses?

Sometimes the market will go nuts, and you won't be able to get out as quickly as you'd like. In these situations, those tiny chances of losing everything kick in, and good money management offers the most protection.

On more ordinary trading days, be sure to supplement your position size and capital protection efforts with ordinary trading tools: trade planning and use of stop and limit orders.

Accounting for opportunity costs

Opportunity cost is the value you give up because you choose to do something else. In trading, each dollar you commit to one trade is a dollar that you cannot commit to another trade. Thus, each dollar you trade carries some opportunity cost, and good traders seek to minimize this cost. During the course of the trading day, you may see several great trades, and some opportunities will show up before you are ready to close out a different trade.

Because a money-management system holds back some of your capital, you are more likely to have funds to take advantage of these opportunities than if you allocate your cash willy-nilly. Your plan may cause you to miss some trades, and that's okay. If you believe that you are missing too many, though, you may want to experiment with another system to see whether it gives you better results. Whatever you do, don't ignore money management.

REMEMBER

If you have committed all your capital to one trade, you miss out on the second. That alone is a good reason to keep some money on the table each time you trade.

Examining Styles of Money Management

Over the years, traders have developed many different ways to manage their money. Some money-management strategies are rooted in superstition, but most are based on different statistical probability theories. The underlying idea is that you should never place all of your money in a single trade. Instead, you should put in an amount appropriate given the level of volatility. Otherwise, you risk losing everything too soon.

TIP

Calculating position size under many of these formulas is tricky stuff. That's why brokerage firms and trading software packages often include money-management calculators. Check Chapter 15 for more information on the brokers and Chapter 13 for more on different software and research services.

In the following sections, we offer a sampling of the many different money-management methods available. Other methods are out there, and none is suitable to all markets all the time. If you trade both options and stocks, you may want to use one system for option trades and another for stock trades. And if that's your situation, you have one big money-management decision to make before you begin: how much money to allocate to each market!

Limiting portions: Fixed fractional

Fixed-fractional trading assumes that you want to limit each trade to a set portion of your total account, often between 2 and 10 percent. Within that range, you trade a larger percentage of money in less risky trades and a smaller amount of money for more risky trades. (In other words, this method isn't all that "fixed," but no one asked us to pick a name for the system!)

Here's the fixed fractional equation for calculating fixed-fractional trade proportions:

$$N = f\left(\frac{equity}{|trade\ risk|}\right)$$

N is the number of contracts or shares of stock you should trade, *f* is the fixed fraction of your account that you have decided to trade, *equity* is the value of your total account, and *trade risk* is the amount of money you could lose on the transaction. Because trade risk is a negative number, you need to convert it to a positive number to make the equation work. Those vertical bars in the equation (| |) are the sign for absolute value, and that means that you convert the number between them to a positive number.

Here's an example that uses the equation. Assume that you've decided to limit each trade to 10 percent of your account, you have a $20,000 account, and you are looking at contracts with a value of $3,500. You want to set your trade based on the assumption that the contracts go to zero, to look at the worst-case scenario. Plugging the numbers into the equation and doing the math gives you

$$0.57 = 0.10\left(\frac{20,000}{|-3,500|}\right)$$

Of course, you probably can't trade 0.57 of a contract, so in this case, you would have to round up to one.

Protecting profits: Fixed ratio

Developed by a trader named Ryan Jones, the *fixed-ratio* money-management system is used in trading options and futures. The idea behind fixed-ratio trading is to help you increase your exposure to the market while protecting your accumulated profits.

To find the optimal number of options or futures contracts to trade, you use this equation:

$$N = 0.50\left(\sqrt{1+8\left(P/\Delta\right)}+1\right)$$

N is the number of contracts or shares of stock that you should trade, P is your accumulated profit to date, and δ (delta) is the dollar amount you would need before you could trade a second contract or another lot of stock. (Don't confuse this delta with the delta used to measure volatility; see the sidebar "Measuring volatility" for more information.)

For example, the minimum margin for Chicago Mercantile Exchange E-mini S&P 500 futures contract, which gives you exposure to the Standard & Poor's 500 stock index, is $3,500. Until you have another $3,500 in your account, you can't trade a second contract. If you use fixed-ratio money management to trade this future, your delta is $3,500.

Here's an example that uses fixed-ration calculation. Assume your delta is $3,500 and that you have $10,000 in account profits. If you plug in the numbers and calculate, you see that you should trade 2.94 contracts:

$$2.94 = 0.50\left(\sqrt{1+8\left(10,000/3,500\right)}+1\right)$$

What this means is that you can trade only one or two contracts, nothing in between. That's one of the imperfections of most money-management systems.

Sticking to 10 percent: Gann

William Gann developed a complicated system for identifying securities trades. Part of his system was a list of rules for managing money, and many traders follow that if nothing else.

TIP

The primary rule is this: Divide your money into ten equal parts and never place more than one 10 percent portion on a single trade. This strategy helps control your risk, whether or not you use Gann. (We discuss Gann in Chapter 9.)

Finding the ideal percentage: Kelly criterion

The Kelly criterion lets you determine the ideal percentage of your portfolio to put at risk. To calculate how much of your portfolio to put at risk, you need to know what percentage of your trades are expected to win, the return from a winning trade, and the ratio performance of winning trades to losing trades. The shorthand that many traders use for the Kelly criterion is edge divided by odds, and in practice, the formula looks like this:

$$\text{Kelly \%} = W - \left(\frac{1-W}{R}\right)$$

W is the percentage of winning trades, and R is the ratio of the average gain of the winning trades relative to the average loss of the losing trades.

To see this formula in action, consider a system that loses 40 percent of the time with a loss of 1 percent and that wins 60 percent of the time with a gain of 1.5 percent. (Look familiar? We used this same example at the beginning of the chapter.) Plugging that info into the Kelly formula, the right percentage to trade is 33.3 percent:

$$\text{Kelly \%} = W - \left(\frac{1-W}{R}\right) = 0.60 - \left(\frac{1-0.60}{0.015/0.010}\right) = 33.3\%$$

In this situation, as long as you limit your trades to no more than 33 percent of your capital, you should never run out of money. The problem, of course, is that if you have a long string of losses, you can find yourself with too little money to execute a trade. Many traders use a "half-Kelly" strategy, limiting each trade to half the amount indicated by the Kelly criterion, as a way to keep the trading account from shrinking too quickly. They are especially likely to do this if the Kelly criterion generates a number greater than about 20 percent, as it does in this example.

TECHNICAL
STUFF

This money-management method emerged from statistical work done at Bell Laboratories in the 1950s. The goal was to figure out the best ways to manage signal-noise issues in long-distance telephone communications. Very quickly, the mathematicians who worked on it saw that it could be applied to gambling, and in no time, the formula took off. In fact, a math professor, Edward O. Thorpe, used the Kelly criterion with great success to win big at blackjack in Las Vegas in the early 1960s, which led to a change in casino rules.

In a casino, the rules are against you. If you find an edge, in no time, you'll be asked to leave, and the rules may be changed. In the financial markets, the odds are even or slightly in your favour, so you have a better opportunity to make money by practising your strategies.

Doubling down: Martingale

The *martingale* style of money management is common with serious casino gamblers, and many traders apply it as well. It's designed to improve the amount of money you can earn in a game that has even odds. Most casino odds favour the house (roulette wheels used to be evenly black and red, but casinos found that they could make more money if they inserted a green slice for zero, thus throwing off the odds). Day trading, on the other hand, is a zero-sum game, especially in the options and futures markets. For every winner, there is a loser, so the odds of any one trade being successful are even. The martingale system is designed to work in any market where the odds are even or in your favour.

Under the martingale strategy, you start with a set amount per trade, say $2,000. If your trade succeeds, you trade another $2,000. If your trade loses, you double your next order (after you close or limit the first trade) so that you can win back your loss. (You may have heard gamblers talk about *doubling down?* Well, this is what they're doing.)

REMEMBER

Under the martingale system, you always come out ahead *as long as you have an infinite amount of money to trade.* See the problem? You can run out of money before you have a trade that works. The market, on the other hand, has almost infinite resources because of the huge volume of participants coming and going all over the world. In short, you're at an enormous disadvantage. As long as you have a disadvantage, thoughtful money management is critical.

Letting a program guide you: Monte Carlo simulation

If you have the programming expertise or buy the right software, you can run what's called a *Monte Carlo simulation,* named for the famous casino town. In this calculation, you enter in your risk and return parameters and your account value and let the program run. It then returns the optimal trade size. The system is not perfect; it can't incorporate every market situation that you'll face, and it has the fractional trade problem that the other systems do. But it has one big advantage: It can incorporate random changes in the markets in ways that simpler money-management models cannot.

There are different schools of thought about the statistical theories that go into a Monte Carlo simulation. Fortunately, you don't have to know them to use the system's estimates of the return in the market to help you determine your position sizes as the market changes.

TIP

A Monte Carlo simulation is more dynamic than most of the other money-management systems, but it isn't as easy to use. For that reason, it isn't a do-it-yourself project unless you have extensive experience creating these programs. If you are interested, you need to find a suitable program. Many brokerage firms include Monte Carlo simulation packages in their day trading platforms.

Considering past performance: Optimal F

The *Optimal F* system of money management was devised by Ralph Vince, and he's written several books about this and other money-management issues (see the appendix for more information). The idea is that you determine the ideal fraction of your money to allocate per trade based on past performance. If your Optimal F is 18 percent, then each trade should be 18 percent of your account — no more, no less. The system is similar to the fixed-fraction and fixed-ratio methods discussed earlier but with a few differences.

To find the number of shares of stock, *N*, to trade under Optimal F, you use this equation:

$$N = \frac{\left(F \times \dfrac{equity}{risk} \right)}{price}$$

F is a factor based on the basis of historical data, *risk* is the biggest percentage loss that you experienced in the past, *equity* is the amount of money in your account, and *price* is the current price. Using these numbers, you can find the contracts or shares you need to buy.

Here's an example: Assume your account has $25,000, your biggest loss (risk) was 40 percent, your *F* is 30 percent, and you're looking at a stock trading at $25 per share. Plug in the numbers and calculation to find that you should buy 750 shares:

$$750 = \frac{\left(0.30 \times \dfrac{25,000}{0.40} \right)}{25}$$

The Optimal F number itself is a mean based on historical trade results. The risk number is also based on past returns, and that's one problem with this method: It kicks in only after you have some trade data. A second problem is that you need to set up a spreadsheet to calculate it (so read Ralph Vince's book if you want to try it out). Some traders only use Optimal F in certain market conditions, in part because the history changes each time a trade is made, and that history doesn't always lead to usable numbers.

How Money Management Affects Your Return

Describing why you need money management is one thing, but showing you how it works is more fun. And because Ann loves making spreadsheets (we all need a hobby, right?), she pulled one together to show you how different ways of managing your money may affect your return.

In Figure 7-2, Ann started with the expected return assumptions that she used in the earlier example: 40 percent of the time a trade loses, and it loses 1 percent. The trade wins 60 percent of the time, and winning trades are up 1.5 percent. She picked a hypothetical account of $20,000 and set up mock trades using these expected return numbers. Then she compared the performance of martingale and Kelly money management to betting the whole account each time.

As the calculations in Figure 7-2 show, you end up with the most money from trading the entire account. That doesn't mean you always get the most money this way, just that that's how the numbers worked out in this case, given the 60/40 win ratio and a 3/2 winning size/losing size ratio. (Keep in mind that if you were using a Kelly or martingale system, you'd probably be doing something with the rest of the account rather than just letting it sit there.)

REMEMBER

This is just an example, applying some different strategies to different hypothetical returns. We're not recommending any one system over another. The best system for you depends on what assets you're trading, your personal trading style, and how much money you have to trade.

Martingale: Starting with 10% and Doubling Losses

	Performance	Intial Account Value	% Traded	Amount Traded	Ending Account Value	% Change
Trade 1	1.5%	$ 20,000	10%	$ 2,000	$ 20,030	
Trade 2	1.5%	$ 20,030		$ 2,000	$ 20,060	
Trade 3	-1.0%	$ 20,060		$ 2,000	$ 20,040	
Trade 4	-1.0%	$ 20,040		$ 4,000	$ 20,000	
Trade 5	1.5%	$ 20,000		$ 8,000	$ 20,120	
Trade 6	1.5%	$ 20,120		$ 2,000	$ 20,150	
Trade 7	-1.0%	$ 20,150		$ 2,000	$ 20,130	
Trade 8	-1.0%	$ 20,130		$ 4,000	$ 20,090	
Trade 9	1.5%	$ 20,090		$ 8,000	$ 20,210	
Trade 10	1.5%	$ 20,210		$ 2,000	$ 20,240	1.20%

Kelly: Trading 33%

	Performance	Intial Account Value	% Traded	Amount Traded	Ending Account Value	
Trade 1	1.5%	$ 20,000	33%	$ 6,660	$ 20,100	
Trade 2	1.5%	$ 20,100	33%	$ 6,693	$ 20,200	
Trade 3	-1.0%	$ 20,200	33%	$ 6,727	$ 20,133	
Trade 4	-1.0%	$ 20,133	33%	$ 6,704	$ 20,066	
Trade 5	1.5%	$ 20,066	33%	$ 6,682	$ 20,166	
Trade 6	1.5%	$ 20,166	33%	$ 6,715	$ 20,267	
Trade 7	-1.0%	$ 20,267	33%	$ 6,749	$ 20,199	
Trade 8	-1.0%	$ 20,199	33%	$ 6,726	$ 20,132	
Trade 9	1.5%	$ 20,132	33%	$ 6,704	$ 20,233	
Trade 10	1.5%	$ 20,233	33%	$ 6,738	$ 20,334	1.67%

Betting Everything

	Performance	Intial Account Value	% Traded	Amount Traded	Ending Account Value	
Trade 1	1.5%	$ 20,000	100%	$ 20,000	$ 20,300	
Trade 2	1.5%	$ 20,300	100%	$ 20,300	$ 20,605	
Trade 3	-1.0%	$ 20,605	100%	$ 20,605	$ 20,398	
Trade 4	-1.0%	$ 20,398	100%	$ 20,398	$ 20,194	
Trade 5	1.5%	$ 20,194	100%	$ 20,194	$ 20,497	
Trade 6	1.5%	$ 20,497	100%	$ 20,497	$ 20,805	
Trade 7	-1.0%	$ 20,805	100%	$ 20,805	$ 20,597	
Trade 8	-1.0%	$ 20,597	100%	$ 20,597	$ 20,391	
Trade 9	1.5%	$ 20,391	100%	$ 20,391	$ 20,697	
Trade 10	1.5%	$ 20,697	100%	$ 20,697	$ 21,007	5.04%

© John Wiley & Sons, Inc.

FIGURE 7-2: How money management affects your return.

Planning for Your Profits

In addition to determining how much to trade each time you place an order, you need a plan for what to do with the profits that accumulate in your account. That's as much a part of money management as calculating your probability of ruin and determining trade size.

Are you going to add the money to your account and trade it as before? Leverage your profits by trading them more aggressively than your core account? Pull money out and put it into long-term investments? Or a combination of the three? The following sections explore some of your options.

Compounding interest

Compound interest is a simple concept: Every time you get a return, that return goes into your account. You keep earning a return on it, which increases your account size some more. You keep earning a return on your return, and pretty soon, the numbers get to be pretty big.

To benefit from that compounding, many traders add their profits back into their accounts and keep trading them as a way to build account size. Although day traders earn little to no interest (which is compensation for loaning out money — say, by buying bonds), the basic principle holds: By returning profits to the trading account to generate even more profits, the account should grow over time.

TIP

This practice of keeping profits in the account to trade makes a lot of sense for smaller traders who want to build their accounts and take more significant positions over time.

Pyramiding power

Pyramiding involves taking trading profits and borrowing heavily against them to generate even more profits. Traders usually do this during the day, using unrealized profits in trades that are not yet closed as collateral for loans used to establish new positions. If the new positions are profitable, the trader can keep borrowing until it's time to close everything at the end of the day.

WARNING

Pyramiding works great as long as the markets are moving in the right direction. If all the positions in the pyramid remain profitable, you can make a lot of money during the course of the day. But if one of those positions turns against you, then the structure collapses and you end up with a call on your margin.

Figure 7-3 starts with an initial trade of $2,000 and assumes a return of 10 percent on each transaction — not realistic, necessarily, but it makes for a nice chart. If the profits from each trade are used as collateral for borrowing, and if that 10 percent return holds all day, then the trader can make 17 percent by pyramiding those gains. If a reversal hits before the end of the trading session and the positions lose 10 percent, then pyramiding magnifies the losses — assuming your broker would let you keep borrowing. After all, the borrowed money has to be repaid regardless of what happens in the market.

Pyramiding magnifies returns
Assume that you need to maintain 25% margin

	Initial Trade Equity	Amount Borrowed	Total Trade Size	Profit at 10% Return
First trade	$ 2,000	$ -	$ 2,000	$ 200
Second trade	$ 200	$ 600	$ 800	$ 80
Third trade	$ 80	$ 240	$ 320	$ 32
Fourth trade	$ 32	$ 96	$ 128	$ 13
Fifth trade	$ 13	$ 38	$ 51	$ 5
Sixth trade	$ 5	$ 15	$ 20	$ 2

Return on initial $2,000 trade: $ 332
Percentage return: 17%

. . . And pyramiding magnifies losses

	Initial Trade Equity	Amount Borrowed	Total Trade Size	Profit at 10% Return
First trade	$ 2,000	$ -	$ 2,000	$ (200)
Second trade	$ 200	$ 600	$ 800	$ (80)
Third trade	$ 80	$ 240	$ 320	$ (32)
Fourth trade	$ 32	$ 96	$ 128	$ (13)
Fifth trade	$ 13	$ 38	$ 51	$ (5)
Sixth trade	$ 5	$ 15	$ 20	$ (2)

Return on initial $2,000 trade: $ (332)
Percentage return: -17%

FIGURE 7-3:
Pyramiding
magnifies returns
and losses.

© John Wiley & Sons, Inc.

REMEMBER

Pyramiding is not related to a pyramid scheme. In trading terms, *pyramiding* is a way to borrow against your profits to generate even bigger profits. A *pyramid scheme* is a fraud that requires participants to recruit new members, and fees paid by the new members go to the older ones. Eventually, the pyramid collapses because recruiting new members gets too difficult and those at the bottom get nothing. Be aware that some investment frauds have been structured as pyramid schemes. Steer clear of deals that sound fabulous and require you to recruit others.

Pyramiding increases your trading risk but also your expected return. It's a useful way to grow a portion of your trading account, especially when the market is favouring your trading system. This technique is good for medium-sized accounts, which have enough money that, if a pyramid were to collapse on you, you'd still have enough to stay in the market.

Making regular withdrawals

Because day trading can be so risky, many traders look to diversify their total financial risk. One way to do this is to pull money out of the trading account to put into a less volatile long-term investment. Many traders routinely pull out a percentage of their profits and put that money into government bonds, a low-risk mutual fund, or real estate. None of these investments is as glamorous or exciting as day trading, but that's the point: Trading is hard work, and anyone can lose money any day, no matter how big his account is or how much money he's made so far. By moving some money out, a trader can build a cushion for a bad trading stretch, prepare for retirement, and have some money to walk away for a short period or even forever. Having money in low-risk investments can greatly reduce the stress and the fear that go with trading.

TIP

The larger the account, the easier it is to pull money out, but even smaller traders should consider taking 5 or 10 percent of each quarter's profits and moving them into another type of investment. Many brokerage firms can set up automatic withdrawal plans that zap money from your trading account to a stock or bond mutual fund if you don't trust yourself to do it.

Chapter **8**

Planning Your Trades and Trading Your Plans

This chapter may be one of the most important chapters in this book. Day trading isn't a mad frenzy of order entry, nor it is a software package that you can buy, set, and forget. If you want to be successful, you have to put some time and attention into your trading. Before you trade, you need to think through what you want to do and how to do it. Afterward, you want to evaluate what you did and whether to do the same thing next time.

The best traders have plans for their trades. They know in advance how they want to trade and what they expect to do when they face the market. They may, at times, find themselves deviating from their plans, due to luck or circumstance or changing markets, but in those cases, they understand why they're trying something else. Even experienced day traders make notes about their trades. In fact, the planning is what allows a novice day trader to stay in the game long enough to become experienced.

Trading comes in many flavours, and many of those who call themselves day traders are actually doing other things with their money. More than a few are actually gambling. If you know in advance what you want to do, not only will you be less likely to panic or follow fads, but you'll also be in a better position to take advantage of opportunities in a way that suits your personality, trading skills, and goals. You'll be more likely to make money because you'll see when the market is moving your favour. And that's why this entire chapter is devoted to planning.

REMEMBER

Failing to plan is planning to fail. And if you can't remember that right now, don't worry. We repeat it several times.

Starting to Plan Your Trades: Just the Basics, Please

A good trader has a plan. She knows what she wants to trade and how to trade it. She knows what her limits are before she places the order. She's not afraid to take a loss now in order to prevent a bigger loss in the future, and she's willing to sit out the market if nothing is happening that day. Her plan gives her the discipline to protect her capital so that she has money in her account when the opportunities present themselves.

In this section, we cover the components of trade planning. When you start trading, you'll probably write notes each day to form a trading plan that covers what you expect for the day, what trades you hope to make, and what your profit goals and loss limit are. As you develop experience, trade planning may become innate. You develop the discipline to trade according to plan without needing to write it all down — although you may find it useful to tape a list of the day's expected announcements to your monitor.

REMEMBER

Like a business plan, a trading plan is flexible. The markets don't know what you've planned, and you'll probably end up deviating on more than one occasion. The key thing is knowing *why* you deviated: Was it because of the information that you saw when you were looking at your screen, or was it because you became panicky?

What do you want to trade?

The first step in your trading plan should also be addressed in your business plan: What do you want to trade? Many traders work in more than one market, and each market is a little different. Some trade different products simultaneously, whereas others choose one for the day and work only on that.

Chapters 4 and 5 cover the different assets that day traders can work with in great detail. You can refer to them if you're just starting out. What assets fit your style, your expertise, and your risk levels? For example, many farmers trade commodities futures both to manage their own risk and to apply their knowledge of agriculture to short-term profits. If your expertise is technology, commodities may not be as good a fit for you. Everything flows from your asset choices.

You need to figure out which markets give you the best chance of getting a profit that day, and this changes regularly. Some days, no trades will be good for you in one market, and you'll be better off sitting out. If you're too antsy to sit out, then find another market to keep you busy so that you don't trade just to stay awake. (Of course, many traders report that the big money opportunities are in the slower, less glamorous markets.)

REMEMBER

As a day trader, you're self-employed. You don't answer to a boss, and you don't have to trade on any particular day if you don't want to. So if you have a headache, if no good trades are available to you, or if recent losses have gotten you down, take the day off and do something fun.

When will you be trading?

You want to find assets that are trading when you are. That sounds obvious, right? Well, it's so obvious that it should be in your plan.

Although global markets seem to be operating 24 hours a day these days, they really don't. Breaks in trading sessions occur, and market holidays in different countries close markets. Even assets that trade well in overnight markets trade differently in them because the participants in them are different. For instance, the interests of currency traders in Asia are somewhat different from those of currency traders in Europe if only because their profit accounting will take place in different currencies, which means that currency trading will be different during the Asian business day than during the European business day.

Hence, you need to consider what is happening when you'll be trading. It's particularly important if you don't trade at the same time every day or if you trade something like currency where one region's business day may be ending and another day beginning while you're trading.

And so, determine if this asset is one you want to trade today, and if you want to work with it all day or for only part of the day.

How do you want to trade?

Figuring out how to trade an asset involves a lot of considerations: What is your mood today? What will other traders be reacting to today? How much risk do you want to take? How much money do you want to commit? These considerations represent the nitty-gritty stage of trade planning that can help you manage your market day better.

Beginning the day with a morning review

Before you start trading, take some time to determine where your head is relative to the market. Is today a day that you can concentrate? Are things happening in your life that may distract you, are you coming down with the flu, or were you out too late last night? Or are you raring to go, ready to take on whatever the day brings?

Your mindset will influence how aggressively you want to trade and how much risk you want to take. Acknowledge it up front or live in denial until the losses come in.

You have to pay attention to do well in the markets, but you also have to know when to hang back during the day's activities. For example, many traders find that their strategies work best at certain times of the day, such as at the open or before major news announcements.

After you determine your own mindset, think about what people will be reacting to that day. Check the newswires to gather information. Then figure out the answers to these questions:

>> Are big news announcements scheduled for today? At what time? Do you want to trade ahead of the news, or do you want to wait and see what the market does?

>> Did something happen overnight? Will that event affect trading on the open, or is it already in the markets? Do you want to trade on the open or wait?

>> Are any major markets closed today? Holidays vary around the world, and a closed market (because it's a monarch's birthday or a religious holiday) can affect the market environment.

>> What are the other people — those who trade the same future, commodity, stock, or currency that you do — worried about today? How are they likely to respond? Do you want to go with the market or strike a contrary position?

TIP

The financial news websites all offer a good overview of upcoming events every day. Make a point of checking them before you get started to see what might be happening that will affect your trading day.

Drawing up a sample order

After you have a sense of how you're going to tackle the day, determine how much you're going to trade. Following are the key considerations:

>> **Do you want to be long or short?** That is, do you want to bet that the asset you are trading is going up in price or down?

>> **Do you want to borrow money?** If so, how much? Borrowing — also known as *margin* or *leverage* — increases your potential return as well as your risk. (We discuss margin, leverage, and short selling in Chapter 6.)

Some contracts, such as futures, have built-in leverage. As soon as you decide to trade them, you're borrowing money.

>> **How much money do you want to trade?** Think about this both in dollars and as a percentage of your total account size. (We discuss money management in detail in Chapter 7.)

With these items detailed, you're in good shape to get started for the day.

Figuring out when to buy and when to sell

After you get insight into what the day may be like and how much money you want to allocate to the markets, your next step is to figure out when you'll buy and when you'll sell. Ah, but if deciding when to buy and sell were easy, do you think we'd be revising a book on day trading? No. Ann would be too busy taking private surfing lessons in front of her beachfront mansion on Maui, while Bryan would be lazing around on a boat in front of his newly built cottage on Lake Winnipeg.

The very best traders aren't selling trading advice, because they're already retired. Everyone else is figuring it out as they go along, with varying degrees of success.

Many traders rely on *technical analysis*, which involves looking at patterns in charts of the price and volume changes. Other traders look at news and price information as the market changes rather than looking at price patterns. (You can find a discussion of this in Chapter 9.) Still others care only about very short-term price discrepancies (covered in Chapter 10). But the most important thing, no matter what approach you prefer, is that you *backtest* and simulate your trading before you commit real dollars. That way, you have a better sense of how you'll react in real market conditions. You can find information about backtesting in Chapter 14.

Setting profit goals

When you trade, you want to have a realistic idea how much money you can make. What's a fair profit? Do you want to ride a winning position until the end of the day, or do you want to get out quickly after you make enough money to compensate for your risk? This question has no one single answer because so much depends on market conditions and your trading style. In this section are some guidelines that can help you determine what's best for you.

THE LANGUAGE OF MONEY

Profits are discussed differently in different markets, and you may as well have the right lingo when you write your plan:

- **Pennies:** Stocks trade in decimal form, so each price movement is worth at least a penny — one cent. It's an obvious way to measure a profit.

- **Pips:** A *pip* is the smallest unit of currency that can be traded. In foreign exchange markets (forex), a pip is generally equal to one one-hundredth of a cent. If the value of the euro moves from $1.1934 to $1.1935, it has moved a pip.

  Note: Do not confuse a pip in the forex market with an investment scheme known as *PIP,* sometimes called People in Profit or Pure Investor. (The fraud also operates as *HYIP,* for High Yield Investment Program.) PIP has been promoted as a trading system with a guaranteed daily return, but it's really a pyramid scheme that takes money from participants and returns little or nothing. You'd think they'd be shut down by now, but no — we've warned about them in every edition of this book, and yet, they are all over the Internet, often on sites that claim that they will find you the legal ones. There is no such thing. You can get more information from the SEC's website, `www.sec.gov/oiea/investor-alerts-bulletins/ia_primebankscam.html`.

- **Points:** A *point* is a single percentage. A penny is a point, as is a 1 percent change in a bond price. A related number, a *basis point,* is a percent of a percent, or 0.0001.

- **Teenies:** Many securities, especially bonds and derivatives on them, trade in increments of 1/8 of a dollar. Half of an eighth is a sixteenth, also known as a *teeny*.

- **Ticks:** A *tick* is the smallest trading increment in a futures contract. It varies from product to product. How much it works out to be depends on the contract structure. For the S&P/TSX Composite Index Mini Futures (SCF), one tick value equals five index points, and each index point represents $5. That means the tick value is equal to $25. The value of an SCF futures contract is calculated by multiplying the current level of the contract by the tick value. For the CME Group's E-Mini S&P 500 contract, a tick is equal to $12.50, calculated as a 0.25 change in the underlying S&P 500 index multiplied by $50 multiplier. A tick on an E-Mini soybean contract is $1.25, calculated as 1/8 cent on a bushel of soybeans in a contract covering 1,000 bushels. You can get information on the tick size of contracts that interest you on the website of the offering exchange.

Your profit goals can be sliced and diced a few different ways. The first is the *gain per trade* on both a percentage basis and an absolute basis. The second is the *gain per day* on both a percentage basis and an absolute basis. What do you have to do to reach these goals? How many successful trades will you have to make? Do you have the capital to do that? And what is right for the trade you are making right now, regardless of what your longer-term goals are?

No one ever lost money taking a profit, as the cliché goes. (The trading business is rife with clichés, if you haven't noticed.) The newer you are to day trading, the more sense it makes to be conservative. Close your positions and end your day when you reach a target profit and then make note of what happens afterward. Can you afford to hold on to your positions longer to make a greater profit?

Setting limits on your trades

Setting a *loss limit* along with a profit goal is a good idea. For example, many futures traders have a rule to risk two ticks in pursuit of three ticks. That means that they'll sell a position as soon as it loses two ticks in value and as soon as it gains three ticks in value. And for anything in between? Well, they close out their positions at the end of the days the result is profit even smaller than three ticks or a loss smaller than two. It's a boring strategy that usually has small profits, but a small profit is better than a negative one.

Even traders who don't have a rule as specific as losing two ticks in pursuit of three often set a limit on how much they'll lose per trade. They know that there is no shame in a loss, only in wishing and hoping that it would magically reverse. Other traders use computer programs to guide their buys and their sells, so they sell their positions automatically. Brokers make setting limits easy by giving customers the choice of a stop order or a limit order to protect their positions.

You want to limit your loss per trade *as well as* your loss per day. If today is not a good one, close up shop, take a break, and come back fresh tomorrow.

Stop orders

A *stop order* is an order to buy or sell a security as soon as a security moves beyond the current market price. A *stop buy* order is set above the current market price, and it is used to manage a short position. A *stop sell* order is set at a price below where the market is now, and it is used to protect a profit or limit a loss on a security that you already own. If you want to make sure you sell a block of stock when it falls below $30 per share, for example, you can enter a stop order at $30 (telling your broker "Sell Stop 30"). As soon as the stock hits or goes below $30, the broker sells it, even if the price goes to $29 or $31 before all the stock is sold. This is often known as a *stop loss* order.

A version of a stop, known as a *trailing stop*, is used to help protect a profit. You can enter a trailing stop order at the current market with a stop loss price below the current market price. It would be set to trail, or automatically increase, as the stock price does. If you bought a block of stock at $30 with a trailing stop of $5, for example, the stop would kick in at $25. But if your trade was a good one and the stock went from $30 to $35, the stop would trail with it and rise to $30, a price $5 below the current market value.

Limit orders

A *limit order* is an order to buy or sell a security at a specific price or better: lower than the current price for the buy order (because you want to buy low, naturally), higher than the specific price for a sell order (because you want to sell high).

If you want to make sure you sell a block of stock when it's at $30 per share, for example, you can enter a limit order at $30 (telling your broker, "Sell Limit 30"). As soon as the stock hits $30, the broker sells it, continuing to place the order as long as the price stays at $30 or higher. If the price goes even a penny below $30, the limit is no longer enforced, and the broker stops selling your position. After all, no buyers are going to want to pay an above-market price just so you can get your order completed!

Stop-limit orders

A *stop-limit* order is a combination of a stop order and a limit order. It tells the broker to buy or sell at a specific price or better but only after the price passes a given stop price. If, for example, you want to make sure you sell a block of stock when it falls below $30 per share but you also want to make sure you sell it only when you'd have a loss, you can enter a stop order at $30 with a limit of $29 (telling your broker, "Sell 30 Limit 29"). As soon as the stock hits $30, the broker sells it as long as the price stays above $29. If it goes below $29, the broker stops selling.

Stop-limit orders help you get out without maximizing your losses; the danger, of course, is that the stock goes to $6 and you could have gotten out at $28 without the stop-limit order.

Are you confused? Well, the differences may be confusing, but understanding them is important to helping you manage your risks. That's why Table 8-1 gives you a handy breakout of the different types of orders.

TABLE 8-1   ## Different Types of Orders

Buy Orders			
	Stop Order	Limit Order	Stop-Limit Order
Order instructions	Buy Stop 30	Buy Limit 30	Buy Stop 30 Limit 31
Market Price ($)	Action after the stock hits $30		
28.50	Nothing	Buy	Nothing
29.00	Nothing	Buy	Nothing
29.50	Nothing	Buy	Nothing
30.00	Buy	Buy	Buy
30.50	Buy	Nothing	Buy
31.00	Buy	Nothing	Nothing
31.50	Buy	Nothing	Nothing
28.50	Sell	Nothing	Nothing
29.00	Sell	Nothing	Sell
29.50	Sell	Nothing	Sell
30.00	Sell	Sell	Sell
30.50	Nothing	Sell	Nothing
31.00	Nothing	Sell	Nothing
31.50	Nothing	Sell	Nothing

Order cancels other

Also known as *one cancels other* or OCO, an *order cancels other* order is used with a limit and a stop-loss to set a trading bracket in a volatile market. The limit sets an automatic exit point when your position hits your price target, and the stop-loss kicks in if your trade moves against you in order to limit your losses. The broker will execute only the relevant order, cancelling the other order when that happens. If not, the other half of the order will be hanging out, waiting to be executed, causing you headaches.

Order sends other

Depending on whom you talk to, OSO stands for *order sends order, order sends other*, or *one sends other*. They all mean the same thing: When one order is executed, another order is automatically entered into the system — and not a moment before. You use an OSO to enter a limit order or a stop-loss order as soon as your order to open a long or short position is executed.

What if the trade goes wrong?

No matter how in tune you feel with the market, no matter how good your track record, and no matter how disciplined you are with setting stops, stuff is going to happen. Just as you can make more money than you plan to, you can also *lose* a lot more. If you day trade, you have to accept that you're going to have some really bad days.

So what do you do? You suck it up, take the loss, and get on with your life. Yes, the market may have blown past your stops. That happens sometimes, and it's hard to watch real dollars disappear into someone else's account, someone you will never know. Still, close your position and just remember that tomorrow is another day with another chance to do better.

WARNING

Don't hold in hopes of making up a loss. The market doesn't know what you own and will not reward your loyalty and best hopes.

TIP

After you take the loss and clear your head, see whether you can learn something for next time. Sometimes a loss can teach you valuable lessons that make you a smarter, more disciplined trader in the long run.

A SAMPLE TRADING PLAN

A trading plan may only be good for a short time, but having an idea of what to expect in the market and how you'll react goes a long way toward keeping trading discipline, which improves your likelihood of long-run profits. What does such a plan look like? Well, here's a sample to get you started.

What I'm Trading Today

Today I'll be trading the S&P/TSX Composite Index Mini Futures. They closed down yesterday, but I'm expecting an uptick in the market today as companies report good earnings, so I am going to trade on the long side. My plan is to start the day buying two contracts with stop orders to sell if they decline more than three ticks each. These contracts will remain open until the end of the day unless the stop is reached. I will add a third contract if the market shows momentum in the morning and a fourth contract if it shows momentum in the afternoon. These two additional contracts can be long or short, depending on the market direction, although it is unlikely that the purchasing manager or home sales surveys will have a large effect on the market's direction. I will close all positions at the end of the day, if not sooner.

Because the margin on each contract is $3,500, my maximum exposure today will be approximately 28 percent of my total account, with no contract accounting for more than 7 percent of my account.

Today's Expected News Announcements

Before the open: Earnings announcements from TD (expect $0.62), SHOP (expect $0.74)

10:00 a.m.: ISM Index — survey of purchasing managers — market expects 51.0

10:00 a.m.: Pending Home Sales — market expects up 0.5 percent

After the close: Earnings announcements from CSU (expect $8.27), MFC (expect $1.29)

5:00 p.m.: U.S. employment — market expects to add 200,000 jobs

5:00 p.m.: Canadian employment — market expects to add 10,000 jobs

My Profit and Loss Goals for the Day

My profit goal is five ticks or $62.50 per contract traded for a target of $250 if I acquire my planned maximum of four contracts, but I plan to ride my profits until the end of the day. If all four contracts decline in value, I will close when they fall three ticks apiece, for a maximum loss of $37.50 per contract or $150 for the day.

Tip: Set up a basic form or spreadsheet with all this information so that it's easy to fill out each morning. It might look like this:

What I'm trading today:

Assets: _____

Leverage: _____

Limits: _____

(continued)

(continued)

Expected news announcements:

Time: _____ Item: _____

Time: _____ Item: _____

Time: _____ Item: _____

Time: _____ Item: _____

Profit and Loss Goals: _____

Closing Out Your Position

By definition, day traders only hold their investment positions for a single day. Closing out at the end of the day is important for a few reasons:

>> Closing out daily reduces your risk of something happening overnight.

>> Margin rates — the interest rates paid on money borrowed for trading — are low and in some cases zero for day traders, but the rates go up on overnight balances.

>> Good trade discipline is what can keep you from making expensive mistakes.

But like all rules, the single-day rule can be broken and probably should be broken sometimes. In this section, we cover a few longer-term trading strategies that you may want to add to your trading business on occasion.

Swing trading: Holding for days

Swing trading involves holding a position for several days. Some swing traders hold overnight, while others hold for days or even months. The longer time period gives more time for a position to work out, which is especially important if the position is based on news events or if it requires taking a position contrary to the current market sentiment. Although swing trading gives traders more options for making a profit, it carries some risks because the position can turn against you while you are away from the markets.

REMEMBER

A tradeoff always exists between risk and return. When you take more risk, you do so in the hopes of getting a greater return. But when you look for a way to increase return, remember that you have to take on more risk to do it.

Swing trading requires paying attention to some basic fundamentals and news flow. It's also a good choice for people who have the discipline to go to bed at night instead of waiting up and watching their position in hopes that nothing goes wrong.

Position trading: Holding for weeks

A *position trader* holds a stake in a stock or a commodity for several weeks and possibly even for months. This person is attracted to the short-term price opportunities, but he also believes that he can make more money holding the stake for a long enough period of time to see business fundamentals play out. Position trading increases the risk and the potential return because a lot more can happen over months than minutes.

Investing: Holding for months or years

An *investor* is not a trader. Investors do careful research and buy a stake in an asset in the hopes of building a profit over the long term. It's not unusual for investors to hold assets for decades, although good ones sell quickly if they realize that they've made a mistake or if the story changes. (They want to cut their losses early, just as any good trader should.)

Investors are concerned about the prospects of the underlying business. Will it make money? Will it pay off its debts? Will it hold its value? They view short-term price fluctuations as noise rather than as profit opportunities.

Many traders pull out some of their profits to invest for the long term (or to give to someone else, such as a mutual-fund manager or hedge fund, to invest). Doing so is a way of building financial security in the pursuit of longer goals. This money is usually kept separate from the trading account.

Maxims and Clichés That Guide and Mislead Traders

In this section, we cover a few of the many maxims traders use to think about their trading, such as

>> The stock doesn't know you own it.

>> Failing to plan is planning to fail.

>> Your first loss is your best loss.

A lot more are out there. Clichés are useful shorthand for important rules that can help you plan your trading. But they can also mislead you because some are really obvious — too obvious to act on effectively. Yes, everyone knows that you make money by buying low and selling high, but how do you tell what low is and high is? Here's a run-through of some clichés that you'll come across in your trading career, along with our take on what they mean.

Pigs get fat, hogs get slaughtered

Trading is pure capitalism, and people do it for one primary reason: to make money. Sure, a ton of economic benefits come from having well-functioning capital markets, such as better price prediction, risk management, and capital formation. But a day trader just wants to make money.

Get too greedy, however, and you're likely to get stupid. You start taking too much risk, deviating too much from your strategy, and getting careless about dealing with your losses. Good traders know when it's time to take a profit and move on to the next trade.

This maxim is one of those obvious but tough-to-follow ones. After all, when do you cross the line from being a happy little piggy to a big fat greedy hog that's about to be turned into a pork belly? Just know that if you're deviating from your trading plan because things are going so great, you may be headed for some trouble.

Here's a cliché that's related to "Pigs get fat, hogs get slaughtered": "Bears get fat, bulls get fat, and hogs get slaughtered." In other words, a savvy trader can make money whether the market is up or down, but a greedy trader runs into trouble.

In a bear market, the money returns to its rightful owners

A *bull* market is one that charges ahead; a *bear* market is one that does poorly. Many people erroneously think of themselves as trading geniuses because they make money when the entire market is going up. Making money by day trading was easy with Internet stocks in 1999, but it wasn't so easy in 2000 when the bubble burst. And when the markets turn negative, those people who really understand trading and who know how to manage risk are able to stay in until things get better, possibly even making nice profits along the way.

The corollary cliché for "In a bear market, the money returns to its rightful owners," is "Don't confuse brains with a bull market." When things are going well, watch out for overconfidence. It may be time to update your business and trading plans, but it's not to time cast them aside.

The trend is your friend

When you day trade, you need to make money fast. You do not have the luxury of waiting for your unique, contrary theory to play out. An investor may be buying a stock in the hopes of holding it for decades, but a trader needs things to work now.

REMEMBER

Given the short-term nature of the market, short-term sentiment is going to trump long-term fundamentals. People trading today may be wrong about the direction of foreign exchange, interest rates, or stock prices, but if you are closing out your positions tonight, you need to work with the information in the market *today*. In the short run, traders who fight the market lose money.

There are two problems with the maxim "The trend is your friend." The first is that by the time you identify a trend, it may be over. Second, sometimes, going against the herd makes sense because you can collect when everyone else realizes their mistake. In such a situation, the psychology of trading comes into play. Are you a good enough judge of human behaviour to know when the trend is right and when it's not?

Buy the rumour, sell the news

Markets react to information. That's ultimately what drives supply and demand. Although the market tends to react quickly to information, it can overreact, too. Lots of gossip gets traded in the markets as everyone looks to get the information they need to gain an advantage. And despite such things as confidentiality agreements and insider-trading laws, many rumours turn out to be true.

These rumours are often attached to such news events as corporate earnings. For whatever reason — good news, analyst research, a popular product — traders may believe, for example, that the company will report good quarterly earnings per share. That's the rumour. If you buy on the rumour, you can take advantage of the price appreciation as the story gets more play. When the earnings are actually announced, one of two things will happen:

>> The earnings will be as good as or better than rumoured, and the price will go up. The trader can sell into that and make a profit.

>> The earnings will be worse than rumoured, everyone will sell on the bad news, and the trader will want to sell to get out of the loss.

Of course, if the rumour is *bad*, you want to do the opposite: sell on the rumour and buy on the news. The problem with "Buy the rumour, sell the news" is that rumours are often wrong, and there may be more opportunities to buy on bad news when other traders are panicking, thus driving prices down for a few minutes before sanity sets in. But this rule is one of those that everyone talks about, whether or not they actually follow it.

Cut your losses and ride your winners

We mention earlier in this chapter that you need to cut your losses before they drag you down. No matter how much it hurts and no matter how much you believe that you're right, you need to close out a losing position and move on.

But the opposite — that you should ride your winners — is not necessarily true. Although good traders tend to be disciplined about selling winning positions, they don't use stops and limits as rigorously on the upside as they may on the downside. They're likely to stick with a profit and see how high it goes before closing out a position.

Note that this conflicts a little with the "Pigs get fat, hogs get slaughtered" maxim. (Trading maxims can be so contradictory!) To prevent overconfidence and sloppiness from greed, ride your winners *within reason.* If your general discipline is to risk three ticks on a futures contract to make five, and a contract goes up six ticks before you can close it out, you may want to stick with it. But if you also close out at the end of every day, don't give in to the temptation of keeping that position open just because it's still going up. Keep to your overall discipline.

You're only as good as your last trade

The markets churn on every day with little regard for why everyone trading right now is there. Prices go up and down to match the supply and the demand at any given moment, which may have nothing to do with the actual long-term worth of an item being traded. And it certainly has nothing to do with how much you really, really want the trade to work out.

One of the biggest enemies of good traders is overconfidence. Especially after a nice run of winning trades, a trader can get caught up in the euphoria and believe that he finally has the secret to successful trading under control. While he's checking the real estate listings for that beachfront estate in Maui, BAM! The next trade is a disaster. Does that mean that the trader is a disaster, too? No, it just means that the markets won this time around.

Most day traders work in zero-sum markets, where for every winner, there's a loser. Hence, not everyone can make money every day. The challenge is to maintain an even keel so as not to be distracted by confidence when the trading is going well or by fear when the trading is going poorly. The next trade is a new trade.

If you don't know who you are, Wall Street is an expensive place to find out

The best traders know their limits. They know what gets them excited, what gets them angry, and what they need to watch out for. They haven't necessarily figured it out in front of a screen, either. Instead, they've looked back on their lives and realized how to apply their strengths and weaknesses to trading. If you are new to trading, consider your own capabilities when designing a trading plan and think carefully about the things that are likely to trip you up. By thinking about those things, you can pay attention and act accordingly.

If you wait to trade with real money to find out your tolerances for risk and stress, you're going to lose a lot of real money first.

There are old traders and bold traders, but no old, bold traders

Trading has a huge survival bias, meaning that the most experienced traders are also the best traders because the worst traders got washed out early on. The sure-fire route to losing your trading capital is to make a few big bets. The older traders know that they have to watch what they do. They have to plan for the risks they want to take and understand when to close out their risks. After all, if you want excitement, go to Vegas. If you want to make the ranks of the old traders, plan your traders and trade your plan.

2

Developing Your Strategy

Discover the most popular technical analysis techniques.

Get familiar with market indicators.

Find out how to eliminate emotion when trading.

Apply day trading techniques to long-term investing.

Investigate some of the different services that can help your trading.

Evaluate your profits, performance, and progress.

Chapter **9**

Picture This: Technical Analysis

In some ways, day trading is easy. Open up an account with a brokerage firm and off you go, buying and selling securities! But how are you going to know when to buy and when to sell? That's not a simple matter. Most day traders fail because it's easy to place the order but hard to know whether the order is the right one.

Traders use different research systems to evaluate the market and have access to tools that can help them figure out when a security is likely to go up in price and when it is likely to go down. Two primary types of investment research systems exist: technical analysis and fundamental analysis. *Technical analysis,* which is widely used by day traders, looks at the supply and demand for a security and how it shows up in price data. Fundamental analysis, which is less commonly used by day traders, looks at the financial and operational factors that affect a security's value. This chapter tells you what you need to know about each.

WARNING

Don't be fooled by anyone offering to sell you a guaranteed system for making money in day trading. Anyone with a surefire system has already made a fortune and retired to a private island in a tropical climate. He or she is too busy enjoying drinks with umbrellas in them to share that trading system with you.

Comparing Research Techniques Used in Day Trading

Day traders need to make decisions fast, and they need to have a framework for doing so. That's why they rely on research. But what kind? Most day traders rely heavily on *technical* research, which is an analysis of charts formed by price patterns to measure the relative supply and demand for the security. But some people use fundamental analysis to help inform their decisions, too. Even though you'll mostly use technical analysis in day trading, taking the time to find out a bit about fundamental analysis can help you understand what longer-term traders and investors are doing in the market.

REMEMBER

Research systems fall into two categories:

>> **Fundamental research looks at the specific factors that affect a security's value.** What's the relationship between the trade deficit and futures on two-year treasury notes? What's the prediction for summer rainfall in Ontario, and how will that affect December corn futures? How dependent is a company on new products to generate earnings growth?

>> **Technical research looks at the supply and demand for the security itself.** Are people buying more and more shares? Is the price going up a lot as they buy more, or does the price go up just a little bit? Does it seem like everyone who is likely to buy has already bought, and what does that mean for the future price?

Knowing what direction your research is

Securities are affected by matters specific to each type and by huge global macro-economic factors that affect every security in different ways. Some traders prefer to think of the big picture first, whereas others start small. And some use a combination of the two approaches. Neither is better; each is simply a different perspective on what's happening in the markets.

Top-down research

With a *top-down* approach, the trader looks at the big economic factors: interest rates, exchange rates, government policies, and the like. How will these things affect a particular sector or security? Is this a good time to buy stocks or short interest-rate futures? The top-down approach can help evaluate the prices in big market sectors, and it can also help determine what factors are affecting trading in a subsector. You don't have to trade stock market index futures to know that the outlook for the overall stock market will have an effect on the trading of any specific company's stock.

Bottom-up research

Bottom-up analysis looks at the specific performance of the asset. It looks at the company's prospects and then works backward to figure out how it will get there. What has to happen for a company's stock price to go up 20 percent? What earnings does it have to report, what types of buyers have to materialize, and what else has to happen in the economy?

Examining fundamental research

Day traders do very little fundamental research. Sure, they know that demand for ethanol affects corn prices, but they really want to know what the price will do right now relative to where the price was a few minutes ago. How new agriculture legislation might affect ethanol prices in six years doesn't figure into day trading.

Knowing a little bit about the fundamentals — those basic facts that affect the supply and demand for a security in all markets — can help the day trader respond better to news events. It can also give you a better feel for when *swing trading* (holding a position for several days) will generate a better profit than closing out every night. But knowing a lot can drag a day trader down.

WARNING

Fundamental analysis can actually *hurt* you in day trading, because you may start making decisions for the wrong reasons. If you know too much about the fundamentals, you may start considering long-term outlooks instead of short-term activity. For example, many people buy S&P 500 and S&P/TSX Composite Index-tracking funds for their retirement accounts because they believe that in the long run, the market will go up. That does not mean that people should trade E-mini S&P futures or an S&P exchange-traded fund today, because a lot of zigzagging can happen between now and the arrival of the long-run price appreciation.

Fundamental research falls into two main categories: top-down and bottom-up. As we mention earlier, top-down starts with broad economic considerations and then looks at how those will affect a specific security. Bottom-up looks at specific securities and then determines whether those are good buys or sells right now.

TIP

If you love the very idea of fundamental research, then day trading is probably not for you. Day trading requires quick responses to price changes, not a careful understanding of accounting methods and business trends. A little fundamental analysis can be helpful in day trading, but a lot can slow you down.

Looking closer at technical analysis

Information about the price, time, and volume of a security's trading can be plotted on a chart. The plots form patterns that can be analyzed to show what happened. How did the supply and demand for a security change, and why? And what does that mean for future supply and demand? Technical analysis is based on the premise that securities prices move in trends and that those trends repeat themselves over time. Therefore, a trader who can recognize a trend on the charts can determine where prices are most likely to go until some unforeseen event comes along that creates a new trend.

Technical analysis shows the strength of supply and demand in the market. It offers clues about behaviour and psychology, which is valuable information for a day trader. In markets with highly uncertain fundamental values, like cryptocurrency, the charts will give you the best sense of where an asset's price is moving.

TIP

Most traders rely on software to spot patterns because it makes them easier to find and to act upon. Remember that the vast volume of short-term trading takes place by computer algorithm. You can't beat them, so join them.

The basic element of technical analysis is a *bar*, which shows you the high, low, open, and closing price of a security for a given day. It looks like the one shown in Figure 9-1.

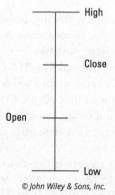

High

Close

Open

FIGURE 9-1:
A bar displays
high, low, open,
and closing.

Low

© *John Wiley & Sons, Inc.*

In most markets, every day generates a new *bar* (many traders talk about bars instead of days, and they aren't talking about where they go after work). A collection of bars, with all their different high, low, open, and close points, is put together into a larger *chart*. Often, a plot of the volume for each bar runs underneath, with the result looking like Figure 9-2.

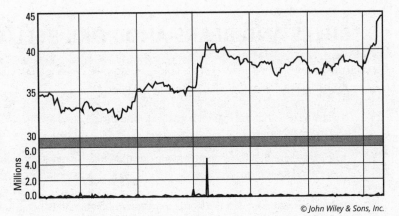

FIGURE 9-2:
A plot of volume underneath a year's worth of bars.

Many patterns formed in the charts are associated with future price moves. Technical analysts thus spend a lot of time looking at the charts to see whether they can predict what's going to happen. Many software packages (some of which are discussed in Chapter 14) send traders signals when certain technical patterns occur so that the traders can place orders accordingly.

REMEMBER

Technical analysis is a way to measure the supply and demand in the market. It's a tool for analyzing the markets, not predicting them. If deciphering the meaning of the data were that easy, everyone would be able to make money in the markets.

Price changes

Market observers debate *market efficiency* all the time. In an efficient market, all information about a security is already included in the security's price, so there's no point to doing any research at all. Few market participants are willing to go that far, but they concede the point that the price is the single most important summary of information about a company. That means that technical analysis, looking at how the price changes over time, is a way of learning about whether a security's prospects are improving or getting worse.

Volume changes

The basic bar shows how price changed during the day, but adding *volume* information tells the other part of the story: how much of a security was demanded at that price. If demand is going up, then more people want the security, so they are willing to pay more for it. The price tells traders what the market knows; the volume tells them how many people in the market know it.

Using Technical Analysis

Technical analysis helps day traders identify changes in the supply and demand for a security that may lead to profitable price changes ahead. It gives traders a way to talk about and think about the market so that they can be more effective.

Most brokerage firm quote systems generate charts, sometimes with the help of additional software that automatically marks the chart with trendlines. Technical traders look for those trendlines. Before placing an order to buy or sell, a trader needs to know whether the security's price is going up and whether that trend is going to continue.

One interesting aspect of technical analysis is that the basics hold no matter what market you're looking at. Technical analysis can help you monitor trends in the stock market, the bond market, the commodity market, and the currency market. Anywhere people try to match their supply and their demand to make a market, technical analysis can be used to show how well they're doing it.

First things first: Should you follow a trend or deviate from it?

The next sections go into all sorts of detail about how to spot a trend, but the key thing to understand as a day trader is whether you should follow a trend or not. Sometimes a trend is good to follow, but sometimes deviating from it is better.

Remember when you were a kid wanting to do something that all your friends were doing and your mother would invariably say, "If all your friends jumped off of a bridge, would you have to jump off, too?"

Well, Mom, guess what? If the bridge were on fire, the escape routes blocked by angry mobs, and the water just a few feet down, then yes, it would be A–OK to jump off the bridge like everyone else. Likewise, if someone were paying us good money to jump and we knew we weren't likely to get hurt on the way down, we'd be over the railing in a flash. Sometimes being a follower is good. But if there were no fire and no angry mob, and we couldn't swim, we might not be so hasty to leap.

Trend following is like those mythical childhood friends on that mythical home-town bridge. Sometimes, you should join the crowd. Other times, deviating is best. When should you follow and when should you deviate? Well, that depends. You need to know what you're trading and what the other people trading that asset are considering when they place their orders. That's why a good understanding of what trends are and how they work can help you.

Finding trends

A technical analyst usually starts off by looking at a chart and drawing lines that show the overall direction of the price bars for the period in question. Rather than plot the graph on paper or print out the screen, she probably uses software to draw the lines. Figure 9-3 shows what this basic analysis looks like.

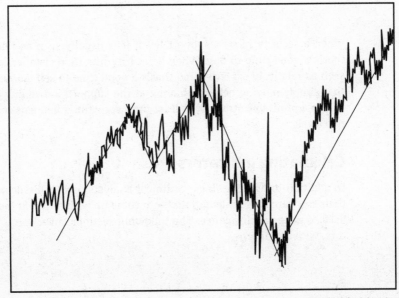

FIGURE 9-3: Basic analysis of trends in price bar changes draws lines showing the general movement.

© John Wiley & Sons, Inc.

With the basic trendlines in place, the trader can start thinking about how the trends have played out so far and what may happen next.

Drawing trendlines

As shown in the preceding section, the most basic trendline is a line that shows the general direction of the trend. And that's a good start, but it doesn't tell you all you need to know. The next step is to take out your ruler, or set your software, to find the trendlines that connect the highs and the lows. Doing so creates a channel that tells you the *support level* (the trendline for the lows) and the *resistance level* (the trendline for the highs), as Figure 9-4 shows. Unless something happens to change the trend, securities tend to move within the channel, so extending the line into the future can give you a sense of where the security is likely to trade.

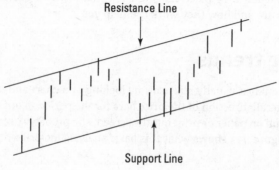

FIGURE 9-4: Drawing trendlines to identify channels.

© John Wiley & Sons, Inc.

When a security hits its support level, it is usually seen as relatively cheap, so that's a good time to buy. When a security hits its resistance level, it is usually seen as relatively expensive, so that's a good time to sell. Some day traders find that simply moving between buying at the support and selling at the resistance can be a profitable strategy, at least until something happens that changes those two levels.

Calculating indicators

In addition to drawing lines, technical analysts use their calculators — or have their software make calculations — to come up with different *indicators*, numbers used to gauge performance. The following sections cover some common indicators, with definitions.

PIVOT POINTS

A *pivot point* is the average of the high, low, and close price for the day. If the next day's price closes above the pivot point, that sets a new support level, and if the next day's price is below the pivot point, that sets a new resistance level. Hence, calculating pivot points and how they change may indicate new upper and lower stops for your trading.

TIP

For markets that are open more or less continuously, such as foreign exchange, the close price is set arbitrarily. The usual custom in Canada and the United States is to use the price at 4 p.m. Eastern time, which is the closing time for the Toronto and New York stock exchanges.

MOVING AVERAGES

Looking at all those little high-low-open-close lines on a chart will give your bifocals a workout. To make the trend easier to spot, traders calculate a *moving average* by averaging the closing prices for a given time period. Some traders prefer to look at the last 5 days; some at the last 60 days. Every day, the latest price is added, and the oldest price is dropped to make that day's calculation. Given the wonders of modern computing technology, pulling up moving averages for almost any time period you want is easy. The average for each day is then plotted against the price chart to show how the trend is changing over time. Figure 9-5 shows an example of a 10-day moving average chart.

FIGURE 9-5:
A price chart showing a 10-day moving average.

© John Wiley & Sons, Inc.

Traders use the moving average line to look for crossovers, convergences, and divergences. A *crossover* occurs whenever the price crosses the moving average line. Usually, buying is a good idea when the price crosses above the moving average line, and selling is a good idea when the price crosses below it.

To use *convergence* and *divergence* in analysis, the trader looks at moving averages from different time periods, such as 5 days, 10 days, and 20 days. Figure 9-6 shows what convergence and divergence look like.

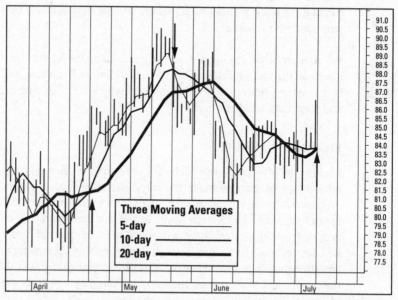

FIGURE 9-6: Moving average convergence and divergence.

TIP

When two or three of the moving average lines converge (come together), that means that the trend may be ending. That often makes it a good time to buy if the trend has been down and a good time to sell if the trend has been up. If two or three of the moving average lines split up and diverge, the trend is likely to continue. That means it's probably a good time to buy if the trend is up and sell if the trend is down.

REMEMBER

A moving average is a lagging indicator. It sums up trading activity in the last 5, 10, 30, or 60 days, which means that the line smooths out changes in the trend that may affect future prices, giving you a more accurate picture of the overall trend over the time period.

Observing trend phases

Price trends tend to move in cycles that can be seen on the charts or observed in market behaviour. Knowing the phases of a trend can help you better evaluate what's happening. Here is a summary of some phases of a trend:

- » **Accumulation:** This is the first part of the trend, where traders get excited about a security and its prospects. They start new positions or add to existing ones.

- » **Main phase (also called *continuation*):** Here, the trend moves along nicely, with no unusual price action. The highs get higher on an uptrend, and the lows get lower on a downtrend. A trader may make money — but not big money — following the trend here.

- » **Consolidation (also called *congestion*):** This phase indicates a sideways market. The security stays within the trend but without hitting higher highs or lower lows. It just stays within the trading range. A consolidation phase is good for scalpers, who make a large volume of trades in search of very small profits. It can be boring for everyone else.

- » **Retracement (also called *correction* or *pullback*):** Retracement is a secondary trend, a short-term pullback away from the main trend to the support level. Retracements create buying opportunities, but they can also kill day traders who are following the trend.

- » **Distribution:** In the distribution phase, traders don't think that the security can go up in price any more. Hence, they tend to sell in large volume.

- » **Reversal:** At this point, the trend changes. It's time to sell if you've been following an uptrend and buy if you've been following a downtrend. Many reversals follow classic patterns, which are discussed later in this chapter.

Those ever-changing trends

Although technical traders look to follow trends, they also look for situations where the trend changes so that they can find new profit opportunities. In general, day traders are going to follow trends, and swing traders — those who hold securities for a few days or even weeks — are going to be more interested in identifying changes that may play out over time.

Monitoring momentum

Following the trend is great, but if the trend is moving quickly, you want to know so that you can get ahead of it. If the rate of change on the trend is going up, then rising prices are likely to occur.

To calculate momentum, take today's closing price for a security, divide that by the closing price ten days ago, and then multiply the result by 100. This gives you a *momentum indicator*. If the price didn't go anywhere, the momentum indicator is 100. If the price went up, the indicator is greater than 100. And if the price went down, the indicator is less than 100.

In technical analysis, trends are usually expected to continue, so a security with a momentum indicator above 100 is expected to keep going up, all else being equal. But that "all else being equal" is the sticky part. Technical analysts usually track momentum indicators over time to see whether the positive momentum is, itself, a trend. In fact, momentum indicators are a good confirmation of the underlying trend.

REMEMBER

Momentum is a leading technical indicator. It tells you what is likely to happen in the future, not what has happened in the past.

Momentum trading is usually done with some attention to the fundamentals. When key business fundamentals, such as sales or profits, are accelerating at the same time that the security is going up in price, the momentum is likely to continue for some time. You can find out more about momentum trading and investing in Chapter 12.

Finding breakouts

A *breakout* occurs when a security price passes through and stays above — or below — the resistance or support line, which creates a new trend with new support and resistance levels. A one-time breakout may just be an anomaly (what technicians sometimes call a *false breakout*), but pay attention to two or more breakouts. Figure 9-7 shows what breakouts look like.

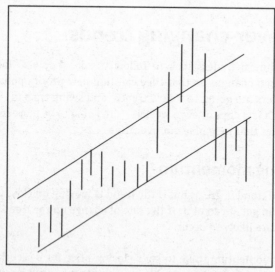

FIGURE 9-7:
A breakout indicates a new trend.

© John Wiley & Sons, Inc.

When a true breakout occurs, a new trend starts. That means an upward breakout is accompanied by rising prices, and a downward breakout is accompanied by falling prices.

False breakouts can wreak havoc for a day to two of trading. With a false breakout, some traders buy or sell, thinking that the trend will continue. When they see that it doesn't, they then turn around and reverse their positions at a loss. During these times, the ability to size up the intelligence of the other traders in the market can come in handy.

Good technical analysts look at several different indicators to determine whether a change in trend is real or just one of those things that goes away quickly as the old trend resumes. For example, they may look at short interest or overall market volatility.

Reading the Charts

How long does it take to find the trend? How long does it take for the trend to play out? When do you act on it? Do you have minutes, hours, or days to act?

Because markets tend to move in cycles, technical analysts look for patterns in the price charts that give them an indication of how long any particular trend may last. In this section, we show you some of the common patterns that day traders look for when they do technical analysis. Alas, some patterns are obvious only in hindsight, but knowing what the patterns mean can help you make better forecasts of where a security price should go.

This section provides just an introduction to some of the better-known (and cleverly named) patterns. Technical analysts look for many others, and you really need a book on the subject to understand them all. Check out the appendix for books that provide more information on technical analysis so that you can get a feel for how you can apply it to your trading style.

Wave your pennants and flags

Pennants and *flags* are chart patterns that show *retracements*, short-term deviations from the main trend. With a retracement, no breakout occurs from the support or resistance level, but the security isn't following the trend, either. Because there is no breakout, the trend is more short-term.

Figure 9-8 shows a pennant. Notice how the support and resistance lines of the pennant (which occur within the support and resistance lines of a much larger trend) converge almost to a point.

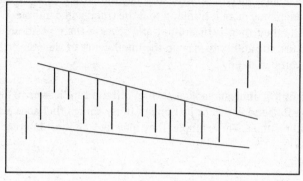

FIGURE 9-8:
In a pennant, support and resistance begin to converge.

Figure 9-9, by contrast, is a flag. The main difference between a flag and a pennant is that the flag's support and resistance lines are parallel.

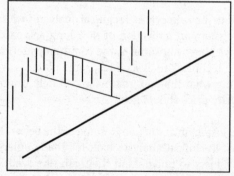

FIGURE 9-9:
A flag, like a pennant, usually indicates falling volume.

Pennants and flags are usually found in the middle of the main phase of a trend, and they seem to last for two weeks before going back to the trendline. They are almost always accompanied by falling volume. In fact, if the trading volume isn't falling, you are probably looking at a *reversal* — a change in trend — rather than a retracement.

Not just for the shower: Head and shoulders

The *head and shoulders* formation is a series of three peaks within a price chart. The peaks on the left and right (the shoulders) should be relatively smaller than the peak in the center (the head). The shoulders connect at a price known as the *neckline,* and when the right shoulder formation is reached, the price plunges down.

The head and shoulders is one of the most bearish technical patterns, and Figure 9-10 shows an example.

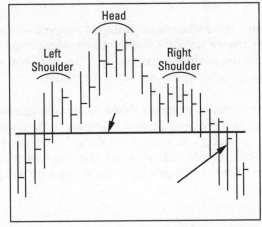

FIGURE 9-10: In a head and shoulders formation, the price goes down after the right shoulder formation.

© John Wiley & Sons, Inc.

The head and shoulders formation seems to result from traders holding out for a last high after a security has had a long price run. At some point, though, the trend changes, because nothing grows forever. And when the trend changes, the prices fall.

An upside-down head and shoulders sometimes appears at the end of a downtrend, and it signals that the security is about to increase in price.

Drink from a cup and handle

When a security hits a peak in price and falls, sometimes because of bad news, it can stay low for a while. But eventually, the bad news works itself out, the underlying fundamentals improve, and the time comes to buy again. The technical analyst sees this scenario play out in a *cup and handle* formation, and Figure 9-11 shows you what one looks like.

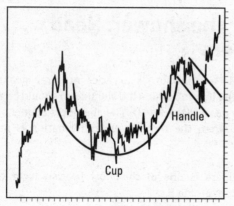

FIGURE 9-11:
A cup and handle formation is a long-term trend.

© John Wiley & Sons, Inc.

The handle forms as those who bought at the old high and who felt burned by the decline take their money and get out. But other traders, those who haven't the same history with the security, recognize that the price will probably resume going up now that those old sellers are out of the market.

A cup and handle formation generally shows up over a long period of trading — sometimes as long as a year — and many subtrends occur during that time. As a day trader, you'll probably care more about those day-to-day changes than the underlying trend taking place. Still, if you see that cup formation and the hint of a handle, you can interpret that as a sign that the security will probably start to rise in price.

Mind the gap

Gaps are breaks in prices that show up all the time, usually when some news event takes place between trading sessions that causes an adjustment in prices and volume. Whether the news is about an acquisition, a product line disappointment, or a war that broke out overnight, it's significant enough to change the trend, and that's why traders pay attention when they see gaps.

A gap is a break between two bars, as shown in Figure 9-12.

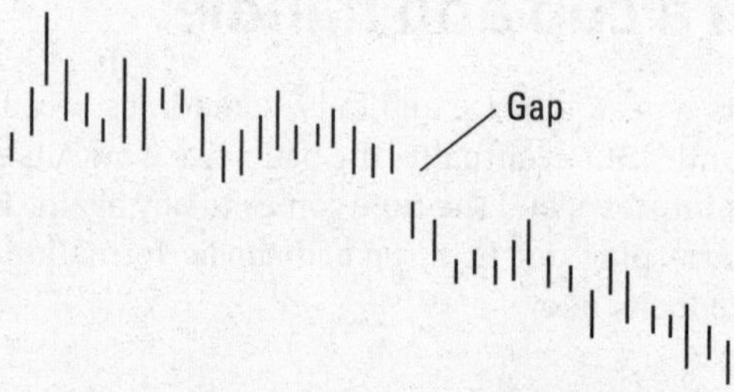

Gap

FIGURE 9-12:
A gap down often means it's time to sell.

© John Wiley & Sons, Inc.

Gaps are usually great signals. A security that gaps up at the open usually means a strong uptrend is beginning, so it's time to buy. Likewise, if the security gaps down, that's often the start of a downtrend, so it's better to sell.

WARNING

Day traders can get sucked into a gap, a situation known as a *gap and crap* (or *gap and trap,* if you prefer more genteel language). Many traders view the security going up in price as a great time to sell, so the day trader who buys on the gap up immediately gets slammed by all the selling pressure. For that reason, some day traders prefer to wait at least 30 minutes before trading on an opening gap, while others rely on their knowledge of the buyers and sellers in a given market to decide what to do.

Grab your pitchforks!

A *pitchfork* is sometimes called an *Andrews pitchfork* after Alan Andrews, the technical analyst who popularized it. This pattern identifies long-run support and resistance levels for subtrends by creating a channel around the main trendline. Figure 9-13 shows what a pitchfork looks like.

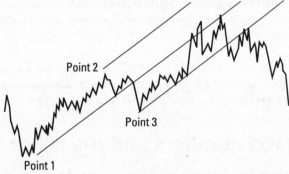

FIGURE 9-13:
A pitchfork makes a channel around the main trendline.

© John Wiley & Sons, Inc.

The upper line shows the resistance level for upward subtrends, and the lower line shows the support level for lower subtrends. The middle line forms a support and a resistance line, depending on which side of it trading takes place. If the price crosses above the midline, it can be expected to go no higher than the highest line. Likewise, if the price crosses below the midline, it can be expected to go no lower than the lowest line.

Considering Different Approaches to Technical Analysis

Technical analysts tend to group themselves under different schools of thought. Each approaches the charts differently and uses them to glean different information about how securities prices are likely to perform. In this section, we offer an introduction to a few of these approaches. If one strikes your fancy, you can look in the appendix for resources to help you learn more.

Dow Theory

Charles Dow, the founder of *The Wall Street Journal,* developed the *Dow Theory.* The theory and the market indexes that are part of it helped sell newspapers; they also helped people make money in the markets. The Dow Theory is the basis for the traditional technical analysis described in this chapter.

Dow believed that securities move in trends, that the trends form patterns that traders can identify, and that those trends remain in place until some major event takes place that changes them. Further, trends in the Dow Jones Industrial Average and the Dow Jones Transportation Average can predict overall market performance.

Not all technicians believe that the Dow Jones Industrial Average and Dow Jones Transportation Average are primary indicators in the modern economy, but they rely on the Dow Theory for their analysis, and they still read the *Journal.*

Fibonacci numbers and the Elliott Wave

Remember back when you had to take standardized tests, you'd often have to figure the next number in a series? Well, here's such a test. What's the next number in this series? (*Hint:* This is not a phone number in Chad.)

0, 1, 1, 2, 3, 5, 8, 13, 21

If you answered 34, you're right! The series is known as the *Fibonacci numbers,* sometimes called the *Fibonacci series* or just the *Fibs.* You find this number by adding together the preceding two numbers in the series, starting with the first two digits on the number line. $0 + 1 = 1$; $1 + 1 = 2$; $1 + 2 = 3$; and so on into infinity. Furthermore, when the series gets well into the double digits, the ratio of one number to the one next to it settles at 0.618, a number known as the *golden ratio,* which means that the ratio of the smaller and the larger of two numbers is the same as the ratio of the larger number to the sum of the two numbers. In nature, this is the proportion of a perfect spiral, like that found on a pinecone and a pineapple.

Ralph Elliott was a trader who believed that over the long run the market moved in waves described by the Fibonacci series. For example, Elliott believed that three down waves and five up waves would characterize a bull market. He also believed that support and resistance levels would be found 61.8 percent above lows and below highs. Under the Elliott Wave system, if a security falls 61.8 percent from a high, it's a good time to buy.

Elliott believed that these waves ranged from centuries to minutes, so both traders and investors use the system to identify the market trends that suit their time frames. Others think it's highly unlikely that the human activity in the stock market would follow the same natural order as the ratio of the spiral on a mollusk shell.

Japanese candlestick charting

Traders in the Japanese rick futures market developed candlestick charts in the 18th century, and the charts have carried through into the present. The basic charts are similar to the high-low-close-open bars that we talk about earlier in this chapter, but they are shaped a little differently to carry more information. Figure 9-14 shows an example of a candlestick.

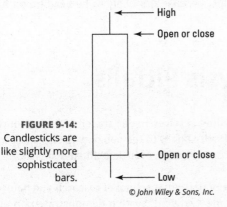

FIGURE 9-14: Candlesticks are like slightly more sophisticated bars.

© John Wiley & Sons, Inc.

The length of the rectangle (the so-called *candle,* also known as the *body*) between the open and the close prices gives a sense of how much volatility the security has, especially relative to the high and low prices above and below the rectangle (the so-called *wick,* also known as the *shadow*). The shapes and colours create different patterns that traders can use to discern the direction of future prices. (Most technical-analysis packages colour the candlesticks green on up days and red on down days, to make finding trends even easier.)

The Gann system

William Gann supposedly made $50 million in the stock and commodities markets in the first half of the 20th century by using a system that he may or may not have taught to others before his death. A lot of mystery and mythology surrounds the Gann system; some traders rely on what they perceive to be his method, whereas others dismiss it, in part because Gann relied on astrology to build his forecasts.

The *Gann system*, as it is defined nowadays, looks at the relationship between price and time. If a security moves one point in one day, that's a 1×1 Gann angle, and that's normal trading. If a security moves two points in one day, it is said to create a 2×1 Gann angle, which is bullish. An angle of less than 1×1 is bearish.

Furthermore, Gann recognized that the market moves back and forth while in a general upward or downward cycle, but some of those fluctuations are more positive than others. Just as the system looks for price movements over time with even proportions (1×1, 2×1, and so on), it also looks for orderly retracements. When a security moves back 50 percent, say from a low of $20 to a high of $40 and then back to $30, it would be a good time to buy under the Gann system.

TIP

Many traders swear by the 50 percent retracement guide — even those who think that Gann is an otherwise crazy system. This may be the origin of one hoary trading chestnut: Buy whenever a price dips, because it's likely to be heading on its way back up.

Avoiding Technical Analysis Pitfalls

A lot of people make a lot of money selling services to day traders. They produce videos, organize seminars, and (ahem) write books to tell you how to be a success. But in the financial world, success is a combination of luck, skill, and smarts.

TIP

Before you commit wholeheartedly to any particular school of research and before you plunk down a lot of money for some "proven" system demonstrated on an infomercial, think about who are you are and what you are trying to do. Despite all the books and all the seminars and all the business-school debates, every form of research has its drawbacks. Keep them in mind as you develop your day trading business plan.

If it's obvious, there's no opportunity

Many day trading systems work much of the time. For example, a security gaps up, meaning that, due to positive news or high demand, the price jumps from one trade to the next (refer to Figure 9-12 for a gap formation). This is good, and the security is likely to keep going up. So you buy the security, you make money. Bingo! But here's the thing: Everyone is looking at that gap, everyone is assuming that the stock will go up, so everyone buys, and that bids up the security. The profit opportunity is gone. So maybe you're better off going short? Or avoiding the situation entirely? Who knows? And that's the problem. Looking for obvious patterns like gaps tells you a lot about what is happening in the market, but only your own judgment and experience can tell you what the next move should be.

Overanalyzing the data

Technical analysis is a useful way to gauge market psychology. That's what it was designed to do. However, when it was developed, most traders were human beings, with all their crazy human emotions. Nowadays, you aren't trading against a person. In almost all cases, you will be trading against machines that do what they are programmed to do. They don't suffer from doubt, fear, or greed — but you do. The market is an aggregation of everyone in it, but you don't want to assign human emotions to nonhumans.

When trying to determine the mood of the market, you can easily start overanalyzing and working yourself into a knot. Should you follow the trend or trade against it? But if everyone trades against it, would you be better off following it?

Instead of puzzling over what's really going on, develop a system that you trust. Do that through backtesting, simulation, and performance analysis. Chapter 14 has plenty of advice on how to use these techniques. The more confident you feel in how you should react given a market situation, the better your trading will be.

Success may be the result of an upward bias

Under the efficient markets theory, all information is already included in a security's price. Until new information comes into the market, the prices move in a random pattern, so any security is as likely to do as well as any other. In some markets, like the stock market, this random path has an *upward bias,* meaning that as long as the economy is growing, companies should perform well, too; therefore, the movement is more likely to be upward than downward, but the magnitude of the movement is random.

If price movements are random, some people are going to win and some are going to lose, no matter what systems they use to pick securities. If price movements are random with an upward bias, then more people are going to win than lose, no matter what systems they use to pick securities. Some of those who win are going to tout their systems, even though random chance was really what led to their success.

REMEMBER

Technical analysis is a useful way to measure the relative supply and demand in the market, and that in turn is a way to gauge the psychology of those who are trading. But it's not perfect. Before you plunk down a lot of money to learn a complex trading system or to subscribe to a newsletter offering a can't-miss method of trading, ask yourself if the person selling it is smart or just lucky. A good system gives you discipline and a way to think about the market relative to your trading style. A bad system costs a lot of money and may have worked for a brief moment in the past, with no relevance to current conditions.

Chapter **10**

Following Market Indicators and Tried-and-True Day Trading Strategies

D ay traders put their research to work through a range of different strategies. All strategies have two things in common: They're designed to make money, and they're designed to work in a single day. And the best ones help traders cut through the psychology of the market.

In this day and age, most trading takes place via computers. Of course, human beings often direct the trading, but the machines are doing the work. Short-term profit potentials can be very small. As much as they want to be dispassionate, human traders get sucked into hope, fear, and greed — the three emotions that ruin people every day. To complicate matters, many markets, such as options and futures, are zero-sum markets, meaning that for every win, someone has to lose. Some markets, such as the stock market, have a positive bias, meaning that winners outnumber losers in the long run, but that doesn't mean that'll be the case today.

With thin profit potential and so much emotional upheaval, making money in the long run as a day trader can be tough. This chapter may help. In it, we cover some common day trading strategies, and we discuss some of the cold analysis that goes into figuring out the psychology of the markets.

Psyching Out the Markets

For every buyer, there's a seller. (There has to be, or no transaction will take place.) The price changes to reach the point where the buyer is willing to buy the security and the seller is willing to part with it. This interaction is basic supply and demand. The financial markets are more efficient at matching supply and demand than almost any other market in existence. There are no racks of unsold sweaters at the end of the season, no hot new cars that can't be purchased at any price, no long lines to get a table. The prices change to match the demand, and those who want to pay the price or receive the price are going to make a trade.

Despite the ruthless capitalistic efficiency underlying trading, the markets are also dominated by human emotion and psychology. All the buyers and all the sell–ers look at the same information, but they reach different conclusions. There's a seller out there for every buyer, so the trader looking to buy needs to know why the seller is willing to make a deal.

Why would someone be on the other side of your trade?

>> **The other trader may have a different time horizon.** For example, long-term investors may sell on bad news that changes a security's outlook. A short-term trader may not care about the long-term outlook if the selling in the morning is overdone, creating an opportunity to buy now and sell at a higher price in the afternoon.

>> **The other trader may have a different risk profile.** A conservative investor may not want to own shares in a company that's being acquired by a high-flying technology company. That investor will sell, and someone with more interest in growth will buy. A trading algorithm may place a trade to manage the risk on another trade.

>> **The other trader may be engaging in wishful thinking, acting out of fear, or trading from sheer greed.** He or she may not be thinking rationally about what is happening, creating an opportunity for you.

> » ***You* may be engaging in wishful thinking, acting out of fear, or trading from sheer greed.** You may be the irrational trader, making mistakes that cost you. Hey, it happens to the best of us sometimes, but the more aware you are of your emotional tendencies, the better you can trade past them.

REMEMBER

Don't try to psych out the trader on the other side. You won't face the same traders each time you trade, and more likely than not, the trader you're facing is a machine. Worry about yourself instead.

Betting on the buy side

Every market participant has his or her own set of reasons and rationales for placing an order today. In general, though, although many reasons to sell exist — to pay taxes, generate cash for college tuition, or meet a pension obligation, among many others — there's only one reason to buy: You think the security is going up in price.

For that reason alone, traders often pay more attention to what is happening to buy orders than to sell orders. To get a sense of who is projecting a profit, traders look at the number of buy orders coming in, how large they are, and at what price. We cover volume and price indicators in more detail later in the chapter.

TIP

Because there are so many good reasons to sell but only one good reason to buy, the market can take a long time to recognize bearish (pessimistic) sentiment indicators. Even if you see that prices should start to go down in the near future, you have to consider that the market today can be very different from what you see coming up. And as a day trader, you only have today.

Avoiding the projection trap

If you took a peek at some of the technical analysis charts in Chapter 9, you may have noticed that you can see what you want to see in some price charts. And if you thought a little about fundamental analysis, you may have seen that interpreting information the way you want to is just as easy. Instead of looking objectively at what the market is telling them, some traders see what they want to see. That's one reason why knowing your system and using your limits are so important.

The best traders are able to figure out the psychology of the market almost by instinct. They can't necessarily explain what they do — which makes it hard for those trying to learn from them. But they can tell you this much: If you can rationally determine why the person on the other side of the trade is trading, you can be in a better position to make money and avoid the big mistakes brought on by hope, fear, and greed.

Taking the Temperature of the Market

For decades, most traders were rooted on the floors of the exchanges. They had a good sense of the mood of the market because they could pick up the mood of the people in the pits with them. They often knew their fellow traders well enough to know how good they were or the needs of the people they were working for. It made for a clubby atmosphere, despite all the shouting and arm waving. It wasn't the most efficient way to trade big volume, but it allowed traders to read the minds of those around them.

Now, almost all trading is electronic, without the paper and the jackets and the excitement. Professional traders, who work for brokerage firms or fund companies, trade electronically, but along long tables (known as trading desks) where they sit next to colleagues trading similar securities. Even though everyone is trading off a screen, they share a mood and thus a sense of what's happening out there. Some day traders can replicate this camaraderie by working for a proprietary trading firm, but most traders work alone at home, with nothing but the information on their screens to tell them what's happening in the market.

Fortunately, ways do exist to figure out what's happening, even when you're just looking at the screen. They include paying attention to price, volume, and volatility indicators, and you're in the right place to find out more about them.

WARNING

Some traders rely on Internet chat rooms to help them measure market sentiment. Doing so can be risky. Some chat rooms have smart people who are willing to share their perspectives on the market, but many are dominated by novice traders who have no good information to share or by people who are trying to manipulate the market in their favour. Check out a chat room carefully before participating.

Pinpointing with price indicators

In an efficient market, all information about a security is included in its price. If the price is high and going up, then the fundamentals are doing well. If the price is low and going lower, then something's not good. And everything in between means something else.

The change in a security's price gives you a first cut of information. Price changes can be analyzed in other ways to help you know when to buy or when to sell.

Measuring a rate of change: Momentum

Momentum, which we discuss in Chapter 12 in greater detail, is the rate at which a security's price is increasing (or decreasing). If momentum is strong and positive, then the security shows both higher highs and higher lows. People want to buy the security for whatever reason, and the price reflects that. Likewise, momentum can be strong and negative. Negative momentum is marked with lower highs and lower lows. No one seems interested in buying, and that keeps dragging the price down.

The exact amount of momentum that a security has can be measured with indicators known as *momentum oscillators*. A classic momentum oscillator starts with the moving average, which is the average of the closing prices for a past time period, say the last ten trading days. Then the change in each day's moving average is plotted below the price line. When the oscillator is positive, traders say that the security is *overbought*; when it's negative, they say that the security is *oversold*. Figure 10-1 shows a momentum oscillator plotted below a price line.

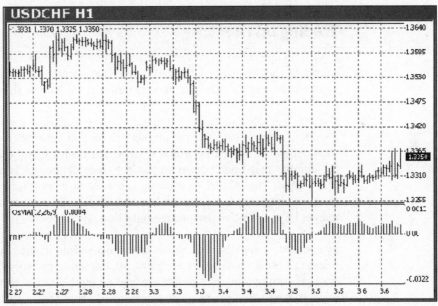

FIGURE 10-1:
A momentum oscillator indicates (no surprise here) momentum.

© John Wiley & Sons, Inc.

If a momentum oscillator shows that a security is overbought (the line is above the center line), too many people own it relative to the remaining demand in the market, and some of them will start selling. Remember, some of these people have perfectly good reasons for selling that may have nothing to do with the underlying fundamentals of the security, but they are going to sell anyway, and that brings the price down. Traders who see that a security is overbought want to sell in advance of those people.

If a momentum oscillator shows that a security is *oversold* (the line is below the center line), the security is probably too cheap. Everyone who wanted to get out has gotten out, and now it may be a bargain. When the buyers who see the profit opportunity jump in, the price goes up.

REMEMBER

The trend is your friend . . . until the end. Although great reasons exist to follow price trends, remember that they all end, so you still need to pay attention to your money management and your stops, no matter how strong a trend seems to be.

TIP

Given that most trends end — or at least zig and zag along the way — some traders look for securities that fit what they call the *1-2-3-4 criterion*. If a security goes up in price for three consecutive days, then it's likely to go down on the fourth day. Likewise, if a security has fallen in price for three days in a row, it's likely to be up on day four. Be sure to run some simulations (see Chapter 14) to see whether this strategy works for a market that interests you.

Trading on the tick

A *tick* is an upward or downward price change. For some securities, such as futures contracts, the tick size is defined as part of the contract. For others, such as stocks, a tick can be anywhere from a penny to infinity (at least in theory).

You can also calculate the tick indicator for the market as a whole. (In fact, most quotation systems calculate the market tick for you.) The tick for the market is the total number of securities in that market that traded up on the last trade minus the number that traded down on the last trade. If the tick is a positive number, that's good: The market as a whole has a lot of buying interest. Although any given security may not do as well, a positive tick shows that most people in the market have a positive perspective right now.

By contrast, a negative tick shows that most people in the market are watching prices fall. Sure, some prices are going up, but unhappy people outnumber happy ones (assuming that most people are trading on the long side, meaning that they make money when prices go up, not down). This shows that the sentiment is negative in the market right now.

Tracking the trin

Trin is short for *trading indicator,* and it's another measure of market sentiment based on how many prices have gone up relative to how many have gone down. Most quotation systems pull up the trin for a given market, but you can also calculate it on your own. The math looks like this:

$$\frac{advances}{declines}$$
$$\frac{advance\ volume}{decline\ volume}$$

The numerator is based on the tick: the number of securities that went up divided by (not less) the number that went down. The denominator includes the volume: the number of shares or contracts that traded for those securities that went up divided by the number of securities traded for those that went down in price. This solution tells you just how strongly buyers supported the securities that were going up and just how much selling pressure faced those securities that went down.

A trin of less than 1.00 usually means that a lot of buyers are taking securities up in price, and that's positive. A trin above 1.00 indicates that the sellers are acting more strongly, which means a lot of negative sentiment is in the market.

Volume

The trin indicator looks at price in conjunction with volume. *Volume* tells you how much trading is taking place in the market. How excited are people about the current price? Do they see this as a great opportunity to buy or to sell? Are they selling fast, to get out now, or are they taking a more leisurely approach to the market these days? This information is carried in the volume of the trading, and it's an important adjunct to the information you see in the prices. Volume tells you whether enough support exists to maintain price trends or whether price trends are likely to change soon.

Force index

The *force index* gives you a sense of the strength of a trend. It starts with information from prices, namely that if the closing price today is higher than the closing price yesterday, that's positive for the security. Conversely, if today's closing price is lower than yesterday's, then the force is generally negative. Then that price information is combined with volume information. The more volume that goes with that price change, the stronger that positive or negative force.

Although many quotation systems calculate force for you, you can do it yourself, too. For each trading day, run this calculation:

Force index = volume × (today's moving average – yesterday's moving average)

In other words, the force index simply scales the moving average momentum oscillator (discussed in the earlier section "Pinpointing with price indicators") for the amount of volume that accompanies that price change. That way, the trader has a sense of just how overbought or oversold the security is on any particular day.

On-balance volume

The *on-balance volume* is a running total of the amount of trading in a security. To calculate the on-balance volume, first look at today's closing price relative to yesterday's and then do one of the following:

>> **If today's close is higher than yesterday's:** Add today's volume to yesterday's on-balance volume.

>> **If today's closing price is less than yesterday's:** Subtract today's volume from yesterday's total.

>> **If today's close is the same as yesterday's:** Don't do anything! Today's balance is the same as yesterday's.

Many traders track on-balance volume over time, and here's why: A change in volume signals a change in demand. The change in demand may not show up in price right away if enough buyers exist to absorb volume from sellers. But if still more buyers are out there, then the price is going to go up. Hence, the volume from even small day-to-day increases in price need to be added up over time. If the volume keeps going up, then at some point, prices are going to have to go up to meet the demand.

On the downside, the volume from small price declines add up over time, too. Over time, this volume may show that very little pent-up interest exists, indicating that prices could languish for some time.

TIP

Many traders look to on-balance volume to gauge the behaviour of so-called *smart money*, such as pension funds, hedge funds, and mutual fund companies. Unlike individual investors, these big institutional accounts tend to trade on fundamentals rather than emotion. They generally start buying a security at the point where the dumb money is tired of owning it, so their early buying may show big volume with little price change. But as the institutions keep buying, the price has to go up to get the smarter individuals and the early institutions to part with their shares.

Open interest

Open interest has a different meaning in the stock market than in the options and futures markets, but in both cases, it gives traders useful information about demand:

>> In the stock market, open interest is the number of buy orders submitted before the market opens. When the open interest is high, people are ready to add shares to their positions or initiate new positions, which means that the stock is likely to go up in price on the demand.

>> In the options and futures markets, open interest is the number of contracts at the end of every day that have not been exercised, closed out, or allowed to expire.

Day traders don't have open interest, because by definition, day traders close out at the end of every day. But some traders keep open interest, either because they think that their position has the ability to increase in profitability or because they're hedging another transaction and need to keep that options or futures position in place. If open interest in a contract is increasing, new money is coming into the market, and prices are likely to continue to go up. This is especially true if volume is increasing at about the same rate as open interest. On the other hand, if open interest is falling, people are closing out their positions because they no longer see a profit potential, and prices are likely to fall.

Volatility, crisis, and opportunity

The *volatility* of a security is a measure of how much that security tends to go up or down in a given time period. The more volatile the security, the more the price fluctuates. Most day traders prefer volatile securities, because they create more opportunities to make a profit in a short amount of time. But volatility can make gauging market sentiment tougher. If a security is volatile, the mood can change quickly. What looked like a profit opportunity at the market open may be gone by lunchtime — and back again before the close.

Average true range

The *average true range* is a measure of volatility that's commonly used in commodity markets, but some stock traders use it, too. It's a measure of how much volatility occurred each day. When averaged over time, this measure shows how much volatility takes place during the period in question. The higher the average true range is, the more volatile a security is.

Many quotation systems calculate the average true range automatically, but if you want to do it yourself, start with finding each day's *true range,* which is the greatest of

>> The current high less the current low

>> The absolute value of the current high less the previous close

>> The absolute value of the current low less the previous close

Calculate those three numbers and then average the highest of them with the true range for the past 14 days.

Each day's true range number shows you just how much the security swung between the high and the low or how much the high or the low that day varied from the previous day's close.

Beta

Beta is the *covariance* (that is, the statistical measure of how much two variables move together) of a stock relative to the rest of the market. The number comes from the *capital assets pricing model,* which is an equation used in academic circles to model the performance of securities. Traders don't use the capital assets pricing model, but they often talk about beta to evaluate the volatility of stocks and options.

What does beta mean?

>> A beta of 1.00 means that the security is moving at a faster rate than the market. You would buy high betas if you think the market is going up but not if the market is going down.

>> A beta of less than 1.00 means that the security is moving more slowly than the market — a good thing if you want less risk than the market.

>> A beta of exactly 1.00 means that the security is moving at the same rate as the market.

>> A negative beta means that the security is moving in the opposite direction of the market. The easiest way to get a negative beta security is to *short* (borrow and then sell) a positive beta security.

The VIX

VIX is short for the Chicago Board Options Exchange Volatility Index. Calculating VIX is complex enough to border on being proprietary, but it's available on many quotation systems and on the exchange's website, `www.cboe.com/products/vix-index-volatility`.

The VIX is based on the implied volatility of options on stocks included in the S&P 500 Index. The greater the volatility, the more uncertainty investors have; the more options that show great volatility, the more widespread is the concern about prospects for the financial markets. In fact, the VIX is often called *the fear index* and is used to gauge the amount of negative sentiment investors have. The greater the VIX, the more bearish the outlook for the market in general. The more bearish the outlook, the more likely the market is to be volatile. And volatility is the day trader's best friend.

Traders can use the VIX to help them value options on the market indexes. (For that matter, traders who want to take a position on market volatility can use options and futures contracts on the VIX, including a mini-sized future, offered by the Chicago Board Options Exchange.) The VIX can also be used to help confirm bullish or bearish sentiment that shows up in other market signals, such as the tick or the on-balance volume measures described earlier. The CBOE also calculates a VIX number on a handful of common stocks, if you are trading those issues or the options on them.

In addition to the VIX, the exchange also tracks the *VXN* (volatility on the Nasdaq 100 Index) and the *VXD* (volatility on the Dow Jones Industrial Average). For a decade, Canada did have its own volatility index, the S&P/TSX 60 VIX, but it was decommissioned in January of 2020. According to the TSX, a new version of this index is coming to market, but so far, no additional details have been released. In any case, the VIX has long been the preferred volatility index for the majority of Canadian traders.

Volatility ratio

The *volatility ratio* tells traders what the implied volatility of a security is relative to the recent historical volatility. This ratio shows whether the security is expected to be more or less volatile right now than it has been in the past, and it's widely used in option markets. The first calculation required is the *implied volatility,* which is backed out using the Black-Scholes model, an academic model for valuing options. When you plug in to the model certain variables — time until expiration, interest rates, dividends, stock price, and strike price — the implied volatility is the volatility number that then generates the current option price. (You don't have to perform these calculations yourself because most quotation systems generate implied volatility for you.)

After you have the implied volatility, you can compare it to the historical volatility of the option, which tells you just how much the price changed over the last 20 or 90 days. If the implied volatility is greater than the statistical volatility, the market may be overestimating the uncertainty in the prices, and the options may be overvalued. If the implied volatility is much less than the statistical volatility, the market may be underestimating uncertainty, so the options may be undervalued.

Measuring Money Flows

Money flows tell you how much money is going into or out of a market. They are another set of indicators telling you where the market sentiment is right now and where it may be going soon. Money-flow indicators combine features of price and volume indicators to help traders gauge the market. Although amounts spent to buy and sell have to match — otherwise, the market wouldn't exist — the enthusiasm of the buyers and the anxiousness of the sellers show up in the volume traded and the direction of the price change. Just how hard was it for the buyers to get the sellers to part with their positions? And how hard will it be to get them to part with their positions tomorrow? That's the information contained in money-flow indicators.

The most basic money-flow indicator is the change in closing price multiplied by the number of shares traded. If the closing price was higher than the closing price yesterday, then the number is positive; if the closing price today was lower than the price yesterday, then the number is negative. Other indicators out there use midpoint values and don't go negative; instead, the numbers range from higher to lower. Whether positive or negative, a high money flow indicates strong buying activity, and that indicates that a positive price trend is likely to continue.

Accumulation/distribution index

In trading terms, *accumulation* is controlled buying, and *distribution* is controlled selling. This kind of buying and selling doesn't lead to big changes in securities prices, usually because the action was planned. No one accumulates or distributes a security in a state of panic.

But even if the buying and selling activity isn't driven by madcap rushes in and out of positions, it's still important to know whether, on balance, the buyers or the sellers have the slight predominance in the market, because that may affect the direction of prices in the near future. For example, if a security has been in an upward trend but more and more down days occur with increasing volume, the sellers are starting to dominate the trading, and the price trend is likely to go down.

To determine the accumulation/distribution index, you use this equation:

$$\frac{accumulation}{distribution} = \frac{(close - low) - (high - close)}{(high - low) \times period's\ volume}$$

Some traders look at accumulation/distribution from day to day, whereas others prefer to look at it for a week or even a month's worth of trading. One way isn't inherently better than the other; it depends on what you trade and how you trade it.

Money-flow ratio and money-flow index

Money flow is closing price multiplied by the number of shares traded. That basic statistic can be manipulated in strange and wonderful ways to generate new statistics carrying even more information about whether the markets are likely to have more buying pressure or more selling pressure in the future.

The first is the *money-flow ratio,* which is simply the total money flow for those days where prices were up from the prior day (days with positive money flow) divided by the total money flow for those days where prices were down from the prior day (which are the days with negative money flow). Day traders tend to calculate money-flow ratios for short time periods, such as a week or ten days, whereas swing traders and investors tend to care about longer time periods, like a month or even four months of trading.

The money-flow ratio is sometimes converted into the *money-flow index,* which can be used as a single indicator or tracked relative to prices for a given period of time. The equation used to figure out the money-flow index looks like this:

$$MFI = 100 - \frac{100}{1 + money\ ratio}$$

If the money-flow index is more than 80, the security is usually considered to be overbought — meaning that the buyers are done buying, and the sellers will put downward pressure on prices. If the money-flow index is less than 20, the security is usually considered to be oversold, and the buyers will soon take over and drive prices up. In between, the money-flow index can help clarify information from other market indicators.

Short interest ratios

Short selling is a way to make money if a security falls in price. In the options and futures markets, one simply agrees to sell a contract to someone else. In the stock and bond markets, short selling is a little more complicated. The short seller borrows stock or bonds through the brokerage firm and then sells them. Ideally, the price falls, and then the trader can buy back the stock or bonds at the lower price to repay the loan. The trader keeps the difference between the security's selling price and its repurchasing price. (The process is described in more detail in Chapter 6.)

People take the short side of a position for only one reason: They think that prices are going to go down. They may want to hedge against this, or they may want to make a big profit if it happens. In the stock market in particular, monitoring the rate of short selling can give clues to investor expectations and future market direction.

The New York Stock Exchange and Nasdaq report the short interest in stocks listed with them. In Canada, IIROC puts out a report that lists the aggregate short positions of all listed securities. The U.S. data is updated monthly, while the Canadian information comes out on the 15th and the last day of every month. (Find the reports here: www.iiroc.ca/industry/marketmonitoringanalysis/Pages/consolidated-short-position-report.aspx.) It takes awhile because brokerage firms must sort out exactly how many shares have been shorted and then report that data. In the U.S., the resulting number, the *short interest ratio*, tells the number of shares that have been shorted, the percentage change from the month before, the average daily trading volume in the same month, and the number of days of trading at the average volume that covering the short positions would take. IIROC only reports the number of shares that have been shorted and the net change from the month before, along with which exchange the stock is listed on (such as TSX, TSXV, CSE, and so on).

REMEMBER

The loans that enable short selling have to be repaid. If the lender asks for the securities back or if prices go up so that the position starts to lose money, the trader is going to have to buy shares to make repayment. The harder it is to get the right number of shares in the market, the more desperate the trader will become, and the higher prices will go.

An increase in short interest shows that investors are becoming nervous about a stock. However, given that short interest is not calculated frequently, the number would probably not give a trader a lot of information about the prospects for the company itself. This doesn't mean short interest doesn't carry a lot of useful information for traders. It does. If the short interest is high, then the security price is likely to go up when all the people who are short need to buy back stock. Likewise, if short interest is low, there will be little buying pressure in the near future.

REMEMBER

High short interest, along with other bullish indicators, is a sign that prices are more likely to go up than down in the near future.

Considering Information That Crops Up during the Trading Day

Technical analysis (covered in Chapter 9) and all the indicators discussed in this chapter offer useful information about what's happening in the markets, but there's one problem: Because so many of those indicators are based on closing prices and closing volume, they aren't much use during the trading day. In fact, many traders read through the information in the morning before the open to sort out what is likely to happen and what the mood of the market is likely to be, but then they have to recalibrate their gauge of the market as information comes to them during the trading day. That information doesn't show up on charts or in neat numerical indicators until the day ends. Fortunately, several sources of information that are updated while the market is open can give a trader a sense of what's happening at any given time.

Price, time, and sales

The most important information for a trader is the current price of the security, how often and in what volume it has been trading, and how much the price has moved from the last trade. This information is the most basic real-time info out there, and it's readily available through a brokerage firm's quotation screens.

Chapter 13 discusses the different quotation services that traders can obtain from their brokerage firms. Although your broker may charge you more to get more detailed quotes, doing so is worth it for most trading strategies. Knowing how the price is moving can give you a sense of whether the general mood of the market is being confirmed or contradicted — information that can help you place more profitable trades.

Order book

High-level price-quote data, such as that available through Nasdaq Basic Canada, Nasdaq Level 2 or Nasdaq TotalView-ITCH, include information on who is placing orders and just how large those orders are. The order book gives you key data because it gives you a sense of how smart the other buyers and sellers are. Are they day traders just trying not to be killed? Or are they institutions that have done a lot of research and are under a lot of performance pressure? Sure, day traders are often very right and institutions are often very wrong, but the information you see in the order book can help you sense whether people are trading on information or on emotion.

An additional piece of information from the order book can help you figure out what's happening in the market now — namely, the presence of an *order imbalance*. An order imbalance means that the number of buyers and sellers doesn't match. This situation often occurs during the open because some traders prefer to place orders before the market opens, whereas others prefer to wait until after the open. These imbalances tend to be small and clear up quickly. However, if a major news event takes place or a great deal of fear exists in the market, large imbalances can occur during the trading day. These imbalances can be disruptive, and in some cases, the exchange stops trading until news is disseminated and enough new orders are placed to balance out the orders.

The order book doesn't show all the orders. Most brokerage firms maintain *dark pools* (also known as *dark books* or *dark liquidity*) for large clients or for their trading desks. Dark pools are collections of orders above or below market prices that aren't advertised except in the pool or on electronic communication networks (also known as ECNs). Traders use this technique to help buy or sell securities without affecting the price and to reduce trading costs. The order is executed only if someone matches it inadvertently rather than the market price changing to meet the changing supply and demand. The bad news for a day trader is that these trades can contribute to market volatility without giving any advance warning.

Quote stuffing

Quote stuffing is the practice of placing a really large number of orders for a security, often at a price significantly above or below the current market price. Almost as soon as the orders are placed, they're cancelled. The transaction is completely handled by computerized trading systems, not people. The people behind the placement of these orders are sometimes referred to as *quote-rate pirates*.

The official idea seems to be to hide customer orders in order to reduce their effect on the market, especially to keep them hidden from other computer trading systems, but in practice, these quotes seem to be a way to lead the market up or down by placing an unusually high or low order out there. Hence, quote stuffing may be outright market manipulation. In some cases, it may simply be that the algorithms in the computer programs place wacky orders for reasons that make sense only to other computer programs. Either way, these orders contribute to market volatility. That may be just the way it goes, unless the orders are placed for nefarious purposes.

Regulators aren't happy with quote stuffing, and it is prohibited — if it's caught.

News flows

Although much of the discussion in this chapter is about the information contained in price, volume, and other trade data, the actual information that comes from news releases is at least as important.

Much of the news is regularly scheduled and much predicted: corporate earnings, Bank of Canada discount rates, unemployment rates, housing starts, and the like. When this information comes in, traders want to know how the actual results compare with what was expected and how this info fits with the overall bullish or bearish sentiment of the market.

The second type of news is the unscheduled breaking event, such as corporate takeovers, horrible storms, political assassinations — and in 2020, a pandemic — or other happenings that were not expected and that take more time for the market to digest. That's in part because these events have the ability to change trends rather than play out against them. In some cases, the markets will halt trading to allow this information to disseminate. (This happened in March 2020, and on more than one occasion, when COVID-19-related fears caused stocks to fall quickly and significantly.) In other cases, traders have to react quickly based on what they know now and what they suspect will happen in the near future.

Many day traders track Twitter and other social-media feeds for information during the trading day, and some brokers include these feeds as part of the services that they offer to their customers. Social media is a permitted way for companies to disseminate information to the market, but it can also be spoofed in such a way as to cause headaches. Even if the tweet is legitimate, it can be used in ways that create havoc. In August of 2018, Elon Musk, the CEO of Tesla Inc., sent out a tweet that he was thinking of taking the company private before the board of directors or other senior executives knew. The story created turmoil in the market — as well as in the company. The SEC ended up charging Musk for securities fraud, though a settlement between the two sides forced Musk to step down as chairman of the board.

TECHNICAL STUFF

What's the difference between risk and uncertainty? *Risk* is something that happens often enough that people can quantify the damage. *Uncertainty* is something that may happen, but no one can figure out the likelihood. A fire that knocks out power to Midtown Manhattan sometime in the next ten years is a risk; the invasion of the planet by aliens from outer space is uncertainty.

WARNING

News can happen at any time. It can change a trend and throw all your careful analysis into disarray. For this reason, careful analysis is no substitute for risk management. Watch your position sizes and have stops in place so that you exit when you need to.

Identifying Anomalies and Traps

Traders can be superstitious, and that superstition shows up in different anomalies and traps that affect the mood of the market even when there is no logical reason for their existence. You want to be aware of them, because they can affect trading.

An *anomaly* is a market condition that occurs regularly but for no good reason. It can be related to the month of the year, the day of the week, or the size of the company involved. A *trap* is a situation where the market doesn't perform the way you expect it to given the indicators that you are looking at. You have a choice: Go with what the market is telling you or go with what your indicators are telling you.

REMEMBER

To a long-term investor, perception is perception. When perception is different from reality, an opportunity exists to make money. To a short-term trader, perception is reality because it affects what happens before everyone figures out what's real.

Bear traps and bull traps

Traders talk about getting caught in traps, which neatly fits the language of bulls and bears. When they stumble into a trap, they're stuck moving against the market, which causes them big trouble. After all, day trading is about identifying trends and moving with them. You only have a few hours to work before the time comes to close out. In this section, we list a few common traps to help you identify and, we hope, avoid them.

TIP

The best antidote for a trap is to take your loss and move on to the next trade.

Chart traps

Look at some of the sample charts in Chapter 9. If you look at actual price charts created in the market every day, you may notice that sometimes it's difficult to determine whether a breakout is false or real and whether a trend is changing or just playing out with a smaller subtrend. A ton of subjectivity goes into reading charts, and some days you read them wrong. You think you're ahead of the market when you're actually just trading against it. Ouch!

Some traders try to work around these types of chart traps by automating their trading. Several different software packages are available that can scan the market and identify potential trading opportunities. But even the best software misreads the market on some occasions, which is why you need to monitor your positions and make sure you stick to your loss limits.

Contrarian traps

In Chapter 1, we note that about 80 percent of day traders lose money. So maybe you're thinking that the way to make money is to just do the opposite of what everyone else is doing. But the reason that day traders lose money isn't so much that they're wrong about the trend; it's because they're sloppy in their trading and don't limit their losses. (That's why so much of this book is about the business of trading rather than the actual mechanics of placing buy and sell orders.)

In a *contrarian trap*, the trader has made the decision to trade against the market, and that's exactly what happens: He or she loses money because the market is moving in the opposite direction. Taking a contrary position doesn't work too well in day trading. In most cases, you have to go with the flow, not against it, to make money in a single day's session. The market is always right in the short term.

A lot of people make money with a contrarian strategy, but they need to pay attention to avoid the traps.

Calendar effects

Many trading anomalies follow time periods — which is not completely unexpected — because many economic and business trends follow the calendar. Companies report their results quarterly. Most close their books for tax purposes at the end of the year. Investors are also evaluated quarterly. Retail sales follow holiday seasons, demand for commodities follows the growing season, and fuel demand varies with the weather. Whatever you decide to trade, you need to do enough *fundamental* research (the study of the business and economic factors that affect the security) so that you know how your chosen securities move over time.

But some of the calendar effects — the January effect, the Monday effect, and the October effect — make little logical sense, yet they still influence trading.

The January effect

Many years ago, the stock market would go up in the early part of January. Why? No one was entirely sure, but the guess is that people tended to sell at the end of December for tax reasons and then buy back those securities in January. It may also be that in the new year everyone is flush with excitement and ready to see the market go up, so they put money to work and start buying.

REMEMBER

If stocks go up in January, then you can get a jump on the market by buying in December, right? And that would make prices go up in December. To get a jump on the December rally, you could buy in November. And that's exactly what people started to do, and the once-pronounced January effect is now weak to nonexistent. (People still talk about it, though, sometimes calling it the *December effect.*) In an efficient market, people eventually figure out these unexplained phenomena and then trade on them until they disappear. Use these anomalies as a way to gauge psychology, not as hard and fast trading rules.

The Monday effect

The market seems to do more poorly on Monday than on the other days of the week. And no matter what the evidence shows (the research is ambiguous, and the findings vary greatly based on the time period and the markets examined), many traders believe this to be true, so it has an effect. Why? There are two thoughts. The first is that people are in a bad mood on Monday because they have to go back to work after the weekend. The second is that people spend all weekend analyzing any bad news from the end of the prior week and then sell as soon as they get back to the office.

TECHNICAL STUFF

The 2008 stock market crash happened on a Monday. Over the previous weekend, the different regulatory agencies decided to allow the old-line brokerage firm of Lehman Brothers to fail. The firm failed to open on Monday, September 15, and the rest of the market went into a tailspin.

The October effect

The stock market has had two grand crashes and one smaller but profound one in October:

>> **October 29, 1929:** On this day, known as Black Tuesday, the Dow Jones Industrial Average declined 12 percent in one day as market speculators caught up with the less rosy reality of the economy. This crash kicked off a general decline that contributed to the Great Depression of the 1930s.

>> **October 19, 1987:** This day, known as Black Monday, saw the Dow Jones Industrial Average decline 23 percent. No one is really sure why this crash happened, but it did.

>> **October 13, 1989:** On this day, the Dow Jones declined 7 percent in the last hour of trading when a leveraged buyout for United Airlines fell through.

Because of these crashes, many traders believe that bad things happen in October, and they act accordingly. Of course, bad things happen in other months. The crash in the Nasdaq market that marked the end of the 1990s tech bubble took place in March 2000, but no one talks about a March effect. The 2008 crash took place in September, while the COVID-19 market meltdown happened in March. Bottom line: Markets move up and down all the time.

Chapter **11**

Eliminating Emotion with Program Trading

n a way, day trading is simple. You see an indicator showing that a trend is starting. You place a trade. Then, when the trend is over or you hit your loss limit, you close out the trade.

Ah, but there are two challenges. The first is identifying an indicator or trend in enough time to trade on it. The second is fighting your emotions so that you actually execute the trade and then close it out — and not execute a completely different trade, or be too overcome with doubt to place the trade, or wish and hope that the loss will magically reverse itself.

Many traders find that the way to make trading work is to do it automatically. They set up their accounts to scan for indicators, and then they place the trades for them. Some traders trust their systems enough to have them do it all for them, whereas others prefer to place the trades themselves but appreciate the reminders.

Think of this chapter as a continuation of Chapter 10. A *trading program*, also known as an *algorithm*, an *expert advisor*, or a *trading robot* — works off of the indicators discussed there. Whether or not you actually use programs, understanding how they work can help you approach the markets better.

This chapter doesn't provide you with a magic money-making machine. In fact, be suspicious of anyone who offers to sell you a trading program that's a sure thing. This chapter does give you some ideas for when to trade and how to take your emotions out of the game.

Creating Your Own Trading Program

Developing a trading algorithm can help you distill your strategy, and it can execute even when you're nervous about pulling the trigger. However, the program is only as good as the programmer. If you write a bad program, you'll get bad trading. Also, market conditions change — a program that worked for a while may need to be tweaked or even scrapped all together.

Before you start programming, you want to spend time with the markets looking at indicators and seeing how the assets that you want to work with trade. And before we get into the soft chewy center of this chapter, make sure you do two hard things: have a plan and know the limitations.

Recognizing what you want to automate

Take out a sheet of paper and a pen, and write out the steps of your ideal trade from start to finish. Answer the following:

>> What are you looking for?

>> What will you do when you see it?

>> What is your loss limit?

>> When will you close it?

Answering these questions can move you toward making your trading more systematic, whether or not you decide to turn to a robot to execute the trades for you.

Here's an example:

1. Scan for the 5-day moving average crossing above the 50-day long-term moving average.

2. When that happens, place an order to place 5 percent of trading capital in that stock.

3. Hold until the stock trades on two downticks in a row or at the end of the day.

You can't write a program until you can write out step by step what you want to do. And, really, you shouldn't trade at all until you can do that.

Knowing the limitations of robots

Robots only do what they're programmed to do. A robot designed to clean carpets can't wash dishes. A robot programmed to trade badly can't trade well. Trading algorithms are only as good as they were designed to be, and they can't respond to changes in market conditions by themselves. You can't set the program to run and then walk away from it.

Yes, the big hedge funds and brokerage firms rely on algorithmic trading. They also hire people with PhDs in computer science to help them. Some hedge funds do such things as locate their servers on the floors of the exchange to speed execution, and they program in artificial intelligence to adapt to changes. You can't keep up.

Programming, the Day Trading Way

Most modern day traders find that they need to program their trades. In other words, they need to determine what they're trading, identify the signals they use to buy and sell securities, and set their trading platform to execute the orders automatically. Instead of working on your reflexes, you do the work of planning and testing.

REMEMBER

Of course, a program is only as good as its inputs, and even the biggest of the big trading firms have had huge losses because of trading glitches.

You don't need to be a software engineer to develop trading programs. Many of the charting services offer program templates that you can follow or adapt; the brokerage firms that work with day traders offer trading platforms that can be programmed without too much effort, usually by clicking on icons or inserting widgets of prewritten code.

Start by writing out your process step by step with a pen on paper before you attempt to convert it to code. Then look at what may be available from your broker or different trading platforms before moving on to programming your trades yourself.

The next sections give you some sense of what products are on the market and how they can be used to help automate your trading and take emotion out of the game.

Looking at basic brokerage offerings

Most brokers who cater to day traders offer automating scanning and signaling. These services allow you to specify parameters that you want to know about for your trading. You'll receive a notice whenever the system detects your parameter in the market so that you can trade. These services can speed up your trading, but they still rely on you to execute the suggested trade.

You can use stop and limit orders to help with automating your trading, especially in enforcing loss limits.

Beyond that, some brokerage firms offer the ability to develop simple algorithms using their scanning and signaling services. These services are usually basic "if, then" commands, but they can go a long way to help you get started.

In addition, your broker may offer tutorials and other tools to help you figure out how to use its platform to trade more effectively.

Adding a trading platform

If you have a complex algorithm in mind, you may want to work with a trading platform that works with your brokerage firm's order entry system and allows you to do some serious programming.

Many of these systems use Python or a proprietary programming language to help you create algorithms that work for you. They can allow you to do almost anything you want.

The key, of course, is that you know what you want to do. Having more programming power isn't going to help you trade better unless you know how to trade and how to program.

Finding trading modules

Not everyone writing day trading programs is an expert computer programmer. They get help! Some vendors sell completed programs and promise that you can make money from them. That's possible. Other traders create modules for different trading platforms that they give away or sell, and you can use them to build out your own programs. Each module is a chunk of code that lets you do one thing, and if you put a few together, you end up with a complete trade.

Finally, plenty of videos and tutorials are available online that have instructions on how to program for your trading. They can help you hone your skills. All of them need to be tested, which is what leads into the next section.

Backtesting Once, Backtesting Twice

We bring up a lot of trading maxims in this book, but this time, here is a popular programming maxim to remember:

> Garbage in, garbage out.

Having a program doesn't necessarily mean that you're going to trade well, and a program that works for a while may not work forever. That's why you have to test it.

REMEMBER

Backtesting is the process of running a trading program through historical data to see how it would have performed. It not only helps you see if the program works, it also helps you pinpoint areas where it doesn't perform well so that you can refine it. You may note that it works better in some types of market conditions than others — more information you can use to hone your trading skills. Almost all brokers and trading platforms offer backtesting services to their day trading customers, because it's that critical.

You can also run your program on current market conditions without trading actual money, a process known as *paper trading* or *simulation trading*. It's a way to see how your program works in current conditions.

Ultimately, though, the true test will be putting it to work in actual trading with actual dollars. You may find some additional glitches and have to start over again.

Trade programming is iterative. To some people, the opportunity to test and refine is part of the fun. Chapter 14 goes into this process in more detail, but for now, know that it's a necessary component of algorithmic trading.

Building on Some Standard Strategies

Day trading, whether done by person or machine, relies on some basic strategies. Trading algorithms build off charts, technical indicators, and common strategies; they don't bring some new secret sauce to the table.

In this section, we review the strategies that traders use to play off the information they receive from their different signals.

Range trading

Range trading, sometimes called *channel trading*, starts with an understanding of the recent trading history of a given security. Getting this history involves looking at the charts (see Chapter 9) to identify typical highs and lows during the day as well as the typical difference between these two prices. With this information, you simply buy low and sell high. When the security dips in price, you place the order to buy; when the security rises, you place the order to sell.

Most range traders use stops and limits to keep their trading in line with what they see. A *stop* limits the loss if the security keeps dropping below your entry point, and the *limit order* gets you out at a profit if the security moves to the top of the range.

REMEMBER

Range trading works in a normal market with just enough volatility to keep the price wiggling around during the day but not so much that it breaks out of the range and starts a new trend.

Contrarian trading

Momentum traders buy securities when prices are rising and sell when prices are falling. These traders figure that something that goes up in price will continue to go up and something going down will continue to go down. Momentum trading (refer to Chapter 12) is one strategy, and it works well for many traders, especially in a strong bull market.

Contrarian trading, on the other hand, is just the opposite of momentum trading, and it can work well, too. The logic behind a contrarian strategy is that nothing goes up forever; for that matter, nothing falls forever, either. The contrarian trader looks for assets that have been rising in price and sells them; she prefers to buy things that have been falling. The point is to sell what seems to be overpriced and buy what seems to be a bargain. Contrarian traders may just be quick to spot when a trend ends. For example, they may buy on a rumour and sell on the news, jumping out right when everyone else is ready to jump in.

Many people who use this strategy well tend to be bargain hunters in every aspect of their lives. They stock up on frozen vegetables when the grocery store has a once-a-year loss leader, and they sell their apartment if their neighbourhood's real estate gets too hot. They have a nose for value and put that to work during the trading day.

Contrarian traders are fighting the trend, which can work against them some-times. This style favours people who know a market inside and out so that they know when to move against it.

News trading

News trading is possibly the most traditional form of day trading. This type of trader doesn't pay much attention to charts. Instead, he waits for information that will drive prices. This information may come in the form of a company announcement about earnings or new products, a general economic announcement about interest rates or unemployment, or just a lot of rumours about what may or may not be happening in a given industry.

Traders who do well with news trading usually have some understanding of the markets they're working in. They're not hard-core fundamental researchers, but they know enough to know what kind of news would be taken well by the markets and what would be taken poorly. They also have the attention span needed to pay attention to a few different news sources simultaneously, as well as the ability to place the order when the time comes.

The downside of news trading is that really good events may be few and far between; more often, the hype is already built into the price by the time you see it. Also, news trading is difficult to automate, although more and more computer programs draw signals from news and social media feeds. You can't place a limit order to buy when a price level is hit; you have to wait until you see the news and then place the order yourself. Thus, news trading works well only for traders who can commit to placing the order.

Pairs trading

With *pair trading*, a pairs trader looks for two related assets and goes long on the stronger one and short on the weaker. Many pairs traders work with stocks and look for two companies in the same industry, but a pairs strategy can be worked in futures and currency markets, too — going long on metals and short on interest-rate futures, for example, or long on the dollar and short on the euro. The idea is to get the maximum return possible from a trend that affects both assets. For example, if one retail stock does really well, it may be because the company is taking market share from a weaker one. These trades are a little more complex because you have to plan both sides.

Arbitraging for Fun . . . and Profit

The key to success in any investment is buying low and selling high. But what's low? And what's high? Who knows?

In the financial markets, the general assumption is that, at least in the short run, the market price is the right price. Only investors, those patient, long-suffering accounting nerds willing to hold investments for years, see deviations between the market price and the true worth of an investment. For everyone else, especially day traders, what you see is what you get.

REMEMBER

Under *the law of one price*, the same asset has the same value everywhere. If markets allow for easy trading — and the financial markets certainly do — then any price discrepancies are short-lived because traders immediately step in to buy at the low price and sell at the high price. In the following sections, we explore how market efficiency limits arbitrage opportunities and how you can step in when the moment is right.

Program trading offers huge advantages for *arbitrage trading* (trading in order to achieve a riskless profit) because the robot can see a price discrepancy and act on it before many humans would be able to.

Understanding how arbitrage and market efficiency interact

The law of one price holds as long as markets are efficient. Market efficiency is a controversial topic in finance. In academic theory, markets are perfectly efficient, and arbitrage simply isn't possible. That makes a lot of sense if you are testing different assumptions about how the markets would work in a perfect world. A long-term investor would say that markets are inefficient in the short run but perfectly efficient in the long run, so they believe that if they do their research now, the rest of the world will eventually come around, allowing them to make good money.

Traders are in between. The market price and volume are pretty much all the information they have to go on. The price may be irrational, but that doesn't matter today. The only thing a trader wants to know is whether an opportunity exists to make money given what's going on right now.

In the academic world, market efficiency comes in three flavours, with no form allowing for arbitrage:

>> **Strong form:** Everything, even inside information known only to company executives, is reflected in the security's price.

>> **Semi-strong form:** Prices include all public information, so profiting from insider trading may be possible.

>> **Weak-form:** Prices reflect all historical information, so research that uncovers new trends may be beneficial.

Those efficient-market true believers are convinced that arbitrage is imaginary because someone would've noticed a price difference between markets already and immediately acted to close it off. But who are those mysterious someones? They are day traders! Even the most devout efficient markets adherent would, if pressed, admit that day traders perform a valuable service in the name of market efficiency.

Those folks with a less-rigid view of market activity admit that arbitrage opportunities exist but that they are few and far between. A trader who expects to make money from arbitrage had better pay close attention to the markets to act quickly when a moment happens.

Finally, people who don't believe in market efficiency believe that market prices are usually out of sync with asset values. They do research in hopes of learning things that other people don't know. This mindset favours investors more than traders because it can take time for these price discrepancies to work themselves out.

TIP

Because arbitrage requires traders to work fast, it tends to work best for traders who are willing and able to automate their trading. If you are comfortable with programming and relying on software to do your work, arbitrage may be a great strategy for you. Remember that the big players have an advantage.

Taking advantages of price discrepancies

So how can you as a day trader take advantage of what you know about the one-price rule? Suppose that what you see in Toronto is not what you see in London, or that you notice that futures prices are not tracking movements in the underlying asset. How about if you see that the stock of every company except one in an industry has reacted to a news event?

Well, then, you have an opportunity to make money, but you'd better act fast because other people — and other robots — will probably see the discrepancy, too. What you do is simple: You sell as much of the high-priced asset in the high-priced market as you can, borrowing shares if you need to, and then you immediately turn around and buy the low-priced asset in the low-priced market.

TIP

Think of the markets as a scale, and you, the arbitrageur, must bring fairness to them. When the markets are out of balance, you take from the high-priced market (the heavier side of the scale) and return it to the low-priced market (the lighter side) until both even out at a price in between.

If you start with a high price of $8 and a low price of $6 and then buy at $6 and sell at $8, your maximum profit is $2 — with no risk. Until the point where the two assets balance at $7, you can make a profit on the difference between them.

Of course, most price differences are on the order of pennies, not dollars, but if you can find enough of these little pricing errors and trade them in size, you can make good money.

WARNING

Sometimes, the price differences are less than a penny, a situation the traders call *subpennying*. A day trader really can't work with that. To see if subpennying is going on with an asset that you trade, set your price screens to display four decimal places rather than only two.

Scalping, the Dangerous Game

The law of one price is all well and good, but prices change constantly during the day. They go up a little bit, they go down a little bit, and they move every time an order is placed.

Once upon a time, day traders could profit from these movements. The process, known as *scalping*, is not exactly arbitrage. Especially active in commodities markets, scalpers look to take advantage of changes in a security's *bid-ask spread*. This spread is the difference between the price that a broker will buy a security for from those who want to sell it (the *bid*) and the price that the broker will charge those who want to buy it (the *ask* — also called the *offer* in some markets).

In normal trading, the bid-ask spread tends to be more or less steady over time because the usual flow of supply and demand stays in balance. After all, under market efficiency, everyone has the same information, so their trading is consistent and allows the broker-dealers to generate a steady profit. Sometimes, however, the spread is a little wider or narrower than normal, not because of a change in the information in the market but because of short-term imbalances in supply and demand.

A basic scalping strategy looks like this:

>> **If the spread between the bid and the ask is wider than usual,** the ask is higher and the bid is lower than it should be. That's because slightly more people want to buy than to sell, so the brokers charge the buyers higher prices. The scalper uses this as a sign to sell.

>> **If the spread between the bid and the ask is narrower than usual,** the ask is lower and the bid is higher than it would normally be. This situation occurs when sellers slightly outnumber buyers and the broker wants to find buyers to pick up the slack. The scalper would be in there buying — and hoping that the selling pressure is short lived.

The scalper has to work quickly to make many small trades. He may buy at $20.25, sell at $20.50, and buy again at $20.30. He has to have a low *trade cost structure* in place (discussed later in this chapter) or else he'll pay out all his profits and more to the broker. He also has to be sure that the price changes aren't driven by real information, because that makes market prices too volatile to make scalping profitable. Scalping is akin to "picking up nickels in front of a steamroller," some traders say, because of the risk of focusing on small price changes when bigger changes are underway.

WARNING

For years, scalping was a common day trading strategy. It was always tricky business, given how quickly prices could move within a trend. With the presence of so many high-frequency traders, scalping has become downright dangerous, if not impossible. You may have a good program for scalping, but other people probably have better ones — and don't even think of scalping without a program to help you. Nowadays, scalping is like picking up pennies as steamrollers come at you from all sides.

WARNING

Scalping, as defined here, is perfectly legal. However, the word is also used to describe some illegal activities, such as promoting a security in public and then selling it in private. (Another term for this is *pump and dump.*) If a celebrity goes on his Twitter feed and talks about how great a stock is so that the price goes up and then he sells the stock the next day when everyone else is buying, he has committed the crime of scalping.

Understanding Risk Arbitrage and Its Tools

In its purest form, arbitrage is riskless because the purchase of an asset in one market and the sale of the asset in another happen simultaneously — you just let those profits flow right into your account. This situation does occur, but not often, and not in a way that lets most day traders compete with algorithmic traders.

Because so few opportunities for true arbitrage exist, most day traders looking at arbitrage strategies actually practice *risk arbitrage.* Like true arbitrage, risk arbitrage attempts to generate profits from price discrepancies, but like the name implies, risk arbitrage involves taking some risk. Yes, you buy one security and sell another in risk arbitrage, but it's not always the same security and not always at the same time. For example, a day trader may buy the stock of an acquisition target and sell the stock of an acquirer in the hopes of making a profit as the deal nears the closing date.

WARNING

Risk arbitrage usually involves strategies that unfold over time — possibly hours, but usually days or weeks. Pursuing these strategies puts you into the world of swing trading (refer to Chapter 8), which carries a different set of risks than day trading.

In risk arbitrage, a trader is buying and selling similar securities. Much of the risk draws from the fact that the securities are not identical, so the law of one price isn't absolute. Nevertheless, it forms the guiding principle, which is this: If you have two different ways to buy the same thing, then the prices of each purchase should be proportional. If the prices aren't proportional, there's an opportunity to make money. And what day trader doesn't want to make money?

REMEMBER

Return is a function of risk. The more risk you take, the greater the return you expect to make.

Arbitrageurs use a mix of different assets and techniques to create these different ways of buying the same thing. The following sections describe some of their favourites.

Arbitrating derivatives

Derivatives are options, futures, and related financial contracts that draw or derive their value from the value of something else, such as the price of a stock index or the current cost of corn. Derivatives offer a lower-cost, lower-obligation method of getting exposure to certain price changes. In the case of agricultural and energy commodities, derivatives are the only practical way for a day trader to own them. Because they are so closely tied to the value of the underlying security, derivatives form a useful, almost-but-not-quite asset for traders looking for arbitrage situations. A trader may see a price discrepancy between the derivative and the underlying asset, thus noticing a profitable trading opportunity.

Using a derivative in tandem with its underlying security, traders can construct a range of risk arbitrage trades (and you can read more about them later in this section). For example, a trader looking to set up arbitrage on a merger could trade options on the stocks of the buying and selling companies rather than trading the stocks themselves. The more arbitrage opportunities there are, the greater the likelihood of making a low-risk profit.

Levering with leverage

Leverage is the process of borrowing money to trade in order to increase potential returns. The more money the trader borrows, the greater the return on capital that she can earn. Leverage is commonly used by day traders, because most trades with a one-day time horizon carry low returns unless they are magnified through borrowing. (Go to Chapter 6 for detailed coverage of leverage.)

That magic of magnification becomes especially important in arbitrage, because the price discrepancies between securities tend to be really small. The primary way to get a bigger return is to borrow money to do it.

WARNING

Leverage has a downside: Along with improving returns, it increases risk. Because even risk arbitrage strategies tend to have low risk, the risk associated with leverage may be acceptable. Just remember that you have to repay all borrowed money, no matter what happens to prices.

Short selling

Short selling (another topic from Chapter 6) creates another set of alternatives for setting up an arbitrage trade — one that's almost necessary to the process. Short selling allows a day trader to profit when a security's price goes down. The short seller goes to her broker, borrows the security that she thinks will decline in price, sells it, and then buys it back in the market later so that she has the shares to repay the loan. In essence, the trader is selling high (with borrowed money) and buying back low. Assuming she's right and the price does indeed fall, she pockets the difference between the price where she sold the security and the price where she bought it back. Of course, that difference is her loss if the price goes up instead of down. The arbitrageur can use this to bet on assets that are likely to go down in price when another asset goes up.

By adding short selling to the bag of tricks, an arbitrageur can find a lot more ways to profit from a price discrepancy in the market. New combinations of cheap and expensive assets — and more ways to trade them — give a day trader more opportunities to make trades during the day.

Creating synthetic securities

Feeling creative? Well, then, consider creating synthetic securities when looking for arbitrage opportunities. A *synthetic security* is a combination of assets that have the same profit-and-loss profile as another asset or group of assets. For example, a stock is a combination of a short *put option,* which has value if the stock goes down in price, and a long *call option,* which has value if the stock goes up in price.

By thinking up ways to mimic the behaviour of an asset through a synthetic security, a day trader can find more ways for an asset to be cheaper in one market than in another, leading to more potential arbitrage opportunities.

A typical arbitrage transaction involving a synthetic security, for example, involves shorting the real security and then buying a package of derivatives that match its risk and return. Many of the risk-arbitrage techniques covered later in this chapter involve the creation of synthetic securities.

REMEMBER

Complex arbitrage trading strategies require more testing and simulation trading and may possibly involve losses while you fine-tune your methods. Be sure you feel comfortable with your trading method before you commit big time and big dollars to it.

Examining Arbitrage Strategies

You can use the tools of arbitrage — derivatives, leverage, short selling, synthetic securities — in all sorts of ways to generate potentially profitable trades, and that's what this section of the chapter covers. If you decide to do arbitrage, you may discover a few useful strategies to follow. Beware of picking too many: The trader who tries to do too much is the trader who will soon be looking for a new job! Instead, look for an arbitrage strategy that matches your approach to the market and make it your own.

The varieties of arbitrage transactions are listed here in alphabetical order. Some are more complex than others, some generate more opportunities than others, and some work best if you are willing to swing trade (hold for a few days) rather than day trade (close out all positions at the end of the day). Keep in mind that this list is not exhaustive; you can find plenty of other ways to exploit price differences in the market, but some involve more time than a day trader is willing to commit.

TIP

Many arbitrage strategies work best in combination with other strategies, such as news-driven trading. For example, a news announcement may cause people to pay attention to a company's stock, resulting in enough trading activity that day to close a price gap. If you know about the pricing problem ahead of time, you can swoop in and make the arbitrage that day.

Other types of arbitrage are certainly out there. Wherever people pay close attention to the markets and price changes, they find small price differences to turn into large, low-risk profits. If you think you've found an arbitrage strategy not listed here, by all means, go and test it to see whether it will work for you.

Convertible arbitrage

As part of designing their capital structure, some companies issue *convertible bonds* (sometimes called a *convertible debenture*) or *convertible preferred stock*. These securities are a cross between stocks and bonds. Like an ordinary bond, convertibles pay regular income to those who hold them (interest for convertible bonds and dividends for convertible preferred stock), but they also act a little like stock because the holders have the right to exchange the convertible security for ordinary common stock.

Here's an example: A $1,000 convertible bond pays 7.5 percent interest and is convertible into 25 shares of stock. If the stock is less than $40 per share, the convertible holder will prefer to cash the interest or dividend cheques. If the company's stock trades above $40, the convertible holder would make more money giving up the income in order to get the stock cheap. Because of the benefit of conversion, the interest rate on a convertible security is usually below that on a regular corporate bond.

REMEMBER

Because a convertible security carries a built-in option to buy the underlying stock, it generally trades in line with the stock. If the convertible's price gets too high or too low, then an arbitrage opportunity presents itself.

Consider this case: A day trader notices that a convertible bond is selling at a lower price than it should be, given the current level of interest rates and the price of the company's common stock. So he buys the convertibles and sells the common stock short. When the stock's price moves back into line, he collects a profit from both sides of the trade.

ETF arbitrage

An *exchange-traded fund,* or *ETF,* is a security based on a stock market index. It may be a recognized index or one that has been invented by the company that created the ETF to track a particular investment strategy.

ETFs have been designed with a built-in mechanism to keep the price of the funds in line with the underlying securities. A typical ETF has two classes of shareholders. The first are *authorized participants,* which are large trading firms that agree to buy the securities in the ETF. The authorized participants then give the securities to the ETF company in exchange for *creation units,* which are shares of the fund that the authorized participant can hold, sell on the open market, or trade back to the ETF company for the shares. The authorized participant will do whatever had the greatest profit potential, some built-in arbitrage designed to keep the ETF's value in line for the second class of shareholders, the regular ETF traders.

Despite this mechanism, an ETF's value may swing out of line with the underlying index or the underlying fundamentals of the sector that it represents. When this happens, a trader can look for an arbitrage opportunity between the ETF and an index future, between two different ETFs, or between an ETF and a representative stock.

Fixed income and interest-rate arbitrage

Fixed-income securities are bonds, notes, and related securities that give their owners a regular interest payment. They are popular with conservative investors, especially retirees, who want to generate a regular income from the quarterly interest payments. They are considered to be safe, predictable, long-run investments, but they can fluctuate wildly in the short term, which makes them attractive to arbitrageurs.

Interest rates are the price of money, and so they affect the value of many kinds of securities. Fixed-income securities have a great deal of interest-rate exposure because they pay out interest. Some stocks have interest-rate exposure, too. Trading in foreign exchange is an attempt to profit from the changing price of one currency relative to another, and that's usually a function of the difference in interest rates between the two countries. Derivatives have a regular expiration schedule, so they have some time value, and that's measured through interest rates.

With so many different assets affected by changes in interest rates, arbitrageurs pay attention. With *fixed-income arbitrage,* the trader breaks out the following:

>> The time value of money

>> The level of risk in the economy

>> The likelihood of repayment

>> The inflation-rate effects on different securities

If one of the numbers is out of whack, the trader constructs and executes an arbitrage trade to profit from it.

REMEMBER

Buying bonds outright is rarely practical for a day trader. Instead, day traders looking at fixed-income arbitrage and other interest-rate sensitive strategies usually rely on interest-rate futures, offered by the CME Group.

How would such a trade work? Think of a day trader monitoring interest rates on U.S. government securities. He notices that two-year treasury notes are trading at a lower yield than expected — especially relative to five-year treasury notes. He sells futures on the two-year treasury notes and then buys futures on the five-year treasury notes. When the difference between the two rates falls back where it should be, the futures trade will turn a profit.

Index arbitrage

Market observers (even in Canada) talk a lot about the performance of the S&P 500 Index and the Dow Jones Industrial Average. These *market indexes* represent the activity of the market and are widely published for market observers to follow. The performance of the index is based on the performance of a group of securities, ranging from the 3,000 largest companies in the market (the Russell 3,000) to a mere 30 large companies (the Dow Jones Industrial Average).

Sure, an arbitrageur could buy all the stocks, and some hedge funds do just that. But very few people can afford to pursue that strategy. Instead, they get exposure to index performance through the many different securities based on the indexes. Buy-and-hold mutual fund investors can buy funds that hold all the same stocks in the same proportion as the index. Those with shorter-term profits in mind can buy exchange-traded funds, which are baskets of stocks listed on organized exchanges, or they can trade futures and options on the indexes.

Arbitrageurs love the idea of an asset — like an index — that has lots of different securities based on its value because it creates lots of opportunities for mispricing. Unless the index, the futures, the options, and the exchange-traded funds are all in line, some canny day trader can step in and make some money.

Suppose, for example, that the S&P 500 futures contract is looking mighty cheap relative to the price of the S&P 500 Index. A trader can short an exchange-traded fund on the index and then buy futures contracts to profit from the difference.

Merger arbitrage

Every day, companies get bought and sold, and that creates arbitrage opportunities. In fact, one of the better-known arbitrage strategies out there is *merger arbitrage*, in which traders try to profit from the change in stock prices after a merger has been announced. This kind of trade starts with the trader looking at the following details in the merger announcement:

>> The name of the acquiring company

>> The name of the company being taken over (and no matter what PR people say, there are no mergers of equals)

>> The price of the transaction

>> The currency (cash, stock, debt)

>> The date the merger is expected to close

Until the date that the merger actually closes, which may be different from the date in the merger announcement, any and every one of the announced details can change. The acquiring company may learn new information about the target company and change its mind. A third company may jump in and make an offer for more money. The shareholders may agree to support the deal only if they get cash instead of stock. All that drama creates opportunity, both for traders looking for one-day opportunities and for those willing to hold a position until the merger closing date.

Here's an example. Say that Major Bancorp offers to buy Downtown Bank for $50 per share in cash. Major Bancorp's shares will probably fall in price because its shareholders will be concerned that the merger will be a lot of trouble. Downtown Bank's shares will go up in price, but not all the way to $50, because its shareholders understand the risk that the deal won't go through. An arbitrageur would short Major Bancorp and buy Downtown Bank to profit from the concerns. If Overseas Banque decides to step in, the trader may think it a profitable idea to buy Major Bancorp and short Overseas Banque. (If another bidder steps in and places a higher offer for Downtown Bank, then the whole arbitrage unravels — hence, the risk.)

GARBITRAGE

Traders get sloppy when an exciting merger is announced. If one company in an industry gets taken over, the stock in all the companies in the industry will go up, often for no good reason. Some traders get so carried away that they buy the wrong stock entirely, usually because of confusion over ticker symbols. If Lowe's Companies, a hardware chain with the ticker symbol LOW, were to be taken over, chances are good that the stock in Loews Corporation — an insurance company with the ticker symbol L — would also go up. Such bad trading is known as *garbitrage*.

Option arbitrage

Options, which we discuss in more detail in Chapter 5, form the basis of many arbitrage strategies, especially for those day traders who work the stock market. First, many different types of options are available, even on the same security. The two main categories are *puts,* which bet on the underlying security price falling, and *calls,* which bet on the underlying security price rising. Puts and calls on the same security come in many different strike prices, depending on where you want to bet the price goes. Some options, known as *American options,* can be cashed in at any time between the date of issue and the expiration date, and you can exercise others, known as *European options,* only at the expiration date. (To complicate matters, American and European options can be issued anywhere.) With all those choices, the alert arbitrageur is bound to notice a few price discrepancies.

Maybe a day trader notices that on a day when a company has a big announcement, the options exchanges seem to be assuming a slightly higher price for the stock than where the stock is actually trading. He decides to buy the underlying stock as well as a put; he also sells a call with the same strike price and expiration date as the put. This strategy creates a synthetic security (refer to the earlier section "Creating synthetic securities") that has the same payoff as shorting the security, meaning that the trader has pulled off a riskless arbitrage transaction. He effectively bought the security cheap in the stock market and sold it at a higher price in the options market.

Watching Out for Those Pesky Transaction Costs

Pure arbitrage works best in a world where trading is free. In reality, trading costs good money. Sometimes you may notice a price discrepancy that seems to last forever, but you can't work it because the profit wouldn't cover your costs. And that actually may be true for everyone else out there.

In the real world, trading costs money. Consider all the costs of getting started: buying equipment, paying for Internet access, learning how to trade. Add to those costs the costs of doing business that vary with each transaction: commissions, fees, interest, the bid-ask spread, and taxes. You don't make a profit on a trade unless it covers those costs.

REMEMBER

Even if you work with a broker who charges little or no commission and even if your broker charges no interest on day trading margin (loans against your securities account), you can bet that your broker is making money off you. That broker's profit is showing up in the spread and the speed of execution, so arbitrage still has a cost that must be covered, even on a seemingly free account. Trust us, brokerage firms are in business to make money, whether or not their customers do.

Add up those trading costs, and you can find yourself in a frustrating situation: You can see the opportunity staring you in the face, but you can't take it. So the opportunity either sits there, taunting you, or it gets picked off by a trader who has lower costs than you do.

TIP

Does that mean you're out of luck? Not at all. If you know what your costs are, you can avoid unprofitable opportunities and take advantage of profitable ones. When determining how much you have to clear, don't consider your fixed costs, like your office and your equipment. Those expenses don't change with any given trade. (Yes, you have to cover them in the long run to stay in business, but you can ignore them in the short run.) Instead, figure out how much money you give to your broker on any given trade, on an order, per share, or per contract basis. Build that into your program.

Chapter **12**

Day Trading for Investors

I t takes a special person to be a day trader — one who has quick reflexes, a strong stomach, and a short-term perspective on the markets. Not everyone's meant to parcel out his or her workday a minute at a time. Most people do better with a long-term perspective on their finances, looking to match their investments with their goals and thinking about their investment performance over months or years rather than right now.

But patient long-term investors can discover a thing or two from the frenetic day trader, which is what this chapter is all about. Many day trading techniques can help swing traders, position traders, and investors — people who hold positions for days, months, or even decades — improve their returns and make smarter decisions when it comes time to buy or sell. In this chapter, we cover some trading and analysis techniques used by day traders that can help longer-term investors improve their returns. Then we discuss some ways that long-term investors may want to add day trading to their list of tricks as a way to achieve a better total return.

Recognizing What Investors Can Glean from Traders

In theory, investors may be willing to wait forever to see great stock picks play out, but in reality, they only have so much time and money. A company's stock may be ridiculously cheap, but the stock can languish a long time before everyone else catches on and bids the price up. The investor who buys and sells well can add a few extra dollars to his investment return, and who doesn't want that? In addition, some long-term investors will take a day trading flyer on a hot idea. Maybe a few will even want to give day trading a try, especially for those securities they've followed long enough to know how the market reacts to news and whether those reactions are appropriate. For a long-term investor, given the time to test strategies and set limits, day trading in known markets may result in some nice incremental short-term returns.

If you're an investor interested in occasionally (or frequently) day trading, you need to adopt not only a few key day trading strategies but also the key characteristics that make day traders successful.

Being disciplined

Successful day traders have an innate sense of discipline. They know when to commit more money to a trade and when to cut their losses and close shop for the day.

Unfortunately, a lot of long-term investors can get sloppy. They have done so much research and committed so much time waiting for a position to work that they often forget the cardinal rule of the trader: The market doesn't know you're in it. The stock doesn't know you own it, so it's not going to reward your loyalty. Securities go up and down every day for no good reason, and sometimes you are going to make a mistake and will have to cut your losses. There's no shame in that, as long as you take something away from it.

Now, how can you get that discipline? By doing these things:

>> **Develop an investment and trading plan, covered in Chapter 2.** Although investing is probably not your primary occupation, you do want to have in writing what your objectives are and how you plan to meet them given other constraints: time, tax considerations, and risk tolerance.

>> **Carefully evaluate your performance (covered in Chapter 14).** Keep a trading diary so that you know what you're trading and why. Can you find ways to improve? Are you making mistakes that can be avoided?

>> **Set up a sell rule.** A quick way for an investor to improve her trading discipline is to set up a sell rule, a rule that tells her when to cut her losses and move on. For example, if a stock is down 20 percent from where it was purchased or where it traded at the beginning of the year, it may be time to sell, regardless of what you hope it will do.

Traders have to go through these exercises to survive. Investors often skip these steps, but they shouldn't.

Dealing with breaking news and breaking markets

One reason that the markets are so volatile is that they respond to news events. Prices reflect information, changing when any little bit of information comes into the market — even if the info is just that someone wants to buy and someone wants to sell right now. The problem is that sometimes the market participants don't react in proportion to the news they receive. Good traders have an almost innate ability to discern news that creates a buy from news that creates a sell. (You can find out more about market indicators and strategies in Chapter 10.) Sometimes traders want to go with the market, and sometimes they want to go against it.

When your investment idea has been affected by a news announcement, you need to consider how your position — and you — will react. After all, no matter how long your time horizon and how careful your research, things happen to companies: CEOs have heart attacks, major products are found to be defective, financial statements turn out to be fraudulent, and so on. How are you going to respond?

The first point is that you have to respond. The market doesn't know your position, and the market doesn't care. (Have we mentioned that already?) You need to assess the situation and decide what to do. Given the information, is it time to buy, sell, or stay put? Holding your long-term position in the face of long-term news is often okay, but that decision should be an active one, not a fallback. The trick is to be objective, which isn't easy when real dollars are at stake.

REMEMBER

Successful day traders are able to keep their emotions under control and keep the market separate from the rest of their lives. Good investors should be able to do the same.

When evaluating news, day traders look at how the news is different from expectations. Investors can also consider how the news is different relative to the known facts about the company to date. For example, suppose that the Canadian Cold Cooler Company is expected to report earnings of $0.10 per share. Instead, the news hits the tape saying that earnings will be only $0.05 because of accounting charges. The trader may see that the earnings are below expectations and short the shares to play on the bad news. The investor may know that the accounting charges were expected and quickly buy more shares while the price is depressed. The fact that there is a way for a buyer and a seller to match their differing needs is the whole reason that the financial markets exist!

REMEMBER

To a day trader, perception is reality. To a keen-eyed investor, the difference between perception and reality may be an opportunity to make money.

Day traders have to think about the psychology of the market because everything moves so quickly. Investors sometimes forget about psychology because they can wait for logic to prevail. When it comes time to place a buy or sell order, however, understanding the psychological climate that day can give the investor a price advantage, and every bit of profit improvement goes straight to the bottom line.

TIP

Day traders keep their sanity by closing out positions at the end of the day so that they can get on with their lives until the next market opens. Investors, on the other hand, may want to know what's happening to their positions at other times. Many brokerage firms offer mobile-phone alert services, which we think are a terrible idea for a day trader but may not be a bad idea for an investor.

Setting targets and limits

Good day traders set limits. They often place stop and limit orders to automatically close out their positions when they reach a certain price level. They have profit targets in mind and know how much they're willing to risk in the pursuit of those gains.

Good investors should set similar limits. It can be harder for them, because they have often done so much research that they feel almost clairvoyant. Why worry about the downside when the research shows that the stock has to go up?

Well, the research may overlook certain realities. And even with thorough analysis, things change. That's why even the most ardent fundamentalist needs to have a downside risk limit. In most cases, stop and limit orders are bad ideas for a long-term investor because they force the sale of a security during a short-term market fluctuation and force the sale when it's really a good time to buy more. Investors have a different risk profile than day traders, so they need to manage risk differently — but they do still need to manage it.

REMEMBER

With a *stop* order, the broker buys or sells the security as soon as a predetermined price is met, even if the price quickly moves back to where it was before the order took effect. A *limit* order is only executed if the security hits the predetermined level, and it stays in effect only if the price is at that level or lower (for a buy limit order) or at that level or higher (for a sell limit order).

Day traders close out their positions at the end of each day, so they rarely review their limits. A swing trader or an investor, on the other hand, who holds for a longer period of time, needs to review those limits frequently. How much should a position move each month, quarter, or year before it's time to cover losses or cash out with a profit? How has the security changed over time, and do the limits need to change with it?

When the position is working, an investor thinks of letting it ride forever. But, alas, few investments work that long into the future, so the investor also needs to think in term of relative performance. Has the time come to sell and put the money into something else with greater potential?

When managing money, day traders usually think about maximizing return while minimizing the risk of ruin. For an investor, the goal is maximizing return relative to a list of long-term objectives, including a target for risk. But because long-term objectives change, the portfolio has to as well. That means that a position that has been working out fine may have to be changed in order to meet the new portfolio goals. The discussion is starting to get beyond the scope of this book, but the point remains: Like successful day traders, successful investors have a plan for how they will allocate their money among different investments, and they adjust it as necessary.

REMEMBER

Although investing is a long-term proposition and lacks the frenzy of trading, it is still an active endeavour. Instead of putting energy into buying and selling, the investor puts it into monitoring.

Judging execution quality

Day traders rely on outstanding trade execution from their brokers. They need to keep costs as low as possible in order to clear a profit from their trading, especially because their profits are relatively small.

Investors may have a greater likelihood of making a profit, given that they are waiting for a position to work out rather than closing it out every night. Even then, better execution leads to better profits. The magnitude of the few extra cents may be smaller relative to the entire profit, but it still counts.

Looking at total execution costs

Your broker makes money three ways. The first is on the commission charged to make the trade. The second is on the *bid-ask spread* (also called the *bid-offer*), which is the difference between the price that the broker buys the security from customers and the price that the broker sells it to customers. The third is any price appreciation on the security between when the broker acquired it and when the firm sold it to the customer. Because three sources of profit are available, some brokers don't even charge commission. But note that the broker can still make money — lots of money — even without a commission.

TIP

When choosing a broker, consider *total execution costs,* not just commission. Some brokers offering deep commission discounts make money from high levels of trading volume, but others make their money from execution.

Improving execution

The broker has a few tricks for improving execution. The first is to invest heavily in information systems that can route and match orders, because even the slightest delay can make a difference if the markets are moving. The second is to have a large enough customer base to be able to match customer orders quickly. Third, and most important, is to decide that execution is a strategic advantage it can use to keep customers happy. Many brokerage firms would rather concentrate on research, financial planning, customer service, or other offerings to keep customers happy instead of offering excellent execution.

In general, a firm that offers low commissions and emphasizes its services to active traders has better execution than a firm that emphasizes its full-service research and advisory expertise. But there are exceptions, and in some cases, the exceptions vary with account size.

Brokerage firms use several numbers to evaluate their execution, including the following:

>> **Average execution speed:** This is the amount of time it takes the firm to fill the first share of an order. Firms also track — and sometimes disclose — how long filling an entire order takes, on average.

>> **Price relative to National Best Bid or Offer:** At any time, there is a list of bid and ask prices in the market, and your broker may not have the best spread. For U.S. securities, the National Best Bid or Offer, defined by Securities and Exchange Commission regulation, is the best price in the market. You may not be able to get this price for all sorts of reasons, usually because of the number of shares you want to buy or sell. For example, if the best bid is for 100 shares and you want to sell 500, you won't be able to get all of the order filled. Brokerage firms track and report how close the price you received was to the best bid or offer at the time.

>> **Price improvement:** Most brokerage firms buy and sell securities for their own accounts. In fact, working as a trader at a brokerage firm may be a great alternative to day trading. Because the firm may own the security or want it for its own account, it may give you a slightly better price than what's in the market.

>> **Average effective spread:** This number measures how much the spread between the bid and the offer differed from the National Best Bid or Offer, on average. The lower the average effective spread, the better.

Brokerage firms have to disclose information monthly about the differences between market orders and public price quotes and the size of effective spreads in different securities. You can look up this info to help compare the performance at different firms. Certainly, your results will vary based on what types of securities you're trading, what market conditions are like when you are trading, and how big an account you have with the firm. But investigating the averages for a brokerage firm can help long-term investors decide whether changing firms to improve profits makes sense.

So what can you do to improve your execution? Here are three suggestions:

>> **Ask the brokerage firm for its policies.** The firm should provide this information, as well as give you some of its recent data, so that you can decide whether the total value of the firm's services matches the total cost.

>> **Check out *MoneySense*'s annual review of online brokerage firms.** Costs are a key component of *MoneySense*'s evaluation.

>> **Update your own hardware and Internet connection so that they're as fast as possible.** If you're a day trader, having access to good data is imperative. (See Chapter 2 for more information on your equipment needs.) If you are not a day trader but actively manage your investment account, you may want to consider an upgrade as well. A few seconds can make a difference.

Applying Momentum

Momentum investors look for securities that are going up in price, especially if accompanied by acceleration in underlying growth. In a sense, they are looking for the same thing day traders are — a security that is going to move big — but they have the expectation of making money over a longer period of time. The thought is that a security starting to go up in price will keep going up unless something dramatic happens to change it. In the meantime, plenty of money can be made.

REMEMBER

In momentum investing, instead of buying low and selling high, the goal is to buy high and sell even higher.

Like most investors, a momentum investor starts with careful fundamental analysis, analyzing a security to determine what will make it go up. Then the momentum investor looks for certain technical and market indicators, similar to those described in Chapters 9 and 10 and used by day traders. In addition, some momentum investors rely on chart services, especially the Value Line and William O'Neil charts, to help them identify securities that are likely to have momentum.

Earnings momentum

Earnings momentum is the province of the investor, not the trader. The investor is looking at the earnings that a company reports every quarter to see whether the earnings are going up at a faster rate, say from a steady rate of 10 percent a year to 12, 13, or more. Such an increase often happens because of a new technology or product that turns a decent company into a hot property in the stock and options markets. If the earning growth rate is accelerating, then the underlying price should go up at an accelerating rate, too.

Day traders don't look for earnings momentum, but they do look for price momentum. The two are usually related.

Price momentum

When a security goes up in price, especially at a fast clip with strong demand underneath it, it is said to have *price momentum.* Most day traders are looking for price momentum in order to make a swift profit. Many long-term investors should look for price momentum, too, in order to avoid being stuck with a position for months before it starts to move. After all, patience pays, but it pays even better if your money is working for you while you wait.

Many momentum traders don't care why something is going up in price; they only know that it is going up and that they can profit by being there for even part of the ride. Following are some of the different indicators that these traders look at:

>> **Relative strength:** You can calculate relative strength in different ways, but the basic idea is that a security that's going up faster than the market as a whole is showing momentum and may be a buy.

>> **Moving average convergence/divergence (MACD):** This indicator looks at how the average price of the security is changing over time. Is the indicator staying relatively level, meaning that the price is moving slowly back and forth, or is the indicator gradually going up, meaning that the price is gradually going up, too? If you plot the moving average against the actual price levels, a wide gap means that the security is moving up or down faster than the average, and if it's moving up, you'd probably want to buy it.

>> **Stochastics index:** This index is the difference between the high and the low price for a security over a given time period. Some analysts look at days, some at weeks. The idea is that, if the difference is getting bigger, it may be because the security is moving up or down in price at a faster than normal rate, creating an opportunity for a momentum buyer.

WARNING

At an extreme, momentum investing leads to *bubbles,* like the infamous dot-com bubble in the late 1990s. People were buying the stocks because they were going up, not because they necessarily thought that the businesses were worth much. This run was fun while it lasted, but a lot of people lost a lot of money when reality set in during March and April 2000. What's the next bubble? We have a few ideas, and you probably do, too.

For investors only: Momentum-research systems

Many day traders rely on different research systems to help them identify buy and sell opportunities in the course of a trading day. These systems usually don't work for an investor, simply because investors are less concerned about short-term movements. They wouldn't see the value in systems that scan the market and identify short-term price discrepancies, for example.

However, many investors use their own research services to help identify good buy and sell opportunities. Two of the more popular ones are Value Line and the William O'Neil charts.

Value Line

Value Line (www.valueline.com) is one of the oldest investment-research services. The company's analysts combine price and trading volume information on stocks with financial data. The numbers are crunched through a proprietary model to generate two rankings: a stock's timeliness and its safety. The higher the stock is on the timeliness ranking, the better it is to buy or hold it now. Historically, Value Line's most timely stocks have outperformed the Dow Jones Industrial Average and the S&P 500, so people are willing to pay for access to the company's data. In addition, many libraries subscribe to Value Line's online database, so you may be able to get access that way. (Hey, one of the advantages of being an investor is that you have the time to go to the library to look something up, a marvel to a day trader who's too busy to go and get even a cup of coffee.)

Value Line as a company has had some problems, most notably with fraud related to its mutual-fund business, but the charting system was not part of those charges.

William O'Neil

William O'Neil (www.williamoneil.com) started a company to distribute his technical-analysis system on stocks and the stock market, started a newspaper called *Investor's Business Daily* (www.investors.com), and wrote a book called *How to Make Money in Stocks.* (See the appendix for more information about it.)

The company's data services are available — for a fee — to large institutional investors such as mutual-fund and insurance companies as well as to individuals. Between the book and the newspaper's website, individual investors can find out a lot about identifying momentum to pick good times to buy or sell a stock as well as determine if the system will work for them.

TIP

Many traders — in all securities, not just stocks — find *Investor's Business Daily* to be at least as useful as *The Globe and Mail,* at least for U.S. stocks, because it looks at the markets from a short-term trading perspective rather than from a long-term, business-management angle.

The company's ranking system is based on what it calls CAN SLIM, which is a mnemonic for a list of criteria that a good stock should meet. Note that this system combines both fundamental and technical indicators:

>> **Current quarterly earnings** should be up 25 percent from a year ago.

>> **Annual earnings** should be up 25 percent from a year ago.

>> **New products or services** should be driving earnings growth, not acquisitions or changes in accounting.

>> **Supply and demand,** meaning the number of shares being purchased each day, is going up.

>> **Leader or laggard?** The stock is a leading company in a leading industry and therefore in the best position to do well.

>> **Institutional sponsorship** is in place, meaning that the stock is becoming more popular with mutual funds, pension funds, and other large shareowners.

>> **Market indexes,** such as the Dow, the Nasdaq, and the S&P 500, should all be up.

Of course, not too many stocks out there meet all the CAN SLIM criteria, but the indicators can give an investor a way of thinking about better times to buy (when more criteria are met) or sell (when fewer are being met).

TIP

The most serious momentum investors tend to be swing traders, who hold positions for a few weeks or months. Longer-term investors often rely on some momentum signals, though, such as those on the CAN SLIM list, to help them identify good times to buy a stock that has been languishing.

When an Investor Considers Trading

Many day traders are also long-term investors. Sure, they trade for the short term, but they regularly take some of their profits and put them toward investments that have a longer time frame. It's smart risk management for a business that has a high washout rate. After all, even a short-term trader has long-term goals.

But does it ever make sense for a long-term investor to take up short-term trading? It may, for three reasons: The idea proves itself to be short term, the research shows short-term trading patterns that may be profitable, and fundamental analysis supports short selling (which usually has a shorter time horizon than a buy would to an investor). The following sections explain these reasons in more detail.

WARNING

Don't try riskier trading strategies unless your portfolio can handle the risk. As with full-time day trading, engage in part-time and occasional trading strategies only with risk capital, money that you can afford to lose. Money needed to pay the mortgage this month or pay for retirement in 30 years is *not* risk capital.

The idea has a short shelf life

Certain circumstances turn every long-term investor into a trader once or twice: He buys a security intending to hold it forever, and within a few days or weeks, some really bad news comes out. Or he buys only to see two days later that the company is being sold. That great long-term buy-and-hold idea no longer fits the original parameters, so it's time to sell. Despite the goal of holding forever, the investor decides to get out and move on, even if it's only a day later.

Your research shows you some trading opportunities

Good investors monitor their holdings, and some become intimate with the nuances of a security's short-term price movements even though the objective is to hold the position for the long term. An investor who gets a feel for the trading patterns of a specific holding may want to turn that into swing-trading and day trading opportunities. Yes, doing so adds risk to the portfolio (and the risks of day trading are covered extensively throughout this book), but it can also increase return.

For example, suppose that an investor who is fascinated with technology stocks notices that the stocks always rise in price right before big industry conferences and then fall when the conference is over. She may not want to change any of her portfolio holdings based on this observation, but she may want a way to profit. So she buys call options on big technology companies before the conference and then sells them on the meeting's first day. That short-term trade allows her to capture benefits of the price run-up without affecting her portfolio position.

You see some great short opportunities

Short selling allows a trader to profit from a decline in the price of a security. The trader enters the order, which automatically arranges the loan of a security from the broker followed by a sale in the market. The trader then waits in hopes that the price will go down. When it does, the trader buys the security back at the lower price and repays the loan, keeping the difference between the purchase price and the sale price.

Because the broker charges interest on the loaned securities, short selling can get expensive. Traders who sell short are usually looking for a relatively short-term profit, not necessarily over a single day but over months rather than years.

In addition to the interest, short selling faces another risk, which is that the security can go up in price while the trader is waiting for it to go down. To reduce that risk, most short sellers do careful research, especially about accounting practices, to back up their choices. And who else does careful research? Many long-term investors.

For the investor who loves to do research and has some appetite for risk, short selling is a way to make money from securities that would make terrible long-term holdings because it seems obvious that they aren't going to do well. When these investors come across securities that are headed for trouble, they can short them in the hope of making a nice short-term profit.

» **Supplementing your trading with research**

» **Checking out vendors before you spend your money**

Chapter **13**

Researching Research Services

A lot of people make big money in day trading, but they aren't day traders. They're the people who have profitable businesses selling training services, software, newsletters, and coaching. The problem is, their lessons don't often help their customers make a profit after these education costs are figured in.

Why the discrepancy between the cost of the training and the value it generates for day traders? It could very well be because some traders who buy these services aren't cut out for day trading in the first place; after all, day trading isn't for everyone. In other cases, though, the traders fail to do good research before plunking down the cold cash for training in a system that just wasn't very good.

You've already plunked down the price of this book. Consider that an investment! In this chapter, we cover some of the different services that day traders may want to buy and give you advice on how to determine which ones are worthwhile and which are not. Keep in mind that companies come and go — sometimes changing owners, other times changing focus. Just because it's listed here doesn't mean it's a good company. Do your own research to make sure.

Sometimes the changes end up having nothing to do with trading. For example, one company mentioned in the first edition of this book, InstaQuote, is no more following an acquisition and name change. InstaQuote is now the name of an app for captioning your social media photos, whereas the old trading business has become part of ThomsonReuters REDI, a platform for institutional traders.

Understanding the Trade of Trading

Day trading is a career. Every career takes time to master, and practitioners have to work to keep their skills up as the field changes. You'll probably find that you need some training to get started and more training to be successful, whether you're trading futures, building bridges, or doing heart surgery. The following sections outline some of the training options available to you.

REMEMBER

Let us be frank: Although we put a lot of information in this book about day trading, we don't include everything. This book is a starting point. The fact is, because you can trade so many different assets in so many ways, no one resource can give you all the information you need. A stock trader following a news-based momentum strategy needs different services than a forex trader looking at interest-rate discrepancies. That's why our goal is not to teach you about specifics but to point you to resources that can help you get started and show you how to get the most value from the money you spend.

Enjoying freebies from the exchanges and the regulators

Before you spend more money, check out what several different exchanges and self-regulatory organizations offer for free to help you get started in trading. Through these sources, you can find webinars, online courses, and plenty of reading material that may give you all the information you need to get started. After all, the financial industry wants people to trade — that's how it makes money — and it wants them to be successful, because that keeps the market functioning. (Exchanges are businesses, like any other.) Going through such free material first can give you a great sense of how suitable you are for a given strategy and help you make better decisions about other types of training.

In this section we list a few Canadian and U.S. resources, in alphabetical order, that are particularly good for new day traders.

Chicago Board Options Exchange Education Center

The Options Institute of the Chicago Board Options Exchange offers a series of great online tutorials, classes, practice accounts, and seminars that cover exchange-traded options in great depth. Many are free, although some of the more intensive programs that include live coaching carry tuition charges. The site includes online toolboxes and calculators, not to mention a simulated trading game.

For more information, go to www.cboe.com/education.

CME Group Education

The CME Group, a holding company for several different exchanges, offers extensive and detailed free education programs on just about every aspect of derivatives trading. Whether your interest is currency, grain, or options on futures, the CME Group has videos, online courses, and white papers covering basic vocabulary, advanced trading strategies, and current market commentary. It has a lot of information that you can use, whatever your strategy. And you really can't beat the price!

For more information, go to www.cmegroup.com/education/index.html.

Institute for Financial Markets

The Institute for Financial Markets is a nonprofit organization that provides basic training programs for people working on the options and futures exchanges. Many of its courses are inappropriate for day traders, who aren't going to be licensed and who do not have mandatory continuing education requirements to maintain those licences. But some of the options may be helpful to you, so check them out after you see what the exchanges have to offer. Recent offerings include the basics of derivatives and trading strategies.

For more information, go to www.theifm.org.

Montreal Exchange

Traders who want to find out more about the options market should visit the Montreal Exchange's website and click on the publications tab. You'll find all sorts of in-depth articles with titles such as "Index Options and Correlation Trading" and "Five Ideas in a Challenging Bond Market." There are also several educational guides to options trading (under the education tab), and the site even has a trading simulator where you can try out stock and options trading without putting any money at risk.

For more information, go to www.m-x.ca.

Nasdaq/OMX

Okay, if we're being honest here, we have to admit that the stock exchanges want to promote investing more than trading, because they want companies to issue stock on their exchanges. The kind of high volatility that day traders love puts off some starchy corporate officers. Hence, much of the information on Nasdaq's site is about how to select stocks for the long term. Still, some information here may be useful to a prospective day trader, including data descriptions that can help you with your strategies.

For more information, go to `www.nasdaq.com/investing`.

National Futures Association Investor Learning Center

The National Futures Association is the self-regulatory organization for the agricultural and financial futures exchanges. This site includes tutorials on trading futures and foreign exchange. This organization doesn't have a lot of tutorials, but those it does have are free and comprehensive.

For more information, go to `www.nfa.futures.org/investor/investorlearning center.asp`.

New York Stock Exchange

The New York Stock Exchange, like Nasdaq, wants to court investors rather than traders. Still, the exchange's site has information on trading stocks, bonds, and exchange-traded funds that can make you smarter on those topics without spending a dime.

For more information, go to `www.nyse.com/the-exchange`.

TMX Money

The TMX Group's TMX Money site is particularly useful for Canadian investors. It posts key press releases from a number of companies — helpful for staying on top of your trades — and has a great stock screener tool to help you come up with trading ideas. It's glossary of stock market terms should be a go-to resource for every newbie trader. While it doesn't have as much educational information as it did when we wrote the first edition of this book, it's still worth bookmarking.

For more information, go to `www.tmxmoney.com`.

Hitting the (virtual) road for conferences

There was once a time, way back in 2019, when you could leave your home, get on a plane, and travel to a conference. At the time of writing, in-person conferences are still a no-no thanks to COVID-19. Our last edition of *Day Trading For Canadians For Dummies* sat on shelves for a decade, so we hope, if you're reading this in the future, you're travelling again. Fortunately, a lot of the investing and trading conferences have gone virtual, which, in many ways, is better for traders as they can attend from the comfort of their home. That may make it easier to attend more conferences — especially for Canadians who may not want to shell out U.S. dollars for entry fees and hotels — and gain even more insights than before. (But watch out for Zoom fatigue!)

TIP

Brokerage firms offering many seminars and training programs may have higher commissions than firms offering less service, but the additional expense may be worth it, especially as you're getting started. You can find out more about brokerage firms that work with day traders in Chapter 15.

The Money Show

The Money Show is a series of investment conferences held in different major cities around North America (at least in pre-pandemic times), including Toronto. Some, like the Traders Expo, focus on trading and foreign exchange, whereas others run the gamut. Registration is free, which means that when you're eventually allowed to show up in person people will try to sell you stuff. Although these vendors can be distracting to an established trader, they can be helpful to new traders looking to find out more about all the different software and services available. Just make sure you're getting information, not an opportunity to spend even more money. These conferences also have high-profile speakers, so you can learn from *MoneySense* celebrities. (Did you catch Bryan's session at the 2020 virutal conference? Did you say no?) The Money Show website includes articles, podcasts, and free online courses to help you discover more about trading.

For more information, go to www.moneyshow.com.

The Trading Show Chicago

This show, and its cousins in New York and California, brings together high-level traders and brand-name speakers to discuss the latest in high-tech trading. For the most part, it's aimed at people making research and technology decisions for proprietary trading firms, but a more experienced day trader may well find good information here, too.

You can find details at www.terrapinn.com/conference/trading-show-chicago/index.stm.

Taking training classes

Although not necessary, many day traders try to master the game by enrolling in a training program, ranging from a graduate-level certificate program offered by Northwestern University to video courses hawked on late-night infomercials. No program can guarantee success, nor is any one program right for every trader. Be sure to check out the many programs before you register, because sometimes one company goes out of business and someone else sets up shop under the old name.

REMEMBER

The larger brokerage and research firms offer their own training courses, often at little or no cost. Consider those as a first option, but keep in mind that their introductory sessions may be sales pitches for more products and services. Of course, other training programs may be disguised sales pitches, too. At some point, you're better off trading than training. The markets will school you better than any webinar.

In fact, some long-time traders argue that, instead of spending thousands of dollars on a trading course, you're better off studying the basics on the cheap and then putting the money that would otherwise go to a workshop fee into actually trading, the logic being that your early losses will instruct you on far more than any classroom lecture or slick webinar ever could. Meanwhile, some of the fee-based programs come with a hard sell, and our general rule is that the harder someone tries to sell something, the greater a deal it is for the person doing the selling.

WARNING

Plenty of great and legitimate training firms are out there — as well as a lot of scammers. Run from anyone who guarantees your success, and don't sign up for a training program until you know what you need to study. If the firm wants you to trade using actual money, find out what broker will be holding the account; one common scam is based on the assumption that most beginning day traders lose money, so the operators take the money and let you think you're trading it when, really, you're just playing a game. We include some information about due diligence at the end of this chapter.

Day Trader Canada

Based in Montreal, this company offers courses and education services to Quebecers. Find out how to trade stocks and options and learn (in French) about direct access platforms. If you speak French, you can also get live trading advice.

You can get more information at www.daytradercanada.com.

Investopedia

Here's a little known fact: Investopedia began life in Edmonton as a dictionary of investing terms. It's now New York-based — though it still has an Alberta office — and has expanded into a website with credible information on just about every aspect of the financial markets. It may be the most useful reference on money, trading, and investing.

While the main site is www.investopedia.com, the company also offers a series of courses through its Investopedia Academy on many different aspects of money, from budgeting to advanced options strategies. Some courses and webinars are free. Most are (relatively) low cost and give you access to a live instructor and trading simulations.

For more information, go to http://academy.investopedia.com.

Online Trading Academy

This company operates franchised trading schools around the world, including Toronto, and despite the name, not all of the programs are online (though may more be now). Its courses aren't cheap — $5,000 or so — but the curriculum is serious. The emphasis is on using technical analysis for both trading and investing. If you're ready to commit a week and a lot of money to figuring out how to read charts, you may want to check it out.

The site is at www.tradingacademy.com.

TopstepTrader

A veteran of the Chicago Mercantile Exchange founded TopstepTrader to address the way people learn to trade in electronic markets. (The old method, of working as a runner on the floor of the exchange, no longer works now that the floors are disappearing.) It starts with two weeks of free practice trading. (It also offers paid trading courses.) If you do well enough in the practice account, you can enter its trading combine, which is designed to mimic the National Football League combine: You pay a deposit, which is refunded if your trading adheres to certain risk and other parameters; you receive research and coaching from experienced traders; and your performance is evaluated. If the coaches like what they see, you may be funded to trade for TopstepTrader's parent firm, Patak Trading, or you may be recruited by another firm.

For more information, go to www.topsteptrader.com.

Trading Advantage

Trading Advantage, run by an experienced commodities floor trader, has a ton of training options, ranging from telephone coaching and a virtual trading room to books and videos. Some of the company's programs are designed for experienced professional traders who want to expand their skills or learn new technologies, whereas others work for an average person who wants to get started or who wants to improve his or her trading prowess.

For more information, go to www.tradingadvantage.com.

Getting the Research You Need

Day traders need a trading system, and they often rely on subscription research services. That's fine, as long as those systems are adding value over and above their cost. Unfortunately, advising day traders is big business, and there may be more money in that than in day trading. Before you call the 800 number given in the infomercial, read the advice we give here, which can help you evaluate the service.

There are three main types of outside services:

>> **Price data** are detailed, real-time price quotes from different markets.

>> **Chart services** help traders identify profitable trends.

>> **Strategic research** helps people develop a system for trading or follow a system designed by someone else.

You may need all three, or none, depending on your knowledge of the financial markets and your trading style.

Many day traders find themselves subscribing to price quote and analytical services. The following section is a listing of a handful of popular ones. It's not a definitive list, and including them on this list is not an endorsement. Rather, it's a guide to get you thinking about what you may need and where you can go to get it.

TIP

If you know you need outside pricing and data services, consider that when you select a brokerage firm. Different firms have different software platforms, and some can handle outside data feeds better than others. For more information on choosing a broker, refer to Chapter 15.

(Price) Quote me on that

Many brokerage firms offer day trading services. They all have services that tell you what the prices are for any security at any time, but this doesn't mean that they have all the prices that you need for your strategy. If, for example, you're day trading common stocks, you may need a system that can signal certain price patterns in any of the thousands of stocks trading at any given day. If you're trading options based on the value of underlying stock, you may need that data as well. If you're day trading international securities, you may need real-time data, and your broker may only offer data with a ten-minute delay in some markets.

Besides needing all the prices and related volume and market-maker data, some strategies involve fast trading. Every second counts, and not all brokers can deliver prices fast enough to make scalping profitable. One solution is to get prices from a separate source that offers faster delivery. Other trading strategies don't require real-time prices on huge numbers of securities, but they may involve a detailed analysis of end-of-day prices. To do that, you may need more information than your broker can give you.

The following sections offer information on some of the different price quote and data services out there.

REMEMBER

The quote service can provide the data in real time only if you have enough bandwidth to receive it. Make sure you have the fastest Internet service and modem available in your area and consider having a second way to connect to the Internet if your primary service goes down.

CQG

CQG pulls data from pretty much all of the world's exchanges, making it popular with people who are trading Canadian, U.S., and international securities. It also has data on over-the-counter foreign exchange. Traders can buy historical data for backtesting (see Chapter 14 for more), and they can add charting and order routing capabilities to their CQG package. People who want to do even more number crunching on their own can link the data to their Microsoft Excel spreadsheets.

For more information, go to www.cqg.com.

DTN

Trading fuel or agricultural products? Then you may need more research than most brokers can give you. DTN produces a huge range of data for farmers and drillers, and it has plenty of services for Canadian traders, too. The company, owned by Schneider Electric, provides pricing and research for commodities traders, including meteorological research and hurricane-related energy supply forecasts. Day traders active in stocks or financial futures are more likely to use the company's IQ data feeds, which allow users to track 1,300 prices simultaneously, and ProphetX, software that combines price data with analytics that can track small market movements and can handle displays on several different monitors at once.

For more information, go to www.dtn.com.

eSignal

eSignal offers detailed prices, news, and trading alerts in most financial markets, including Canada, delivered to your computer or your phone. Its charting features are more advanced than those offered by most brokerage firms. Especially useful for traders who are looking at several different stocks, eSignal can help identify trading opportunities using a preferred strategy and scan the market for other stocks that meet specified investment criteria. The company also offers backtesting and real-time strategy testing, end-of-day analysis for traders who don't need real-time data, and add-on signals that support different proprietary trading strategies.

For more information, go to www.esignal.com.

Oanda

Oanda provides both foreign exchange trading services and data. The company, which has offices around the world, including in Toronto, has exchange rates for major currencies and small frontier markets. The data is available — for a price — to those who want to use it with another brokerage firm's platform.

For more information, go to www.oanda.com.

Charting your strategy

Almost all day trading strategies rely on technical analysis, which is the process of identifying buy and sell opportunities based on the supply and demand for a security. Technical analysts look at charts of price and volume changes to identify changes in the trend. We discuss technical analysis in more detail in Chapter 9. Some technical-analysis strategies are complicated and require sophisticated charting. That's why many day traders use software that can turn price data into the information they need to make decisions.

TIP

The symbols and data displays trip up many users of these services. Take the time to find out as much as you can about how the services work before you trade in real time with real money; most of these providers offer seminars or online tutorials that can help. Yeah, many of the features are obvious, but you want to avoid costly mistakes.

MarketDelta

MarketDelta's software provides detailed charting services that match different strategies over several time periods, in colors that make the data stand out. The goal is to make price information more transparent and thus chart information more accurate. The company mostly deals with professionals, but some of its products are suitable for some day traders.

For more information, go to www.marketdelta.com.

Metastock

Metastock has several different charting and analytical packages, including one for foreign exchange trading, another for people who day trade in stocks, and a third for stock investors who are holding for longer than a single day. It even has some fundamental research tools. Traders following specific strategies recommended by different market analysts can purchase add-ons that give them the tools needed to trade effectively and participate in in-person and online user groups. Some brokerage firms offer Metastock tools as an alternative to the broker's proprietary platform.

For more information, go to www.metastock.com.

NinjaTrader

A trading platform for active traders, NinjaTrader can be used instead of the trading software offered by many brokerage firms, including several of firms that deal with day traders. The service is best known for its charting capabilities in the foreign exchange and futures markets, but it can also handle market scanning, automated trade execution, backtesting, and simulation trading. The company operates a website called NinjaTrader Ecosystem (www.ninjatraderecosystem.com) that includes webinars, programming modules, and services that use the NinjaTrader platform.

For more information, check out www.ninjatrader.com.

OmniTrader

OmniTrader is designed to automate technical analysis, especially for stock traders. Traders can use it to set up automatic trading systems or to help them make their own decisions during the trading day. The system also includes money-management tools, as well as simulated trading and backtesting to help you find new strategies.

For more information, go to www.omnitrader.com.

StockTwits

Social media is a great way to keep up with pop stars and find out local bargains, and it has applications for trading, too. StockTwits is a service that is similar to Twitter. It lets members post trade ideas and market data, and it pulls in streams from Facebook, Twitter, and LinkedIn. It's a way of following market sentiment more than anything, but sentiment drives markets. And StockTwits is free.

For more information, go to www.stocktwits.com.

Trade-Ideas

Trade-Ideas is designed for stock traders. The software scans the incoming price data feed to find trading opportunities based on prespecified indicators, and it can also show how much the market is deviating from a trader's style. For traders watching hundreds or thousands of stocks, Trade-Ideas can be a useful addendum to a brokerage firm's offerings.

For more information, go to www.trade-ideas.com.

News, newsletters, gurus, and strategic advice

Trading relies on information so that everyone in the market can evaluate what the right price for a security should be. Most of this information can be found from an analysis of the news and the price data, both of which are readily available from brokerage firms and quote services. But many traders follow explicit philosophies or rely on the insight of certain analysts. Here's a list of some of the bigger ones you'll come across.

Many of these market gurus have good ideas, but don't follow any of them blindly. Their techniques don't work in all markets at all times. Besides, anyone with a truly foolproof plan isn't going to give it away. These newsletters are just part of the ongoing conversation in the markets that help traders make decisions.

Andrew Pyle

Andrew Pyle is a ScotiaMcleod portfolio manager — not a guy you'd typically turn to for day trading advice. But some traders swear by his weekly newsletter. It won't give you strategic tips, but his two-page document presents an excellent overview of the economy and zeros in on specific securities such as bonds, commodities, and currencies.

For more information, go to www.pylegroup.ca.

Briefing.com

If you follow a news-driven trading strategy, you need to know what the news is. Briefing.com offers daily news summaries and live updates on news events and ideas for trades that may suit your style. And unlike the standard news feeds available to anyone with Internet access, it doesn't have any celebrity or human-interest stories to distract you.

For more information, go to www.briefing.com.

Bulding Wealth for Canadians

No, it's not the title for a new *For Dummies* book but rather the name of Gordon Pape's website, which is full of excellent investment advice. Pape is one of the most well known personal finance experts in Canada, and his subscriber-only newsletter ($219.95 for 24 issues) covers everything from gold to company news to ETFs and more. He's not a day trader, so don't expect to find information on the latest charting methods, but if you're interested in the markets, then Pape's a must read.

For more information, go to www.buildingwealth.ca.

Coinbase

This site has carved out a niche in with those who care about cryptocurrency. It has lots of news, information, historical data, and an Initial Coin Offering calendar to help you figure out what's happening with this emerging asset class. If you're interested in crypto, this site is a great starting point.

For more information, go to www.coinbase.com.

Elliott Wave

The *Elliott Wave* is a theory that says markets move in grand cycles over a century or more. Within that grand cycle are subcycles lasting years, months, weeks, days, minutes, and seconds. Given all the layers and analysis required, those who follow the theory usually subscribe to research services to help them. Robert Prechter, one of the leading scholars of the theory, maintains this site.

For more information, go to www.elliottwave.com.

Investing.com

One of this site's many features is a calendar of major economic announcements and trading holidays all over the world, which is a huge help in trade planning. It also has webinars, news, and a strategy tracker that lets you see how different traders are doing. Its pages of technical indicators can help you study and improve your own chart-reading skills.

But we love it for that sweet, sweet economic calendar.

For more information, go to www.investing.com.

School of Gann

The Gann method of technical analysis looks at the slopes of the charts to predict changes. It's a complicated system, so traders who follow it usually rely on newsletters and research services to help them. School of Gann is one that specializes in this system.

For more information, go to www.schoolofgann.com.

TradeTheNews.com

TradeTheNews offers independent traders access to a *squawk box*, the audio news feed and commentary that goes in the background on most professional trading desks. Its staffers work on the floor of different exchanges and provide real-time news and analysis, which is helpful for traders working news-driven strategies.

For more information, go to www.tradethenews.com.

Doing Your Due Diligence

Trading software, training, and research can get expensive, and some services and seminars are outright scams. Even those that are legitimate (and most are) may not be right for you. Before you spend your money, do your research. Start with the free programs offered by the exchanges (listed in the first section of this chapter) so that you have enough knowledge to understand what a trading-services purveyor is trying to do. Then do research and ask questions. To find out where to go and what to ask, read on.

Where to start your research

You have a ton of tools available to you to do your due diligence. A good place to start is the Internet. Go to your favorite search engine and enter the name of the program you're looking at plus the word *scam* or *rip-off* and see what turns up on the third or fourth page of the search.

TIP

Anyone with even a little knowledge of search-engine optimization knows this tip. If your search turns up 50 blog posts with lines like "Why Company X is NOT a scam!!!" well, guess what? Company X probably has something to hide, and if you go to the third or fourth page of the search results, you may find out what it is. Or click on the News tab of your search engine to see what's being reported that may be causing the panic. If something looks skeevy, just move on, because plenty of legitimate vendors that you can work with instead are out there.

Another way to check out a trading service is to search on Reddit.com, a website where people discuss anything and everything. True, some posters have ulterior motives, but the overall conversation leads to a rich database of observations about just about anything. Are those shoes you see advertised online as good as they seem? Is that trading service a scam? Redditors are happy to tell you all about it. You don't have to be a registered user to search and read the site, either.

REMEMBER

You may find out very little about any given research firm from an Internet search or checks with the different regulatory organizations. That doesn't mean the firm in question isn't for real, just that it hasn't caused any concerns so far.

Investment Industry Regulatory Organization of Canada

IIROC regulates all of Canada's online brokerage firms and investment dealers. On its website, you'll find disciplinary notices. Although many are centred around advisers or firms that aren't relevant to day traders, it's possible the broker you want to work with has gotten into some legal trouble. Check out the media releases section to get all the details.

For more information, go to www.iiroc.ca.

Ontario Securities Commission

Canada has different regulators for every province, but if a firm wants clients it'll have to be open for business in Ontario. That means it has to register with the OSC. The following link will take you to a handy page that allows you to check whether a firm is registered.

For more information, go to www.osc.gov.on.ca/en/Investors_check-registration_index.htm.

Securities and Exchange Commission

At www.sec.gov/investor.shtml, the Securities and Exchange Commission offers lots of great information about every aspect of stock and bond investing, with a special emphasis on problems and scams to avoid. Ponzi schemes involving virtual currencies? E-mail pump-and-dump scams? Don't let the information scare you away from the market; use it to evaluate any services that you're thinking of paying for.

Questions to ask

After you do your basic background checks, you're ready to ask some questions about the service providers you're considering. Talk to the customer service reps, and try talking to other traders as well. Here is a list of questions to get you started:

>> Can I get a free trial to check the service out?

>> What training and support do you offer? Do you have a user community?

>> How long will it take me to study the system? Will I need to pay for additional training and coaching, or is your built-in support adequate?

>> Who will be teaching me or advising me, and what is this person's background?

>> How long have you been in business? Why was the company formed?

>> What additional features are available at additional costs? How many customers subscribe to only the basic system?

>> Does this system support my trading style and work with the assets I prefer to trade?

>> Do you screen traders for your program? Do you ask traders to leave? What are the characteristics of those who do well? Of those who don't do well?

>> Can I talk to other customers?

>> Is your software compatible with my broker? With other services I'm using? With my computer's operating system? With my Internet bandwidth?

>> Are your performance numbers actual, or are they hypothetical and based on backtesting? How were the numbers calculated?

REMEMBER

Hypothetical performance is based on an analysis of what would have happened had the system been in place in the past or of what may happen if market conditions cooperate. It can be subject to *data mining*, which means that the system was developed to generate good performance in backtesting, not because it has any logical or theoretical basis.

WARNING

Don't trust any promises of performance. Day trading is a difficult business. Many people wash out because it doesn't suit their personality. Others fail because they don't have enough startup capital, they don't take the time to figure out how to do it, or they simply have a run of bad luck. No one can promise that you'll succeed.

Chapter 14

Testing, Tracking, and Evaluating Performance

Any one trade involves a lot of variables: price bought, price sold, commissions charged, volume traded, and amount of leverage used. And each of these affects your overall performance. In the heat of a trading day, it can be hard to juggle all these factors and determine just how well you did or didn't do. And yet, you can't trade by the seat of your pants, at least not if you want to stay in the game for the long haul.

Performance calculation starts before you trade. You want to test your strategies and see whether they work for you, which requires backtesting and paper trading. You want to keep track of your trades in real time with the help of a trading diary. And then, on a periodic basis (at least monthly), you should review your progress to see how much money you're making and whether you need to change your strategy.

Before You Trade: Testing Your System

Performance measurement starts before the trading does. That's because you want to figure out how you'll trade before you start working with real money. Chapter 4 describes some of the different securities that can be traded on a daily basis, whereas Chapters 9 through 11 cover some of the strategies that day traders use. After you figure out the combinations of securities and strategies you want to use, you want to see whether they would have made you money in the past. Then you should try them to see whether they still work now.

The happy news? You can do all this without risking a dime, except of course for the money you may spend on backtesting and simulation software. You knew there had to be a catch, right? Consider it an investment in the success of your business.

Backtesting

In *backtesting,* a trader specifies the strategy that he or she would use and then runs that strategy through a database of historic securities prices to see whether it would have made money. The test includes assumptions about commissions, leverage, and position size. The results give information on returns, volatility, and win-loss ratios that you can use to refine a trading strategy and implement it well.

Starting with a hypothesis

What trades do you want to do? After you figure out what and how to trade, you can start setting forth what your strategy will be. Will you look for high-momentum, small-cap stocks? Seek price changes related to news events in agricultural commodities? Ride large-cap stocks within their ranges? Arbitrage stock index futures and their options?

After you do your research, you can lay out your strategy as a hypothesis, which may be something like this: "High-momentum, small-cap stocks tend to close up for the day, so I can buy them in the morning and make money selling them in the afternoon." Or this: "News events take at least half an hour to affect corn prices, so I can buy or sell on the news and make a profit." With this statement, you can move on to the test to see whether your hypothesis holds.

WARNING

One of the most valuable parts about backtesting is that you have to be very specific about what your trading rule is. Computers cannot understand vague instructions, and if you find that your trading strategy is too complicated to write out and set into a backtesting program, it's probably too complicated for you to follow.

Running the test

Say you start with something simple: Maybe you have reason to think that pharmaceutical companies that are moving down in price on decreasing volume will turn and close up for the day. The first thing you do is enter that into the software: the industry group and the buy pattern that you're looking for. The results will show whether your hunch is correct and how often and for what time periods.

If you like what you see, you can add more variables. What happens if you add *leverage* (use borrowed money) in your trades? Leverage increases your risk of loss, but it also increases your potential return. How does that affect your trade? Suppose you increase the size of your trades, making fewer but larger ones. Would that help you make more money or less? By playing around with the system, you can get a good sense of the best way to make money with your trade ideas. You can also get a sense of when your rule won't work, which can help you avoid problems.

If your strategy doesn't work in testing, you want to ask yourself why not. Is your theory not as good as you thought, or are the markets different now? And if they are different now, how are they different? Unless you can answer those questions, you're just engaging in wishful thinking, and wishful thinking will destroy any trader, no matter what the test results may be.

Most backtesting software allows for optimization, which means that it can come up with the leverage, position, holding period, and other parameters that will generate the best risk-adjusted return given the data on hand. You can then compare this result to your trading style and your capital position to see whether it works.

WARNING

Backtesting is subject to something that traders call *over-optimization*, mathematicians call *curve-fitting*, and analysts call *data mining*. All these terms mean that the person performing the test looks at a past time where the market performed well and then identifies all the variables and specifications that generated that performance. Although over-optimization sounds great, what often happens is that the test generates a model that includes unnecessary variables and that makes no logical sense in practice. If you find a strategy that works when the stock closes up one day, down two days, then up a third day, followed by four down days when it hits an intra-day high, you probably haven't made an amazing discovery; you've just fit the curve.

REMEMBER

Human beings have evolved to see patterns, even when no pattern exists. It's the same with the market. It's entirely possible that, although the results of your test look great, they only show a random event that happened to work once. You need to keep testing, even after you start trading.

Comparing the results with market cycles

The markets change every day in response to new regulations, interest rate fluctuations, economic conditions, nasty world events, and run-of-the-mill news events. (It's like the joke about weather: If you don't like it now, wait a minute, and it'll change.) Different securities and strategies do better in some market climates than in others.

When you backtest, be sure to do so over a long enough period of time so that you can see how your strategy would work over different market conditions. Here are some things to check:

>> How did the strategy do in periods of inflation? Economic growth? High interest rates? Low interest rates?

>> What was happening in the markets during the time that the strategy worked best? What was happening when it worked worst? How likely is either of those to happen again?

>> How does market volatility affect the strategy? Is the security more volatile than the market, less volatile, or does it seem to be removed from the market?

>> Have major changes occurred in the sector over the period of the test? Examples of these types of changes include new technologies that increase demand for certain commodities or changes in regulation that make industries obsolete. Does this mean that past performance still applies?

>> Have there been changes in the way that the security trades? For example, the bulk of trading in most commodities used to take place in open-outcry trading pits. Now, trading is almost entirely electronic. How do your test results look given current trading technologies?

TECHNICAL STUFF

In the capital assets pricing model, which is a key part of academic finance theory, the market risk is known as *beta*. The value that a portfolio manager adds to investment performance is known as *alpha*. In the long run, conventional finance theory says that the return on a diversified portfolio comes from beta; alpha doesn't exist, so investors can't beat the market in the long run. In the short run, where day traders play, this relationship may not be so strong.

REMEMBER

Remember the maximum maxim in finance: Past performance is not indicative of future results. A strategy may test perfectly, but that doesn't mean it will continue to work. Backtesting is an important step to successful day trading, but it is only one step.

Simulation trading

With a backtested strategy in hand, you may be tempted to start putting real money on the line. Don't, at least not yet. Start with what is known variously as *ghost trading, paper trading,* and *simulation trading.* Sit down in front of your computer screen and start watching the price quotes. When you see your ideal entry point, write it down. When you see your exit point, write it down. (Or use the simulation functions available from many brokers to save yourself the paper and pencil work.) Do exactly what you plan to do with real money, just don't use the money. Then figure out what your performance would be.

If your strategy doesn't generate a lot of trades, you can probably keep track with a pen and paper and then enter the data into a spreadsheet to calculate the effects of commissions and leverage and to analyze the performance on both a percentage and a win–loss basis. How does it look?

For more complex strategies that involve a large number of trades on a large number of securities, you may want to use a trading-simulation software package. These packages mimic trading software. They let you enter the size of your order, let you use leverage, and tell you whether your trade can be executed given current market conditions.

REMEMBER

Markets are affected by supply and demand, and your trade can affect that, which is the biggest drawback of simulation trading: It's difficult to take the market effects of your trade into account in any reliable way, especially if you'll be trading large positions in thinly traded markets.

The results of your trading simulation can help you refine your trading strategy further. Does it work in current market conditions? Are you able to identify entry and exit points? Can you execute enough trades to make your day trading efforts financially worthwhile? Do you want to refine your strategy some more, or are you ready to go with it?

Your tests won't guarantee your results, and they won't show you how you'll react under the real pressure of real markets and real money. However, if your system doesn't work well under perfect conditions, it is unlikely to do better in actual conditions.

TIP

Finding a suitable strategy may take a long time. Some traders report spending months finding a strategy they felt comfortable using. Day trading is a business like any other. Consider this part of the market research and education process that you need to go through, just as you'd spend time doing research before opening a store or training for a new career. Be patient. It's better to do good simulation for months than to lose thousands of real dollars in hours.

Backtesting and simulation software

Several vendors have risen to meet the challenge of backtesting, and it is becoming standard on more and more trading platforms. The list in this section is by no means exhaustive, nor is it an endorsement of their services. It's just a good place for you to start your research.

If you're just getting started with trading, you may want to try a cheaper package just to see how backtesting and simulation work. If you already have an account with a brokerage firm, check to see whether backtesting and simulation are among the services offered. You can always move up to a more sophisticated backtesting package as your needs change or if you start pursuing exotic strategies with unusual securities.

The more sophisticated the package, the pricier it is. If you have the programming expertise or if your strategy is not well represented in current backtesting programs, you may want to create your own system. Many software-savvy day traders write programs using Excel's Visual Basic functions, allowing them to create custom tests that they then run against price databases to backtest strategies. While these are all U.S.-based programs, Canadians will find them useful too.

AmiBroker

AmiBroker (www.amibroker.com) offers a robust backtesting service at a relatively low price. For that reason, it's a popular choice with people who are getting started in day trading and who don't have more expensive services. It also allows users to make sophisticated technical charts that they can use to monitor the markets. One drawback is that you may have to pay extra for the market-price-quote data, depending on what securities and time periods you want to test.

Investor/RT

Developed by a company called Linn Software (www.linnsoft.com), Investor/RT allows you to develop your own tests and create your own programs. It has packages for Macs, which makes it popular with traders who prefer Apple computers. Its users tend to be sophisticated about their trading systems and backtesting requirements; this software isn't really for beginners.

MetaStock

As the name implies, MetaStock (www.metastock.com) is designed for traders who work in stocks, although a MetaStock package is available especially for currency traders, and the regular packages include capabilities for futures and commodities traders. It defines traders as *end-of-day* (those who make decisions about trading tomorrow based on numbers at the end of today's trading) and as *real-time* (those who make decisions during the trading day). Most day traders are real-time traders. The company was once owned by Canada's Thomson Reuters, a major financial-information services company, but it sold the business to Innovative Market Analysis in 2013.

NinjaTrader

NinjaTrader (www.ninjatrader.com) is a popular software package used for managing and programming traders. It includes great backtesting capabilities, too. The platform works with many different brokerage firms, for a fee, but the charting and trade testing capabilities are free. That may be why it's become one of the most popular services for backtesting.

OptionVue

If you trade options, you may want to check out OptionVue (www.optionvue.com), which offers a range of analytical tools on the options markets. The software's BackTrader module, an add-on feature, helps you learn more about options markets, test new strategies, and examine relationships between options and the underlying stocks — really useful information for people working in equity markets.

Tradecision

Tradecision's (www.tradecision.com) trade-analysis software package is a little pricier than most retail trading alternatives, but it offers more advanced capabilities, including an analysis of the strengths and weaknesses of different trading rules. It can incorporate advanced money-management techniques and artificial intelligence to develop more predictions about performance in different market conditions. The system may be overkill for most new day traders, but it can come in handy for some.

TradeStation

TradeStation (www.tradestation.com) is an online broker that specializes in services for day traders. Its strategy testing service lets you specify different trading parameters, and then it shows you where these trades would have taken place in the past, using price charts. That way, you can see what would have happened, which is helpful if you're good at technical analysis. It also generates a report of the strategy, showing dollar, percentage, and win-loss performance over different time periods. It doesn't have a trade-simulation feature.

Trading Blox

The Trading Blox software system (www.tradingblox.com) was developed by professional traders who needed to test their own theories and who didn't want to do a lot of programming to do it. It comes in three versions (and price levels), ranging from basic to sophisticated, and the company boasts that it works with some commercial trading firms. Of course, some of its capabilities may be more than you need when you're starting out.

During the Day: Tracking Your Trades

After you put your strategy to work during the trading day, you can easily let the energy and emotion overtake you. You get sloppy and stop keeping track of what's happening. And that's not good. Day trading isn't a video game; it's a job. Keeping careful records helps you identify not only how well you follow your strategy but also ways to refine it. These records can also show you how successful your trading is, and it makes your life a lot easier when tax time comes around. (Refer to Chapter 18 for more information on what the friendly folks at the CRA expect from traders, besides a cut of their profits.)

Setting up your spreadsheet

The easiest way to get started tracking your trades is with a spreadsheet software program such as Microsoft Excel. Set up columns for the asset being purchased, the time of the trade, the price, the quantity purchased, and the commission. Then set up similar columns to show what happens when the position is closed out. Finally, calculate your performance based on the change in the security's price and the dollars and percentage return on your trade. Figure 14-1 gives you an example.

Trade Tracker
2/1/11

POSITIONS Symbol	Description	Purchase Date	Purchase Time	Purchase Price	Lot Attempted	Lot Filled	Comm.	Total Cost	Sale Time	Sale Price	Sale Quantity	Comm.	Total Proceeds	Gain/Loss in Points	Gain/Loss in Dollars	Gain/Loss in Percent
INTC	Intel	2/1/11	9:31	20.98	1,000	1,000	6.00	(20,986.00)	9:52	21.10	1000	6.00	21,094.00	12	108.00	0.51%
NVDA	Nvidia	2/1/11	9:33	30.38	1000	1,000	6.00	(30,374.00)	9:58	30.87	1000	6.00	30,864.00	49	490.00	1.61%
AKAM	Akamai	2/1/11	9:46	57.44	500	500	3.00	(28,717.00)	10:36	56.60	500	3.00	28,297.00	-84	(420.00)	-1.46%
INTC	Intel	2/1/11	10:18	21.08	1000	1,000	6.00	(21,074.00)	10:40	20.95	1000	6.00	20,944.00	-13	(130.00)	-0.62%
AKAM	Akamai	2/1/11	11:08	55.09	500	200	1.20	(11,016.80)	12:08	55.39	200	1.20	11,076.80	30	60.00	0.54%
NVDA	Nvidia	2/1/11	11:08	30.38	1000	1,000	6.00	(30,374.00)	11:28	30.31	1000	6.00	30,304.00	-7	(70.00)	-0.23%
INTC	Intel	2/1/11	11:11	20.91	1000	1,000	6.00	(20,904.00)	11:45	21.03	1000	6.00	21,024.00	12	120.00	0.57%
NVDA	Nvidia	2/1/11	11:55	30.38	1000	1,000	6.00	(30,374.00)	12:15	30.72	1000	6.00	30,714.00	34	340.00	1.12%
INTC	Intel	2/1/11	12:23	20.93	1000	1,000	6.00	(20,924.00)	12:56	21.07	1000	6.00	21,064.00	14	140.00	0.67%
INTC	Intel	2/1/11	13:08	21.05	1000	1,000	6.00	(21,044.00)	13:52	21.04	1000	6.00	21,034.00	-1	(10.00)	-0.05%
AKAM	Akamai	2/1/11	13:22	55.43	500	500	3.00	(27,712.00)	13:41	55.48	500	3.00	27,737.00	5	25.00	0.09%
INTC	Intel	2/1/11	14:05	21.03	1000	1,000	6.00	(21,024.00)	14:26	21.09	1000	6.00	21,084.00	6	60.00	0.29%
NVDA	Nvidia	2/1/11	14:09	30.52	1000	1,000	6.00	(30,514.00)	15:09	30.54	1000	6.00	30,534.00	2	20.00	0.07%
INTC	Intel	2/1/11	15:05	21.10	1000	1,000	6.00	(21,094.00)	15:59	21.11	1000	6.00	21,104.00	1	10.00	0.05%

Starting Capital: $ 165,239.00
Day's Profit: $ 743.00
Percent Change: 0.45%
Ending Capital: $ 165,982.00
Ratio of winning to losing trades: 10 : 4
Hourly Wage: $ 92.88

Total commissions paid: $ 146.40

© John Wiley & Sons, Inc.

FIGURE 14-1: You can use this sample to make your own trade-tracking spreadsheet.

Some brokerage firms and trading platforms automatically store your trade data for analysis. You can then download the data into your own spreadsheet or work with it in your trading software, making analysis simple. If you make too many trades to keep track of manually, then this feature will be especially important to you.

Pulling everything into a profit and loss statement

If you refer to the bottom of Figure 14-1, you see some quick summary statistics on how the day's trading went: trading profits net of commissions, trading profits as a percentage of trading capital, and the ratio of winning to losing transactions. This information should be transferred into another spreadsheet so that you can track your ongoing success. Figure 14-2 shows an example of a profit and loss spreadsheet.

Profit and Loss

	Initial Capital	Net Profit (Loss)	Ending Capital	Percentage Change	Hourly Wage
1/3/11	$ 161,298	$ 134	$ 161,432	0.08%	$ 16.75
1/4/11	$ 161,432	$ (268)	$ 161,164	-0.17%	$ (33.50)
1/5/11	$ 161,164	$ 450	$ 161,614	0.28%	$ 56.25
1/8/11	$ 161,614	$ (183)	$ 161,431	-0.1 1%	$ (22.88)
1/9/11	$ 161,431	$ 192	$ 161,623	0.12%	$ 24.00
1/10/11	$ 161,623	$ 598	$ 162,221	0.37%	$ 74.75
1/11/11	$ 162,221	$ (168)	$ 162,053	-0.10%	$ (21.00)
1/12/11	$ 162,053	$ 987	$ 163,040	0.61%	$ 123.38
1/16/11	$ 163,040	$ (196)	$ 162,844	-0.12%	$ (24.50)
1/17/11	$ 162,844	$ 59	$ 162,903	0.04%	$ 7.38
1/18/11	$ 162,903	$ (273)	$ 162,630	-0.17%	$ (34.13)
1/19/11	$ 162,630	$ (124)	$ 162,506	-0.08%	$ (15.50)
1/22/11	$ 162,506	$ 689	$ 163,195	0.42%	$ 86.13
1/23/11	$ 163,195	$ (397)	$ 162,798	-0.24%	$ (49.63)
1/24/11	$ 162,798	$ 967	$ 163,765	0.59%	$ 120.88
1/25/11	$ 163,765	$ (387)	$ 163,378	-0.24%	$ (48.38)
1/26/11	$ 163,378	$ 469	$ 163,847	0.29%	$ 58.63
1/29/11	$ 163,847	$ 798	$ 164,645	0.49%	$ 99.75
1/30/11	$ 164,645	$ (129)	$ 164,516	-0.08%	$ (16.13)
1/31/11	$ 164,516	$ 723	$ 165,239	0.44%	$ 90.38
January:	$ 161,298	$ 3,941	$ 165,239	2.44%	$ 24.63
2/1/11	$ 165,239	$ 743	$ 165,982	0.45%	$ 92.88

FIGURE 14-2: A sample profit and loss spreadsheet.

© John Wiley & Sons, Inc.

TIP

Calculate your hourly wage for each day that you trade. Simply take each day's profit and divide it by the number of hours that you worked. That number, more than any other, can help you see whether it makes sense for you to keep trading or whether you'd be better off pursuing a different line of work. If you find that calculating the number daily is too stressful, try doing it monthly.

Keeping a trading diary

As part of your trading spreadsheet or in addition to it, you should track the reasons for every trade. Was the reason for the trade because of a signal from your system? Because of a hunch? Because you saw an opportunity that was too good to pass up? Also track how the trade worked out. Is your trading system giving off good signals? Are you following them? Are your hunches so good that maybe your system needs to be refined? Are you missing good trades because you are following your gut and not the data in front of you?

REMEMBER

Over time, some trading systems stop working because too many people figure them out. If you can watch for that, you can tweak your system as you go. The big guys do this, too; the downside of the high-frequency, algorithmic trading that so many hedge funds use is that the algorithms have to be rewritten all the time.

A *trading diary* gives you information to systematically assess your trading. Start by writing down why you are making a particular trade. Do this when you make the trade. (If you wait until later, you'll forget, and you'll change your logic to suit your needs. That's just what people do, you know?) Enter the information in a spreadsheet, jot something quick on a piece of scratch paper, or keep a notebook dedicated to your trading. Your recording system doesn't have to be fancy, as long as you take the time to make the notes that you can refer to.

TIP

Some traders create a form and make copies of it and then keep a stack on hand so that they can easily fill them out during the day. They even create predetermined indicators that match their strategies and that they can check off or circle. At the end of the day, they collect their diary sheets into a three-ring binder that they can refer back to when the time comes to evaluate their trading strategy and their performance.

Figure 14-3 offers an example of a trading diary. You can customize it for your own trading strategy, including those indicators that matter most to you.

TIP

The trading diary form in Figure 14-3 is just an example. If your trading style is so fast that you don't have time to fill it out, don't fret. Instead, come up with some kind of shorthand that lets you keep a running tally of trades made based on a signal from your system, trades based on your own hunches, and trades based on other interpretations of market conditions. Then match your notes against the trade confirmations from your broker to see how you did.

Trading Diary

Date: _____
Time: _____
Security Name: _____ Symbol: _____ Market: _____

Price entered: _____ Long/short? long short
Quantity: _____ Leverage used? yes no

Indicators:
Price trend is	rising	falling	rangebound
Volume is	rising	falling	steady
Sector is	rising	falling	rangebound
Market is	rising	falling	rangebound

Technical Pattern: _____

Price closed: _____
Quantity: _____
Time: _____

Indicators:
Price trend is	rising	falling	rangebound
Volume is	rising	falling	steady
Sector is	rising	falling	rangebound
Market is	rising	falling	rangebound

Technical Pattern: _____

I initiated this trade because (check one):
_____ The trading system signalled it
_____ I had a hunch (explain below)
_____ The market looked right, even though the signal didn't go off (explain below)
_____ Other (explain below)

I closed out this trade because (check one):
_____ The trading system signalled it
_____ I needed to cut my losses
_____ I had a hunch (explain below)
_____ The market looked right, even though the signal didn't go off (explain below)
_____ Other (explain below)

Explanation and lessons learned:

FIGURE 14-3:
A trading diary should be customized to your own preferences.

_____
_____
_____
_____
_____
_____
_____

© John Wiley & Sons, Inc.

After You Trade: Calculating Overall Performance

Calculating performance seems easy: Simply use the balance at the end of the year and the balance at the start of the year to find the percentage change. But what if you added money to your investment in the middle of the year? What if you took cash out in the middle of the year to buy a new computer? Before you know it, you're left with algebra unlike any you've seen since high school and you're stuck solving it if you want to see how you're doing.

In addition to the increase in your assets, you want to track your *volatility*, which is how much your gains and losses can fluctuate. Volatility is an important measure of risk, especially if your trading strategy relies on leverage.

Reviewing types of return

The investment performance calculation starts by dividing returns into different categories: income, short-term capital gains, and long-term capital gains. Although almost all a day trader's gains come from short-term capital gains, we go over the definitions of each so that you know the differences.

Income

When investors talk about *income returns,* they mean regular payments from their investments, usually in the form of dividends from stock or interest payments on bonds. As a day trader, you may earn income on the cash balance in your brokerage account but probably not from your trading activities.

Capital gains

A *capital gain* is the price appreciation in an asset — a stock, a bond, a house, or whatever it is that you're investing in. You buy it at one price, sell it at another, and the difference is a capital gain. (Unless, of course, you sell the asset for less than you paid, and then you have a capital loss.)

REMEMBER

Income in tax terms is different from income in financial terms. Much of what an investor would consider to be a capital gain, such as the short-term capital gains that day traders generate, the CRA considers to be income.

Calculating returns

Give someone with a numerical bent a list of numbers and a calculator, and she can some up with several different relationships between the numbers. After the asset values for each time period have been determined, rates of return can be calculated. But how? And over how long a time period? The process gets a little more complicated because money is coming in and going out while the asset values move up and down. The following sections outline different calculations you can use to figure out your investment returns.

Calculating compound average rate of return (CAGR)

The most common way to calculate investment returns is to use a time-weighted average. This method is perfect for traders who start with one pool of money and don't add to it or take money out. This is also called the *compound average rate of return* (CAGR). If you are looking at only one month or one year, it's a simple percentage. To calculate performance on a percentage basis, you use this equation:

$$\frac{EOY - BOY}{BOY}$$

EOY represents the end of year asset value, and *BOY* represents the beginning of year value. The result is the percentage return for one year, and to calculate it, you use simple arithmetic.

Now if you want to look at your return over a period of several years, you need to look at the *compound* return rather than the simple return for each year. The compound return shows you how your investment is growing. You are getting returns on top of returns, and that's a good thing. But the math gets a little complicated because now you have to use the root function on your calculator. The equation for compound annual growth looks like this:

$$\sqrt[N]{\frac{EOP}{BOP}} - 1$$

EOP represents the end of the total time period, *BOP* represents the beginning of the total time period, and *N* is the number of years that you're looking at.

The basic percentage rate of return is great; it's an accurate, intuitive measure of how much gain you're generating from your trading activities. As long as you don't take any money out of your trading account or put any money into it, you're set.

Calculating performance when you make deposits and withdrawals

You may be putting money into your account. Maybe you have a salaried job and are day trading on the side, or maybe your spouse gives you a percentage of his income to add to your trading account. You may also be taking money out of your day trading account to cover your living expenses or to put into other investment opportunities. All that money flowing into and out of your account can really screw up your performance calculation. You need a way to calculate the performance of your trading system without considering the deposits and withdrawals to your trading account.

Here's an example: You start day trading on January 1 with $100,000 in your account. On May 1, your income tax refund from last year arrives, and you add $1,000 of the money to your account and start trading with it. On December 1, you take out $5,000 to buy holiday presents. At the end of the year, your account is worth $115,000. How did you do?

As a day trader, you have a few methods at your disposal for calculating your performance when you make withdrawals and deposits:

>> **The Modified Dietz method** loses a little accuracy but makes up for it with simplicity.

>> **The time-weighted rate of return** isolates investment and trading performance from the rest of the account.

>> **The dollar-weighted rate of return** has many flaws but gives a sense of what the account holder has.

Read on to see the return that would be calculated using each of these methods.

MODIFIED DIETZ METHOD

The *Modified Dietz method* is related to the simple percent change formula, but it adjusts the beginning and ending period amounts for the cash inflows and cash outflows. The equation for the Modified Dietz method looks like this:

$$\frac{EOY - BOY - deposits + withdrawals}{BOY + deposits - withdrawals}$$

If you plug in the numbers from the example, you get

$$\frac{115,000 - 100,000 - 1,000 + 5,000}{100,000 + 1,000 - 5,000}$$

Do the math and you see that the result is 19.8 percent.

The advantage of the Modified Dietz method is that it's so easy to do. You can use it when you want a rough idea of how you are doing with your trading but you don't have the time to run a more detailed analysis. The key disadvantage is that it doesn't consider the timing of the deposits and withdrawals. It would generate the same answer if you took out $5,000 in May and put in $1,000 in December, even though the amount of money you would have to trade between May 1 and December 1 would be very different.

TIME-WEIGHTED RATE OF RETURN

The *time-weighted rate of return* shows the investment performance as a percentage of the assets at hand to trade. This method is the standard of trader evaluation, but the math is much more complicated than with the basic percentage change or the Modified Dietz method. You need to calculate the CAGR for each time period and then do a second calculation to incorporate each of those over a longer period. Using the preceding example, you'd calculate one return for the first four months of the year, another for the next seven months, and then a third return for the month of December. These three returns would then be multiplied to generate a return for the year.

The general equation you use to figure the time-weighted rate of return looks like this:

$$\sqrt[N]{\left(1+r_{p1}\right)\left(1+r_{p2}\right)\left(1+r_{p3}\right)\ldots\left(1+r_{pn}\right)}-1$$

N is the total number of time periods that you are looking at, and *rpn* is the return for that particular time period. To make the calculations easier, you can do it in a spreadsheet. Figure 14-4 shows the time-weighted return for this example. As you can see, the result is 18.78 percent, a little below the Modified Dietz return.

	January	May	December
Beginning of Period Account Value	$ 100,000	$ 109,000	$ 123,000
Deposit/(Withdrawal)	$ -	$ 1,000	$ (5,000)
Adjusted Beginning Account Value	$ 100,000	$ 110,000	$ 118,000
Trading Earnings	$ 9,000	$ 13,000	$ (3,000)
End-of-Period Account Value	$ 109,000	$ 123,000	$ 115,000
Period Percentage Return:	9.00%	11.82%	-2.54%
Annual Return:			18.78%

FIGURE 14-4: An example of the time-weighted rate of return calculation.

© John Wiley & Sons, Inc.

TIP

If you plan on adding to or taking money out of your account, you can make your return calculations much easier by setting a regular schedule and sticking to it. Otherwise, you have to do calculations for fractional time periods. It's not impossible, but it's kind of a hassle.

REMEMBER

The time-weighted rate of return gives you the best sense of your trading performance, and its precision more than offsets the complexity of the calculation. You want to look at this number when you are deciding whether to change or refine your strategy.

DOLLAR-WEIGHTED RETURNS

The *dollar-weighted return*, also called the *money-weighted return*, is the rate that makes the net present value of a stream of numbers equal to zero. That calculation is also called the *internal rate of return* or *IRR*, and it is used for other things than just return calculations. You can use it to determine what the return is for a stream of numbers over time and to calculate returns when you're putting money into or taking money out of your trading account. And if you have a financial calculator such as the Hewlett-PackardHP17BII+ or the Texas Instruments BA2+, the calculations are pretty easy.

WARNING

Ah, but there's a catch! Although useful, the dollar-weighted method can misstate returns and occasionally shows nonsensical results if too many negative returns appear in a series. And yes, day traders often have negative returns. If you get a result showing a ridiculously large positive or a ridiculously small negative return (like −15,989.9 percent, for example), you may want to try another calculation.

Figure 14-5 shows the dollar-weighted rate of return using the same data used in the two preceding examples.

	January	May	December
Beginning of Period Account Value	$ 100,000	$ 109,000	$ 123,000
Deposit/(Withdrawal)	$ -	$ 1,000	$ (5,000)
Adjusted Beginning Account Value	$ 100,000	$ 110,000	$ 118,000
Trading Earnings	$ 9,000	$ 13,000	$ (3,000)
End-of-Period Account Value	$ 109,000	$ 123,000	$ 115,000
Period Percentage Return:	9.00%	11.82%	-2.54%
Annual Return:			12.10%

FIGURE 14-5: Calculating the dollar-weighted rate of return.

© John Wiley & Sons, Inc.

The result is 12.1 percent, lower than the other two examples because the dollar-weighted return overstates the withdrawal and the loss in the last month of the year. The withdrawals affect the account's spending power, offsetting the investment performance. But the overall account balance is up more than 12.1 percent, even considering the deposit at the beginning of May. The weight of the cash flows threw off this calculation.

Because of the problems with dollar-weighted returns, professional investors who analyze investment returns usually prefer the time-weighted, compound average approach. Still, the dollar-weighted return has some value, especially for an investor who wants to know how the asset value has changed over time. Because a day trader is usually both an investor and an account owner, the dollar-weighted rate of return can show whether the investment performance is affecting spending power. This measure is particularly useful if you are trying to decide whether to continue day trading.

Just as you have alternatives in calculating your performance, so too does anyone trying to sell you a trading system or training course. Ask questions about the performance calculation method and how cash flows and expenses are handled. The numbers may not look so great once you grade the math behind them.

Determining the risk to your return

Now that you have return numbers from your profit and loss statements and your return calculations, it's time to perform black-belt performance jujitsu and determine your risk levels. We're not going to go into all of the many risk and volatility measures out there, because believe us, the good editors of the *For Dummies* books don't want to proofread all the math. In fact, some of these measures may be more math than *you* want to do. That's okay. Even if you look at just a few measures, you'll have more information than if you ignore them all.

Batting average — er, win-loss percentage

Baseball players are judged by how often they hit the ball. After all, they can't score until they get on base, and they can't get on base without a hit or a walk. The number of hits relative to the number of times at bat is the batting average. It's a simple, beautiful number.

Day traders often calculate their batting average, too, although they may call it their *win-loss percentage* or *win ratio*. It's the same: the number of successful trades to the total number of trades. Not all trades have to work out for you to make money, but the more often the trades work for you, the better your overall performance is likely to be. If you have both good performance and a high batting average, then your strategy may have less risk than one that relies on just a handful of home run trades amidst a bunch of strikeouts.

Standard deviation

Want something harder than your batting average? Turn to *standard deviation*, which is tricky to calculate without a spreadsheet but forms the core of many risk measures out there.

The standard deviation calculation starts with the average return over a given time period. This is the *expected* return, the return that, on average, you get if you stick with your trading strategy. But any given week, month, or year, the return may be very different from what you expect. The more likely you are to get what you expect, the less risk you take. Insured bank savings accounts pay a low interest rate, but the rate is guaranteed. Day trading offers the potential for much higher returns but also the possibility that you could lose everything any one month — especially if you can't stick to your trading discipline.

The explanation is a lot easier to understand after you take a gander at Figure 14-6.

Calculating Standard Deviation

	Percentage Return	Step Two: Subtract expected return from each reported return R-E(R)	Step Three: Calculate the square of each difference (R-E(R))^2
Step One: **Find the expected return**			
January	(0.02)	(0.0211)	0.0004
February	0.01	0.0079	0.0001
March	(0.00)	(0.0040)	0.0000
April	0.09	0.0849	0.0072
May	0.01	0.0082	0.0001
June	0.01	0.0082	0.0001
July	(0.08)	(0.0818)	0.0067
August	0.02	0.0182	0.0003
September	0.03	0.0282	0.0008
October	(0.04)	(0.0418)	0.0017
November	(0.01)	(0.0118)	0.0001
December	0.01	0.0049	0.0000
Total	0.02	Sum of the squares:	0.0176
E(R)	0.0018	Step Four: Average of the sum of the squares	0.0015
		Step Five: Square root of the average of the sum of the squares, also known as standard deviation	0.0383

FIGURE 14-6: Calculating standard deviation.

© John Wiley & Sons, Inc.

As this figure shows, you calculate standard deviation through a series of steps:

1. Take every return over the time period and then find the average.

A simple mean will do. Here, there are 12 months, so we added all 12 returns and then divided by 12.

2. Subtract the average from each of the 12 returns.

This calculation shows how much any one return differs from the average, to give you a sense of how much the returns can go back and forth.

3. Square the differences you found in Step 2 (multiply them by themselves) to get rid of the negative numbers.

When you add those up, you get a number known in statistics as the *sum of the squares.*

4. Find the average of the sum of the squares.

5. Calculate the square root of the average of the sum of the squares.

That square root from this step is the *standard deviation,* the magic number you're looking for.

Of course, you don't have to do all of this math. Almost all trading software calculates standard deviation automatically, but at least you now know where the calculation comes from.

REMEMBER

The higher the standard deviation, the riskier the strategy. This number can help you determine how comfortable you are with different trading techniques you may be backtesting, as well as whether you want to stick with your current strategy.

In academic terms, *risk* is the likelihood of getting any return other than the return you expect. To most normal human beings, there's no risk in getting more than you expect; the problem is in getting less of a return than you were counting on. This is a key limitation of risk evaluation. Of course, a few periods of better-than-expected returns are often followed by a run of worse-than-expected returns as performance reverts to the mean.

REMEMBER

The truism that past performance is no indicator of future results applies to risk as well as to return.

Using benchmarks to evaluate your performance

To understand your performance numbers, you need one more step: what your performance is relative to what else you could be doing with your money. The following sections have the details.

Performance relative to an index

The most common way to think about investment performance is relative to a *market index.* These are the measures of the overall market that are quoted all the time in the news, such as the S&P/TSX Composite Index, the S&P 500 and the Dow Jones Industrial Average. Not only are these widely watched, but many mutual funds and futures contracts also are designed to mimic their performance. That means investors can always do at least as well as the index itself, if their investment objectives call for exposure to that part of the broad investment market.

REMEMBER

One big problem is that day traders often look at the wrong index for the type of investment that they have. They'll compare the performance of trading in agricultural commodities to the S&P/TSX when a commodities index would be a better measure. And the indexes assume that the assets in question are held for the long haul rather than traded every few minutes or every few hours.

If you aren't sure what index to use, check a financial website such as Yahoo! Finance (https://finance.yahoo.com/indices) or check out the Market Lab section of *Barron's* (www.barrons.com), a weekly financial publication put out by Dow Jones & Company, the same people who publish *The Wall Street Journal* and the Dow Jones Industrial Average. Both of these have lengthy lists of different stock, bond, and commodity indexes covering the United States and the world. You can find the one that best matches your preferred markets and use it to compare your performance.

In some cases, your trading practices may overlap more than one index. If so, pick the indexes that are appropriate and compare them only to those trades that match. If you trade 40 percent currencies and 60 percent metals, then you should create your own hybrid index that's 40 percent currencies and 60 percent metals.

Performance relative to your time

In the earlier section "Pulling everything into a profit and loss statement," where we talk about tracking your trades and doing a profit and loss statement, we say that you should calculate your hourly wage. There's a reason for that. Instead of day trading, you could put your money in a nice, simple index mutual fund and take a regular job. If your hourly wage is less than what you can earn elsewhere, you may want to consider doing just that.

Of course, there are benefits to working on your own that don't often show up in your bank account. We say this as freelance financial writers. If you enjoy day trading and if you make enough money to suit your lifestyle, by all means, don't let the relative numbers stop you.

Performance relative to other traders

You probably want to know how you're doing relative to other people who are trading. However, you'll probably never know. No central repository of trading returns exists (although wouldn't it be interesting if the brokerage firms or exchanges could report that?). Some academics have done studies of day trading returns, but they're working with historic data stripped of customer information.

On message boards and at get-togethers, you may hear other traders talk about their returns. Take this information with an entire box of salt. Some people lie. Others exaggerate or obfuscate. Someone who has average or poor returns may want to lie to try to impress others, while those with great returns may not want to call attention to their prowess.

Ignore whatever other traders tell you about their returns. If you are satisfied with your performance relative to your risk and your time, nothing else matters.

3
Day Trading, Incorporated

IN THIS PART . . .

Find the right broker and get familiar with the rules and regulations.

Get the ins and outs on Canadian investment accounts.

Deep dive into day trading tax rules.

» **Choosing from the many brokers available**

» **Watching out for scams**

Chapter 15

Your Key Vendor: Your Broker

You can't day trade without a trading account at a brokerage firm. It's that simple. Although every trader needs one, and although the rates charged are similar, brokerage accounts are not commodities. Not only do different brokers offer different services, but most brokers also have tiers of services available for different types of investors and traders. You aren't just buying a way to execute a trade but rather a set of services.

Some brokerage services will be worth the money and then some to you. Others will be inappropriate for your style. To help you get started on your research, this chapter covers the different types of accounts, with information on their features and benefits. After all, you want to make a good trade from the start!

Choosing a Brokerage

If you are going to trade, you need a brokerage account. What kind of broker you need depends on what you plan to trade (head to Chapters 4 and 5 for some of the basics of different types of securities and where they trade):

>> If you plan to trade stocks, you need a full-service broker that has access to the Toronto Stock Exchange, Nasdaq, the New York Stock Exchange (NYSE), and other major exchanges.

>> If you'd rather trade the stock market through derivatives, then you need a trading account with a broker holding that has access to derivatives exchanges, such as the Montreal Exchange.

TIP

Many day traders pursue two or three strategies, which may require holding different brokerage accounts. Having multiple brokerage accounts isn't unusual. If you are going to trade both grain futures and tech stocks, for example, you may want one account with a futures brokerage and another account with a stock brokerage that offers fast execution.

The following sections tell you what to look for when choosing a brokerage firm.

Getting proper pricing

All brokerage firms offer *price quotes* — a summary of the current bid and offer prices for selling or buying the security in question. But not all these price quotes are the same. Some are offered in *real time*, meaning that you see the prices as soon as your modem can transmit the change to you. Others are delayed, sometimes by seconds, sometimes by minutes. If you're buying a bond with plans to hold it for ten years, the difference in price between now and 15 minutes ago probably isn't material. But if you're looking to day trade in the bond market, using short-term changes in treasury futures, a delay of even 30 seconds may be the difference between your strategy succeeding or failing.

REMEMBER

Almost all day trading strategies need direct access in order to maximize profitability. Direct-access brokers allow you to see the price quotes in real time so that you can act on them immediately, and they allow you to work through different electronic communications networks rather than going through the firm's own traders.

To help you with the pricing, some brokers offer access to *liquidity pools,* also known as *dark pools, dark liquidity,* or *dark books.* These pools are private execution networks that can sometimes wreak havoc with the market, but when used properly, they can improve the pricing on a stock trade. Brokers that participate in these pools may place your order in the liquidity pool, and then your order will be executed only if a matching trade exists. In this situation, the trade happens faster and often with better pricing than it would if it had been executed in the open market.

Unlike those brokerage services aimed at day traders, a traditional retail brokerage offers customers more research and advice and may even offer to improve order execution by waiting until market conditions are more favourable. That's fine for investors but not so good for day traders.

In addition to different levels of market access, brokerage firms offer different types of price quotes with different amounts of detail. Read on for descriptions and pictures to see what you need for your strategy.

REMEMBER

Faster, detailed price quotes are valuable to traders, so brokerage firms usually charge more for them. Don't skimp on price services at the expense of your trading profitability.

Level I quotes

Level I quotes give you the current bid and ask, or bid and offer, prices for a given security. The *bid,* of course, is the price at which the broker buys the security from you, and the *ask* (also called *offer* in some markets) is the price at which the broker offers to sell the security to you. A Level I quote also shows the size of the most recent buy and sell orders.

WARNING

Most brokerage firms offer real-time Level I quotes for free, but these numbers do not have enough detail for day trading.

Level II quotes

Level II quotes not only tell you what the current bid and offer prices are but also who the market makers are — the brokerage firm traders who are buying and selling the security — and what size orders they have at different prices (see Figure 15-1). This information can help you gauge the volatility and direction of trading in the market, which can help you make more profitable trades. Most brokerage firms that specialize in day trading offer Level II quotes in most markets.

SYMBOL	**AMAT**	Applied Materials (NGS)		
LAST SALE	20.15 q	NASDAQ Bid Tick (+)		
NATIONAL BBO	20.15 q	20.16 q	6900 × 3000	

MPID	Bid	Size	MPID	Ask	Size
NSDQ	20.15	3000	NSDQ	20.16	2000
ARCX	20.15	2600	ARCX	20.16	1900
BEST	20.15	1500	TDCM	20.16	1000
NITE	20.15	1400	OPCO	20.17	2100
CINN	20.15	1200	BARD	20.17	1000
BOFA	20.15	1000	CLYP	20.18	2000
AUTO	20.14	5000	SCHB	20.18	1500
LEHM	20.14	1000	NITE	20.18	1100
ABLE	20.14	1000	DAIN	20.18	100
SCHB	20.14	500	TEJS	20.18	100
GSCO	20.14	100	GSCO	20.18	100
RAJA	20.12	1200	MSCO	20.19	1500
TDCM	20.12	1000	JPMS	20.19	100
MONR	20.12	1000	BEST	20.20	1200
SWST	20.12	1000	NFSC	20.20	1000
NORT	20.12	400	FBRC	20.20	800
JPMS	20.12	100	FACT	20.20	100
PERT	20.11	800	UBSW	20.21	1100
PIPR	20.11	100	GSCO	20.21	1000
PRUS	20.10	500	FBCO	20.21	100
FBCO	20.09	1400	LEHM	20.21	100
COWN	20.09	800	RHCO	20.21	100
HDSN	20.09	400	WCHV	20.22	1200
UBSW	20.09	400	GLBT	20.22	1000

FIGURE 15-1:
A Nasdaq
Level II quote.

Source: Nasdaq

TotalView quotes

TotalView quotes show all orders in the U.S. market for a given security, both attributed to market makers and anonymous (see Figure 15-2). This information gives traders the most detailed information about what's happening in the market. Although all this detail may be overkill for some trading strategies, it's vital to the success of most. You'll have a better idea of how much information your trading strategies need after you test them, using the advice in Chapter 14.

Evaluating types of platform

When you have an account with a brokerage firm, you have a way to get information about the markets and place your orders. The conduit is the Internet, but you need a way to get your orders to it. Some brokerage firms have their own software that you can use; others allow you to log in through a website. The following sections detail your options.

SYMBOL	**AMAT**	Applied Materials (NGS)	
LAST SALE	20.15 q	NASDAQ Bid Tick (+)	
NATIONAL BBO	20.15 q	20.16 q	6900 × 3000

Bid Price	Total Depth	Ask Price	Total Depth
20.15	10700	20.16	4900
20.14	56100	20.17	9100
20.13	26300	20.18	13400
20.12	9900	20.19	11200
20.11	1700	20.20	8700

MPID	Bid	Size	MPID	Ask	Size
NSDQ	20.15	3000	NSDQ	20.16	2000
ARCX	20.15	2600	ARCX	20.16	1900
BEST	20.15	1500	TDCM	20.16	1000
NITE	20.15	1400	NSDQ	20.17	6000
CINN	20.15	1200	OPCO	20.17	2100
BOFA	20.15	1000	BARD	20.17	1000
NSDQ	20.14	28500	NSDQ	20.18	5000
BEST	20.14	12500	OPCO	20.18	2500
NITE	20.14	7500	CLYP	20.18	2000
AUTO	20.14	5000	SCHB	20.18	1500
LEHM	20.14	1000	NITE	20.18	1100
ABLE	20.14	1000	TDCM	20.18	1000
SCHB	20.14	500	DAIN	20.18	100
GSCO	20.14	100	TEJS	20.18	100
NSDQ	20.13	10000	GSCO	20.18	100
GSCO	20.13	8800	NSDQ	20.19	5500
SCHB	20.13	7500	NITE	20.19	3000
NSDQ	20.12	2200	MSCO	20.19	1500
BEST	20.12	2000	OPCO	20.19	1000
RAJA	20.12	1200	JPMS	20.19	100
LEHM	20.12	1000	SCHB	20.19	100
TDCM	20.12	1000	BAR	20.19	4000
MONR	20.12	1000	BEST	20.20	1200
SWST	20.12	1000	NFSC	20.20	1000
NORT	20.12	400	NSDQ	20.20	1000
JPMS	20.12	100	FBRC	20.20	800
PERT	20.11	800	SCHB	20.20	500
GSCO	20.11	500	NITE	20.20	100
LEHM	20.11	100	FACT	20.20	100
NSDQ	20.11	100	UBSW	20.21	1100
NORT	20.11	100	GSCO	20.21	1000
PIPR	20.11	100	NITE	20.21	1000
NSDQ	20.10	13500	NSDQ	20.21	500
SCHB	20.10	3500	TDCM	20.21	100
TDCM	20.10	2000	FBCO	20.21	100
PRUS	20.10	500	LEHM	20.21	100
GSCO	20.09	100	RHCO	20.21	100
NSDQ	20.09	2500	LEHM	20.22	5000
RAJA	20.09	2200	WCHV	20.22	1200
FBCO	20.09	1400	GLBT	20.22	1000
MONR	20.09	1000	NSDQ	20.22	500
NITE	20.09	1000	FBRC	20.22	500
COWN	20.09	800	DAIN	20.22	100
HDSN	20.09	400	NITE	20.22	100
UBSW	20.09	400	BEST	20.22	100

Source: Nasdaq

FIGURE 15-2: A Nasdaq TotalView quote is the most detailed available.

Software-based platforms

With a software-based platform, you must download and install the brokerage firm's proprietary system onto your computer. When you're ready to start your trading day, you connect to the Internet first, launch the software to see what's happening, and place your trades. Software systems generally offer more features and analytical tools than web-based platforms, but you can only trade on a machine that has the software loaded on it.

Web-based platforms

With a web-based trading platform, you go to the broker's website and log in to trade. With these types of platforms, you can trade from any computer that has Internet access, which is a boon if you travel or work from several different locations. In exchange, you may give up some of the analytic and backtesting tools offered through software-based platforms.

TIP

Note that web-based platforms may be designed to work on specific web browsers. Given the importance of having a stable connection and full functionality in a fast-moving market, if the firm recommends using Firefox, accept that. Don't cling to a preferred alternative.

WARNING

What about mobile platforms? Some brokerage firms allow you to get price quotes and place trades through a mobile phone. This capability may be useful to some people, especially as a backup system, but relying on it solely is a bad idea for most day traders. Day trading is a business, and that means you need some discipline about setting regular hours and working from a regular workspace. You'll probably need more information to work a trade than will fit on your phone's screen (most day traders work off more than one full-sized screen, in fact). Finally, you need to take a break from the market to maintain balance in your life. If you're making trades at your cousin's wedding, you have a problem.

Opening an account

When you open a brokerage account, you must fill out a lot of paperwork to comply with government and exchange regulations. Basically, these forms help the firm ensure that you're suitable for day trading; that you understand the risks of options, futures, and margin strategies; and that your trading money did not come from ill-gotten gains.

After you complete and sign the paperwork, you need to transfer funds. Write a cheque or set up a wire or Internet transfer from an existing bank, brokerage, or mutual fund account.

Exploring Brokers for Day Traders

Following is a list of brokerage firms with services for day traders. It's arranged by specialty (stocks and options together and then foreign exchange) and alphabetically within each category. This list is not exhaustive. Also keep in mind that every year new firms are formed and existing firms are acquired or merged away, so be sure to do your own research. Also, this list doesn't imply an endorsement of anyone's services.

TIP

Each winter, *The Globe and Mail* (www.globeandmail.com) conducts a survey of online brokerage firms with updates on the latest features and rankings based on such criteria as technology, usability, additional features, customer service, and trading costs. Check it out when you're ready to research.

Brokers for stocks and a bit of the rest

Day traders almost always work through online brokerage accounts. Many firms offering these accounts handle trading in almost all securities. The firms usually belong to all the exchanges, so you can trade almost anything anywhere in the world through them. These brokerage accounts often offer a range of news and charting services to help you plan your trading. In some cases, their offerings may be overkill; you may find them distracting and their services unnecessary. Some may not handle your security of choice well.

REMEMBER

Brokerage firms don't make money just on the commission charged per trade. Other sources of revenue include monthly service charges, fees for real-time quotes, interest on margin loans to customers, and the *spread,* which is the difference between what you pay for a security and what the firm paid to get it. So don't let the commission be the critical factor in deciding among brokerage firms. Think about the services you need and the relative cost to you of different account offerings.

BMO InvestorLine

The Bank of Montreal's InvestorLine is geared toward online investors but also has an active trader component, including access to Level II quotes and margin accounts. As with most bank offerings, you can trade only equities and options, and you need a mimumum $5,000 to open an account. If you make more than 75 trades a quarter or have a mimum account balance of $2 million, you'll get access to BMO Market Pro, a software platform that has more than 100 customizable technical studies, real-time charts, and analytics useful for day traders.

For more information, go to www.bmo.com/investorline.

CIBC Investor's Edge

One benefit of trading with a bank is obtaining access to its extensive research material. CIBC Investor's Edge lets you do all the usual stuff, and it also opens the doors to its CIBC Asset Management and CIBC World Markets reports. In addition, its "stock centre" covers North American companies, and you get access to Morningstar's comprehensive company and ETF reports. If you make more than 150 traders per quarter, you're eligible for a per trade discount on stock and option securities.

For more information, go to www.investorsedge.cibc.com.

Desjardins Online Brokerage

Desjardins Online Brokerage is owned by Desjardins Securities, the brokerage arm of Montreal-based Desjardins Group, the largest credit union in North America. Those who make more than 10 trades a month will get access to its Disnat Direct platform, which offers Level II quotes, real-time streams that update automatically, and access to the company's research services. As well, make more than 30 equity or ETF trades a month and you'll pay just $0.75 per trade.

For more information, go to www.disnat.com.

HSBC InvestDirect

HSBC InvestDirect offers traders easy access to securities on international markets, such as Hong Kong, China, London, Paris, and Frankfurt. Other services provide more research and analysis, and some offer cheaper pricing. (Active traders — those who make 150 trades or more per quarter — are dinged $4.88 for equity and ETF trades.) But if you're keen on international investing, especially Chinese markets, then this could be the right brokerage for you.

For more information, go to www.hsbc.ca/investments/investdirect.

Interactive Brokers

U.S.-based Interactive Brokers, which operates in Canada, is far more focused on day traders than the bank brokerages. It offers stock, options, futures, and foreign exchange trading services, low pricing (between $0.0005 and $0.0035 per share [not per trade] on stock and ETF trades), and a robust IB Trader Workstation software package that gives you access to more than 100 global markets.

For more information, go to www.interactivebrokers.ca.

National Bank Direct Brokerage

Montreal's National Bank Direct Brokerage gives traders plenty of research and technical analysis tools. Use the firm's Market-Q software to get real-time quotes, access to Level II quotes, technical indicators, and more.

For more information, go to www.nbdb.ca.

Qtrade

Vancouver-based Qtrade may be a small, independent firm, but it offers a whole range of investment services. The firm lets you trade the basics — Canadian and U.S. stocks, bonds, GICs, mutual funds, and options — and it allows you to do short selling in a margin account. QTrade also offers a lot of stock-related research, and you can trade more than 100 ETFs commission-free.

For more information, go to www.qtrade.ca.

Questrade

Toronto-based Questrade gives traders the chance to buy and sell equities, options, forex, contracts for difference, gold, and mutual funds. It also has a variety of trading platforms, including Questrade IQ Edge and Questrade Global, the latter of which is ideal for currency and commodity traders. Questrade also offers access to its comprehensive Market Intelligence research tools.

For more information, go to www.questrade.com.

RBC Direct Investing

RBC Direct Investing offers similar options as the other banks — Level II quotes, web and mobile-based trading dashboards, and real-time streaming quotes for stocks and ETFs. One advantage of this service is access to RBC Capital Markets' extensive Canadian and U.S. research. RBC credit card holders can also pay for trading commission using reward points.

For more information, go to www.rbcdirectinvesting.com.

Scotia iTrade

When we wrote the first edition of this book, Scotiabank had just bought E*Trade Canada and renamed it Scotia iTrade. It has envolved quite a bit from the old days, as investors can trade stocks, options, bonds, GICs, and mutual funds, and it provides services for active traders through its Scotia OnLine platform. As with some other brokerages, Scotia iTrade offers a practice trading account that comes with $100,000 fictional dollars.

For more information, go to www.scotiaitrade.com.

TD Direct Investing

It may not be called TD Waterhouse anymore (its name changed in 2012), but it's still one of the better bank brokerage platforms in the country. Day traders who are interested in trading U.S. stocks can have access to its popular think-or-swim trading platform (requires a minimum $25,000 USD deposit) and its Advanced Dashboard, which comes with advanced charting, earnings announcements for Canadian and U.S. companies, and much more.

For more information, go to www.td.com/ca/en/investing/direct-investing.

Brokers for foreign exchange

The foreign exchange, or forex, market is the largest trading market in the world and offers lots of opportunities for day traders to make (or lose) money. Most forex trades take place between banks, corporations, and hedge funds directly, without the use of a broker. If you want to trade foreign currency directly, you need to use a trading firm that is tied in to these networks. Many of the brokers listed in the preceding sections offer forex. The following sections list those that do little else.

CMC Markets

CMC Markets was the first firm to allow individual investors to trade in foreign exchange and contracts for difference. The company has a software- and web-based platform that offers trading shares, commodities, indices, and 65 different currency pairs. It also has extensive technical analysis, research, and education services for its customers.

For more information, go to www.cmcmarkets.ca.

Friedberg Direct

Friedberg Direct, owned by the family-run Friedberg Mercantile Group, offers margin protection and the ability to create detailed account statements. Before you start spending, play with fake money in a demo account.

For more information, go to www.friedbergdirect.ca.

OANDA

Pronounced "O and A," this broker specializes in foreign exchange and mostly works with corporate customers. Despite this, it has no minimum trade size, which makes it popular individual day traders too. It doesn't offer a lot of services, but one that stands out is its analysis of price spreads. It can work with many trading platforms, including MetaTrader.

For more information, go to www.oanda.com.

Watching Out for Brokerage Scams

In Chapter 13, we cover research services, including information on how to investigate and identify any potential scams. We want to revisit it here. We have reason to believe that every broker listed in this chapter is legitimate.

A lot of research and advisory services are out there, and many traders find them to be useful. The best advisors work through a brokerage account. What this means is that you don't keep your money with the advisor, but you subscribe to the advisor's service and execute the trades yourself. Or you find an advisor who works with a particular broker. The advisor places the trade, to be executed in your account so that you can monitor what is happening.

Some popular platforms, like MetaTrader, are software overlays for your brokerage accounts. Instead of using the broker's signaling and charting services, you use the platform's — but the brokerage firm that has custody of your money executes your trades.

The use of a broker separate from the advisor is common in the money management world. You should expect it. Sure, day trading is risky, but it's better to lose money based on your decisions rather than to have it stolen from you.

WARNING

There's a common scam that crops up every few years, and the basis of it is simple: Most day traders lose money, especially when they're starting out. The scam artist offers a day trading advisory service, especially for new traders. You deposit your money and then trade through the service platform. The operator takes your money. You think you're really trading, but really, you're only paper trading. And maybe the advice isn't all that good, so you think you lose everything and no one is the wiser.

The way these scams get caught is that those few traders who actually do make money want their cash back so that they can move up to a platform or broker with more sophisticated services, and they find out the hard way that the money is gone.

REMEMBER

The bottom line: Look for your money to be kept with a brand-name brokerage firm. Check out a list of IIROC approved brokers and investment dealers at www.iiroc.ca/industry/Pages/Dealers-We-Regulate.aspx.

IN THIS CHAPTER

» Looking at a history of day trading and regulations

» Wondering who all these regulators are, anyway

» Considering some basic brokerage requirements

» Handling hot tips

» Trading with other people

Chapter **16**

Regulation Right Now

The financial markets are wild and woolly playgrounds for capitalism at its best. Every moment of the trading day, buyers and sellers get together to figure out what the price of a stock, commodity, or currency should be at that moment given the supply, the demand, and the information out there. It's beautiful.

One reason why the markets work so well is that they are regulated. That may seem like an oxymoron: Isn't capitalism all about free trade, unfettered by any rules from nannying bureaucrats? Ah, but for capitalism to work, people on both sides of a trade need to know that the terms will be enforced. They need to know that the money is in their account and safe from theft. And they need to know that no one has an unfair advantage. *Regulation* creates the trust that makes markets function.

Day traders may not be managing money for other investors, and they may not answer to an employer, but that doesn't mean they don't have rules to follow. They have to comply with applicable securities laws and exchange regulations, some of which specifically address those who make lots of short-term trades. Likewise, brokers and advisers who deal with day traders have regulations that they need to follow, and understanding them can help day traders make better decisions about whom to deal with. In this chapter, you find out who does the regulating, what they look at, and how it all affects you.

How Regulations Created Day Trading

Canada's regulatory system is very different from that in the U.S., though it all stems from the same place. The American system came first, so, naturally, we borrowed many of their rules when forming our own regulatory system. Things have developed significantly since then, and although many similarities exist you'll also find a lot of differences. But first, a quick course in American history is in order so you can see how regulation in fact helped create trading.

With the advent of the telegraph, traders could receive daily price quotes. Many cities had *bucket shops,* which were storefront businesses where traders could bet on changes in stock and commodity prices. They weren't buying the security itself, but were instead placing bets against others. These schemes were highly prone to manipulation and fraud, and they were wiped out after the stock market crash of 1929.

After the 1929 crash, small investors could trade off the ticker tape, which was a printout of price changes sent by telegraph, or wire. In most cases, they would do this by going down to their brokerage firm's office, sitting in a conference room, and placing orders based on the changes they saw come across the tape. Really serious traders could get a wire installed in their own office, but the costs were prohibitive for most individual investors. In any event, traders still had to place their orders through a broker rather than having direct access to the market, so they could not count on timely execution.

TECHNICAL STUFF

Another reason why so little day trading happened back then is that until 1975 all American brokerage firms charged the same commissions. That year, the U.S. Securities and Exchange Commission (SEC) ruled that this amounted to price fixing, so brokers could then compete on their commissions. Some brokerage firms, such as Charles Schwab, began to allow customers to trade stock at discount commission rates, which made active trading more profitable. Some brokerage firms don't even charge commissions anymore. (But don't worry; they get money from you in other ways.)

The system of trading off the ticker tape more or less persisted until the stock market crash of 1987. Brokerage firms and market makers were flooded with orders, so they took care of their biggest customers first and pushed the smallest trades to the bottom of the pile. After the crash, the exchanges and the SEC called for several changes that would reduce the chances of another crash and improve execution if one were to happen. One of those changes was the Small Order Entry System, often known as SOES, which gave orders of 1,000 shares or fewer priority over larger orders.

Similar regulation was developed in Canada at about the same time. Our Order Exposure Rule was created to make sure smaller orders were given the same priority as larger ones. Here, 50 standard trading units or fewer (about 5,000 shares) have to be immediately entered on a market place. Brokers can't fill their larger orders first.

In the 1990s, when Internet access became widely available, this became less of a problem because traders could place orders in real time. But the rule still applies. Brokers could, theoretically, wait to execute Internet orders so they could deal with their 100,000-share trades first. Of course, that would be terrible for business — and with so much competition, fast execution is a selling point. Still, this rule, plus the speed of the Internet, put traders on the same footing as brokers and made day trading look like a pretty good way to make a living.

In 2008, things got crazy with the financial markets coming darn close to a full-on collapse. All that volatility was a lot of fun for those traders who could handle it. The brokerage firms developed larger and more sophisticated trading programs that seemed to work well until a single large order on the afternoon of May 6, 2010, caused everything to go haywire. That so-called "flash crash" exposed the risks created by high-frequency trading programs. At first, no one wanted to blame technology and instead tried to place the blame on traders whose fingers were too big to punch the numbers on their order-entry machines.

REMEMBER

While the Great Recession did usher in a new era of regulation for the world's financial institutions, other than firms creating more sophisticated software and Internet speeds increasing, little has changed for day traders over the last decade.

Who Regulates What?

In Canada, financial markets get regulatory oversight from various bodies, but most of the rules come from the provincial security commissions (such as the Ontario Securities Commission; OSC) and the Investment Industry Regulatory Organization of Canada (IIROC). Both have similar goals: to ensure that investors and traders have adequate information to make decisions, and to prevent fraud and abuse.

Unlike in the United States, which has the Securities and Exchange Commission, Canada has no national regulator. IIROC governs dealers (the institutions whose trading software you're using) across the country, and the securities commissions enforce the provincial Securities Act and Commodity Futures Act. The commissions' mandate, says the OSC's website, is to protect investors from "unfair, improper or fraudulent practices and to foster fair and efficient capital markets and confidence in capital markets."

Both IIROC and Canada's other self-regulatory organization, the Mutual Fund Dealers Association (MFDA), which oversees dealers who sell only mutual funds, police their own members, but the former self-regulatory organization (SRO) does a lot more. IIROC regulates the TSX and other Canadian exchanges, such as the NEO Exchange and the Canada Securities Exchange.

When it comes to equity exchanges, IIROC's main job is to make sure nothing fishy is happening. The organization monitors trading activity and can place halts or delays if market integrity is compromised. It also enforces Universal Market Integrity Rules — the rules in Canada that govern trading.

IIROC also monitors how securities are traded in order to look for patterns that might point to market manipulation or insider trading. It works with brokerage firms to make sure they know who their customers are and that they have systems in place to make certain these customers play by the rules.

Because the stock and corporate bond markets are the most popular markets and have a relatively large number of relatively small issuers, regulators are active and visible. Not just one government is issuing currency — a whole bunch of companies issue shares of stock. When it turns out that one of these companies has fraudulent numbers the headlines erupt, and suddenly everyone cares about what the regulators are up to. That's just the first layer in regulating this market.

TIP

When we first wrote this chapter 12 years ago, there was a lot of talk in the hallowed halls of the Legislature about creating a single national securities regulator in Canada, much like the SEC in the United States. That conversation is still ongoing. Governments have been debating the question of whether Canada needs one for decades, so the chances of it happening soon remain slim. However, if you're reading this book a few years after its publication date, be aware that some of what we've written here may be obsolete.

Provincial securities commissions

Each province has its own agency to ensure the markets work efficiently. Although rules may vary, they all share a common goal: to keep capital markets safe from fraud. Each commission governs its own jurisdiction, but they do work together. The commissions also work with the SEC or other governing bodies when fraud crosses country borders.

The provincial securities commissions have various functions, including:

>> Regulating provincial capital markets by enforcing the provincial Securities Act and, depending on where, the Commodity Futures Act. The commissions ensure that any companies that have securities listed on exchanges in their

jurisdiction report their financial information accurately and on time, so that investors can determine whether investing in the company makes sense for them.

>> Working with various stakeholders — retail investors, pensions funds, dealers, advisers, stock exchanges, alternative trading systems, SROs, and more — in ensuring compliance, investor protection, and keeping fair and efficient markets.

>> Prosecuting firms and individuals who violate securities law. Although the commissions spend a lot of time investigating allegations of misconduct, they hold hearings over takeover bids and other regulatory issues, too.

Investment Industry Regulatory Organization of Canada (IIROC)

IIROC (www.iiroc.ca) was created in 2008 when the Investment Dealers Association and Market Regulation Services merged. The IDA was an SRO that oversaw Canadian dealers, and MRS provided regulation services for Canadian markets. The union has brought better oversight to the industry, making it more difficult for nefarious crooks to take advantage of investors.

The new SRO oversees investment dealers in Canada that trade stocks, bonds, mutual funds, options, forex, and other securities. It also looks after trading activity on debt and equity markets. It has 173 member firms, with thousands of people who are registered to sell securities. IIROC administers background checks and licensing exams, regulates securities trading and monitors how firms comply, and provides information for investors so that they are better informed about the investing process.

IIROC also requires advisers to know as much as they can about their clients, via Know Your Client forms. This includes determining whether an investment strategy is suitable for them. We discuss suitability later in this chapter under "Are you suitable for day trading?" — for now, just know that it's an IIROC function.

TIP

The first thing a day trader should do is check IIROC and MFDA's media release pages and the security commissions' registration sites. Every time a disciplinary hearing against a firm or adviser takes place, the progress of the proceedings is posted on the site. Find out whether the firm you want to trade with has violated any regulations. The security commissions' registrations sites allow you to type in the name of a person or firm and see whether they are in fact registered, what category they're registered in, and if any conditions were attached to that registration. These tools help ensure you're not dealing with a criminal.

Mutual Fund Dealers Association of Canada (MFDA)

Unlike IIROC, which oversees dealers who trade stocks and bonds, the MFDA (www.mfda.ca) represents members who work only with mutual funds. Despite operating under its own set of rules, it shares many of the same goals as IIROC. It regulates operations, standards, and business conduct of its members and tries to improve investor protection. It can fine members for violating rules, and works with authorities when criminal charges are laid.

The MFDA represents 91 firms with more than 78,000 advisers and with about $568 billion in assets under administration. It's highly unlikely the brokerage firm you use will be an MFDA member. Because you're trading more than just mutual funds, you'll be working in an IIROC environment.

The exchanges

It wasn't long ago that each major city had its own exchange. But through mergers and an agreement that Toronto would host a central stock exchange, the TSX became the main exchange in the country. However, depending on what you trade, the TSX is not the only game in town. You'll also find the Toronto Venture Exchange (TSXV), the Montreal Exchange (MX), and other exchanges and alternative trading systems, many of which are mentioned throughout this book.

Canada's main exchanges are owned by the TMX Group. It oversees the TSX, the TSXV, the MX, the TSX Alpha Exchange, and others. The group has outsourced its regulation duties of the TSX, TSXV, and the TSX Alpha Exchange to IIROC, while the MX regulates trading activity in-house.

Brokerage Basics for Firm and Customer

No matter how they are regulated, brokers and futures commission merchants have to know who their customers are and what they are up to. That leads to some basic regulations about suitability and money laundering — and extra paperwork for you. Don't be too annoyed by all the paperwork you have to fill out to open an account, though — your brokerage firm has even more.

Are you suitable for day trading?

Brokerage firms have to make sure the activity surrounding their customers is appropriate. The firms need to know their customers and be sure that any recommendations are suitable. When it comes to day trading, firms want to be sure their customers are dealing with *risk capital* — money they can afford to lose. They also want to be sure that their customers understand the risks they are taking. Depending on the firm, and what you're trying to do, you might have to submit financial statements, sign a stack of disclosures, and verify that you have had previous trading experience.

It's no one's business but your own, of course, except that the regulators want to make sure that firm employees aren't talking customers into taking on risks they should not be taking. Sure, you can lie about it. You can tell the broker you don't *need* the $25,000 you're putting in your account, even if that's the money paying for your child's education. But when it's gone, you can't say you didn't know about the risks involved.

Staying out of the money laundromat

Money laundering is a way to receive money acquired from illegal activities. Your average drug dealer, Mafia hit man, or corrupt politician doesn't accept credit cards, but he really doesn't want to keep lots of cash in his house. How can he collect interest on his money if it's locked in a safe in his closet? And besides, his friends are an unsavory sort. Can he trust them to stay away from his cache? If this criminal fellow takes all that cash to the bank, those pesky bankers will start asking a lot of questions, because they know that most people pursuing legitimate business activities get paid through cheques or electronic direct deposit.

Hence, the felon with funds will look for a way to make it appear that the money is legitimate. It happens in all sorts of ways, ranging from making lots of small cash deposits to engaging in complicated series of financial trades and money transfers, especially between countries, that become difficult for investigators to trace. Sometimes these transactions look a lot like day trading, and that means that legitimate brokerage firms opening day trade accounts should be paying attention to who their customers are.

Fighting money laundering took on urgency after the September 11, 2001 attacks, because it was clear that someone somewhere had given some bad people a lot of cash to fund the preparation and execution of their deadly mission. Several nations increased their oversight of financial activities during the aftermath of the strikes on the World Trade Center and Pentagon. That's why one piece of paperwork from your broker will be the anti–money laundering disclosure. The Financial Transactions Reports Analysis Centre of Canada (FINTRAC) is the government body that looks after money laundering activities, but brokers track this as well. If they suspect a trader is laundering money they'll report it to FINTRAC, which will then investigate.

MONEY LAUNDERING: AL CAPONE OR WATERGATE?

Although some believe that the term *money laundry* dates back to Al Capone's attempts to evade taxes by owning laundries — businesses that had a large number of small cash transactions — the U.S. Federal Reserve Board says the term didn't come into use until the Watergate scandal, when Nixon's campaign staff had to hide the money used to pay the people who broke into his opponent's psychiatrist's office.

In order for your brokerage firm to verify that it knows who its customers are and where their money came from, you'll probably have to provide the following when you open a brokerage account:

>> Your name

>> Date of birth

>> Street address

>> Place of business

>> Social Insurance Number

>> Driver's licence and passport

>> Copies of financial statements

Rules for day traders

Here's the problem for regulators: Many day traders lose money, and those losses can be magnified by the use of *leverage strategies* (trading with borrowed money, meaning that you can lose more money than you have in the quest for large profits; we discuss this in detail in Chapter 6). If the customer who lost the money can't pay up, then the broker is on the hook. If too many customers lose money beyond what the broker can absorb, then the losses ripple through the financial system, and that's not good.

IIROC has a long list of rules that its member firms have to meet in order to stay in business. The organization sets margin requirements and, depending on the type of account, the requirements are stricter to reflect the greater risk. You can read through all the rules by visiting this link: www.iiroc.ca/industry/rulebook/Pages/default.aspx.

REMEMBER

The rules set by IIROC are minimum requirements. Brokerage firms are free to set higher limits for account size and borrowing in order to manage their own risks better.

Tax reporting

If you're a long-term investor receiving dividends, your online broker will send you a slip at the end of the year detailing how much income you've made. Traders will also receive tax forms if they received dividends or interest income — this mostly applies to people who hold overnight positions. Brokers may also send out a summary of trades to help track capital gains and losses. We cover tax issues in Chapter 18.

Hot Tips and Insider Trading

The regulations are very clear for things about suitability and money laundering. You get a bunch of forms, you read them, you sign them, you present documentation, and everyone is happy. The rules that keep the markets functioning are clear and easy to follow.

Another set of rules also keeps markets functioning — namely, that no one has an unfair information advantage. If you knew about big merger announcements, interest rate decisions by the Bank of Canada, or a new sugar substitute that would eliminate demand for corn syrup, you could make a lot of money in the stock market, trading options on interest rate futures, or playing in the grain futures market.

WARNING

Insider trading is a broad term. Any non-public information that a reasonable person would consider when deciding whether to buy or sell a security could apply, and that's a pretty vague standard — especially because the whole purpose of research is to combine bits of immaterial information together to make investment decisions.

Day traders can be susceptible to hot tips, because they are buying and selling so quickly. If these hot tips are actually inside information, though, the trader can become liable. If you get great information from someone who is in a position to know — an officer, a director, a lawyer, an investment banker — you may be looking at stiff penalties. According to the Canada Business Corporations Act, courts can assess civil penalties, while a criminal conviction can land someone in jail for up to ten years.

Insider trading is difficult to prove, so federal regulators use other tools to punish those it suspects of making improper profits. In the United States, Martha Stewart wasn't sent to prison on insider trading charges; she was charged with obstructing justice by lying to investigators about what happened.

Whenever a big announcement is made, such as a merger, the exchanges go back and review trading for several days before to see whether any unusual activities occurred in relevant securities and derivatives. Then they start tracing them back to the traders involved through the brokerage firms to see whether it was coincidence or part of a pattern.

The bottom line is this: You may never come across inside information. But if a tip seems too good to be true, it probably is — so be careful.

Taking on Partners

After your day trading proves to be wildly successful, you might want to take on partners to give you more trading capital and a slightly more regular income from the management fees. You can do it, but it's a lot of work.

If you start trading as a business a good chance exists you'll have to register with your provincial securities commission as a dealer, an investment fund manager, or perhaps something else depending on what you're doing. What triggers registration is complicated. If you're thinking about bringing people on board, it's best to call your securities commission or a lawyer and ask them what you need to do. You may also want to read part 25.1 of the Ontario Securities Act (www.e-laws. gov.on.ca/html/statutes/english/elaws_statutes_90s05_e.htm - BK55) to find out which category you'd fall under.

Registration is not a do-it-yourself project. An error or omission may have tremendous repercussions down the line, from fines to jail time. If you want to take on partners for your trading business, spend the money for qualified legal advice. It will protect you and show prospective customers that you're serious about your business.

Chapter **17**

Choosing the Right Accounts

The U.S. has so many different kinds of investment accounts, it's a wonder how people figure out how to save. In Canada, there are really just four main ones to choose from: the registered retirement savings plan (RRSP), the registered retirement income fund (RRIF), the tax-free savings account (TFSA), and then a non-registered account. There are others, most notably the Registered Education Savings Plan (RESP), which was created to help people save for their child's education. While you can buy and sell stocks, currencies, options, and other investments in a RESP, just don't. It's best to keep your kids' university dollars in more basic ETFs or mutual funds or risk ending up in trouble later when their school bills come due.

When the government created the RRSP, TFSA, and RRIF, they did not have day trading in mind. The RRSP was designed for long-term retirement saving, whereas the TFSA was created to help Canadians save for both long-term and shorter-term needs. We go into more detail on each of these accounts later in this chapter, but the RRIF is what the RRSP turns into in the year you turn 71, when you're then forced to withdraw a certain amount of money from the account every year. You can trade stocks and other securities in these accounts, but there are some limits.

Understanding Investment Accounts

In this section, we'll go through some of the different accounts available to Canadians, but there are a couple universal things to consider before trading in one.

REMEMBER

While we go into more detail in the next chapter, it's important to note that if you day trade, the Canada Revenue Agency (CRA) may say you're running a business rather than just investing, which could result in your trading money getting taxed as income. If you're trading in an RRSP or a TFSA, you could potentially lose all the excellent tax benefits that come with these accounts (and are described below). That could be a problem if you're also using these accounts for long-term savings. (Again, we go into more detail in Chapter 18.)

When it comes to trading in a registered account itself, you're allowed to hold what's referred to as qualified investments. (This applies to all types of registered accounts.) For a security to be qualified, it must typically trade on at least one Designated Stock Exchange as recognized by Canada's Finance Department. That includes the TSX, NYSE, NASDAQ, London Stock Exchange, and about 42 others.

Qualified investments include cash, cash, gold, silver, GICs, bonds, T-bills, mutual funds, ETFs, stocks, currencies, mortgages, annuities, and options. Non-qualified investments include shares of private companies and some real estate. If you own a non-qualified investment in an RRSP you may have to pay a hefty tax penalty upon withdrawal.

REMEMBER

There are also some things you cannot do in a registered account. A big one for traders is use margin. While you can borrow money from a bank and put it into an RRSP, you can't trade with a margin account. You also can't use *uncovered options,* which are options that are sold without the seller owning the underlying securities. If that option is exercised by the buyer, the seller would have to quickly acquire a position in that security. Short selling is also not allowed in a registered account. Keep all of that in mind as you read on and find out about Canada's different investment accounts.

RRSP

The RRSP was introduced in 1957 as a way to get Canadians to save for retirement. Back then you could only contribute up to 10 percent of your income, up to a maximum of $2,500. Now you're allowed to contribute up to 18 percent of your income, up to a maximum $27,830 in 2021. (The max goes up a little bit every year.) It is, by far, the most popular investment account, in large part because any money inside of it is allowed to grow on a tax-deferred basis. You only pay tax on the money when you withdraw it, ideally in retirement.

The RRSP has some key features that are important to understand whether you're a day trader or an investor:

>> You're investing pre-tax dollars into the account, which is why, when you contribute, you receive an income tax refund cheque.

>> Money inside of the account can grow on a tax-deferred basis, which means you do not have to pay any annual taxes on capital gains, dividends, or income. (We talk a lot more about tax in Chapter 18.)

>> When you do withdraw, you're taxed at your marginal rate. The key to the RRSP is to contribute when you're in a high tax bracket — higher earners get more on their tax refund — and remove the money when you're in a low tax bracket, like many people are in retirement.

>> If you pull the money out before you turn 71, you will have to pay a withdrawal tax. It's not exactly a tax in the traditional sense, as the government wants to ensure it gets its portion of your RRSP dollars, so it takes some of the money you remove from the account to prevent you from spending their share. If the government takes too much from you, they will return the difference.

>> You lose contribution room when you withdraw money from an RRSP. So if you have total contribution room of $100,000 and you remove $20,000 from an RRSP account, you will now have only $80,000 of total room.

>> There are two ways you can withdraw without penalty. If you're a first-time homebuyer, you can remove $35,000 from the account under the Home Buyers' Plan, though you must repay those funds within 15 years or will get taxed on any outstanding payments. You can also withdraw $20,000 penalty free to pay for education under the Lifelong Learning Plan. Those funds must be repaid within 10 years.

TFSA

The TFSA was introduced in 2009 by Stephen Harper's Conservative government, who wanted to give Canadians a more flexible savings vehicle than the RRSP. (Politics were at play, too, of course, with the TFSA announcement coming a few months before a Federal election.) The key feature here is that any money inside of a TFSA can grow truly tax-free. You pay no tax when you withdraw or on any capital gains.

The one gripe that many people have with this account is that contribution room is more limited than it is with an RRSP: As of 2020, you can only invest $6,000 a year. (That's up from the original $5,000.) However, if you were 18 in 2009 and have never contributed to your TFSA, then you'll have $69,500 in total contribution room to use. That will increase every year. Not too shabby.

The TFSA is pretty straightforward, but there are some things to keep in mind when using one:

>> You're contributing after-tax dollars in a TFSA, which is why, unlike the RRSP, you do not have to pay tax on any withdrawals.

>> You do not lose contribution room when you withdraw; however, any money that is removed from a TFSA (including money made on a security) cannot be put back into the account until January 1 of the following year.

>> If you get greedy and overcontribute to a TSFA (so if you exceed that total contribution amount), you'll get hit with a 1-percent tax per month on those excess contributions.

RRIF

In the year you turn 71, you must convert your RRSP into a RRIF. You can convert your RRSP into a RRIF at any time prior — and some people in their 60s and even 50s do. The key difference between a RRIF and a RRSP is that you must withdraw from the latter. You can't add any new money into it, though you can still invest what's in there into qualified securities.

What you must withdraw is predetermined. Typically, you need to remove 5.28 percent from your RRSP in the year you turn 71. (That changed to 3.98 percent during the pandemic in 2020 in part because the government didn't want people to have withdraw in a down market. Will that minimum stick beyond 2020? Time will tell.) If you don't need the money to live on, then you can put it in a TFSA, as long as you have contribution room, where it can grow tax-free.

There's not much else to know about the RRIF other than you will have to pay tax on those withdrawals at your marginal income rate, and that the money remaining in the account can continue to grow on a tax-deferred basis. If you've built up a big nest egg, or if you have other sources of income coming in, then you could end up paying a lot in tax when you withdraw. The intention, though, is that you'll be in a lower tax bracket in retirement, so you won't have to fork over too much to the CRA.

Non-registered accounts

Anything goes in a non-registered account. You can use uncovered options, short sell, use a margin account, and do whatever else day traders are wont to do (along as you're not breaking any laws, of course). You do not get tax-free or tax-deferred growth, however. As we explain in the next chapter, you will have to pay tax on capital gains, dividends, and income (such as bond distributions), though the former two are taxed at a lower rate than income.

Deciding on an Account to Use for Day Trading

Many people do actively trade inside of an RRSP or a TFSA (and more so a TFSA because of its flexibility) in part because these are the accounts Canadians are most familiar with. You may have set up an RRSP to use for long-term investing, but as you get more familiar with the markets, you may have decided to trade a stock or two until, before you know it, you're buying and selling frequently.

Day traders, though, should strongly consider sticking with a non-registered account. Here are five reason why:

>> You don't want to lose the tax-advantaged status of your RRSP or TFSA. Having a place to put your money where it can grow tax-free is an integral retirement savings strategy. Don't mess with that.

>> While you can get pretty deep in the trading woods in a registered account — remember you can still trade currencies and even other kinds of options — do you want to be getting all fancy in a long-term savings account? It could be a good idea to keep your trading money and retirement money as separate as possible.

>> With a non-registered savings account, you can do all the buying and selling your heart desires, which means it's the most flexible account for day traders.

>> While we go into more detail on tax in Chapter 18, there's one big tax benefit of using a non-registered account. If you lose money on a trade, you may be able to claim capital losses, which could then offset any possible capital gains taxes you may have to pay. (This is assuming the CRA doesn't say you're in the business of day trading. If they do, you won't be able to claim capital gains and losses.)

>> There's no contribution limit like in an RRSP or TFSA. If you're a high roller and want to put $100,000 into an account, you can do that in a non-registered vehicle.

Chapter **18**

Taxes for Traders

Think day trade returns come without a catch? Think again, because the CRA has plenty of ways to catch you come tax time. Day trading involves strategies that generate both high returns and high tax liabilities, which can eat away at your total return if you're not careful. Depending on how you file, not all of your expenses are deductible. And, even more troubling, although you might think you're day trading the CRA could have a different definition of your activities.

Taxes themselves aren't necessarily bad, because somehow we have to pay for things like roads and schools and health care. But taxes can be devastating to your personal finances if you haven't planned for them. You need to consider the tax implications of your trading strategy right from the start and keep careful records so that you're ready.

WARNING

Tax issues for day traders are complex and change frequently. Check the most recent federal regulations at www.cra-arc.gc.ca and work with an accountant or tax expert who has experience in these matters. This chapter is just a guide. We're reasonably social folks and all, but we're not going on an audit with you.

Are You a Trader or an Investor?

As we show you in this chapter, investors have it good when it comes to tax. They can grow their money on a tax-deferred basis in an RRSP, only paying the CRA when they withdraw in retirement. They also don't have to pay any tax on gains made in a TFSA, and any dividends and capital gains made in non-registered accounts are taxed at lower rates than normal income. If you lose money in a non-registered account, you can claim capital losses and use those losses to offset gains.

Most day traders will not get to take advantage of all these wonderful tax advantages. If you trade full time, expect your earnings to be treated as plain old income. How does the CRA determine whether you're an investor or a trader? You'll be branded as a trader if you meet some (though not necessarily all) of the following criteria:

>> You have a history of extensive buying and selling of securities.

>> You own securities for a short period of time. Again, no specific time frame applies, but you can assume they're talking days, not years.

>> You know a thing or two about or have experience in the securities markets.

>> Trading makes up a part of your regular business activities.

>> You spend a "substantial" amount of time studying markets and looking into potential purchases.

>> You primarily buy on margin or use another type of debt.

>> You've made it known that you're a trader, or are willing to purchase securities.

>> The shares you purchase are speculative or non-dividend-paying investments.

Even if you trade part-time, have other employment, or are new to the day trading game, the CRA could define you as a trader — and therefore will be expecting a heftier tax bill at the end of the year.

Claiming Business Expenses

We delve into more details soon, but there are still some tax advantages for traders. If trading is your business, you can claim business expenses just like any entrepreneur. As well, if you make enough money, you could consider incorporating. (Most accountants recommend this route if you're able to keep at least

$50,000 in the corporation per year.) Income held inside a Canadian corporation does get taxed at a more favourable rate than normal income (rates vary by province), but if you have to pull all that cash outside of the corporation to live on, then you may have to pay regular income taxes on whatever's removed.

Something to keep in mind: You might qualify as a trader for some of your activities and as an investor for others. If this looks to be the case, you need to keep detailed records to separate your trades, and you should use different brokerage accounts to make the difference clear from the day you open the position.

WARNING

Legally, if you day trade, you have to file income tax as though it's your full-time job. Capital gains taxes will not apply. However, lots of traders try to push the boundaries and file capital gains taxes rather than income tax until they're told otherwise, an approach we don't advocate. Talk to your tax adviser about how you should file and the consequences of filing incorrectly.

Hiring a Tax Adviser

You don't have to hire someone to do your taxes, but you probably should. If you're claiming capital gains, day trading will generate a lot of separate transactions to track, and the tax laws are tricky. Mistakes can end up costing you your entire trading profit.

TIP

Do yourself a favour and find a tax expert. You can talk to other traders, get references from the attorneys and accountants you work with now, or even do Internet searches to find people who understand both CRA regulations and the unique needs of people who frequently buy and sell securities, whether or not the CRA calls them traders.

REMEMBER

Anyone can represent clients before the CRA in audits, collections, or appeals, but it's a good idea to hire an accountant, or someone who knows a lot about tax and, preferably, investing.

The many flavours of tax experts

Okay, you're waiting for us to say there's only one flavour, and it's vanilla, right? Wrong. Tax experts fall into several different categories, and knowing which is which can help you determine who is best for you.

Chartered accountants

Chartered accountants are the most educated of the bunch. Although many great accountants exist across all designations, if you want to hire the one whose name is followed by the most prestigious letters, the CA tops the list. CAs need to have a university degree with specific business-related credits before they can take on the Chartered Accountants of Canada's extensive course load.

Certified management accountants

A CMA can do almost everything a CA can (at least for your purposes), but it's an easier designation to obtain. Generally, CMAs focus on managerial accounting and hold jobs in industry and government. But they can help prepare your taxes too.

Certified general accountants

It's the easiest designation to get, but that doesn't mean CGAs are less qualified to help you prepare returns and calculate gains, losses, or income. CGAs often specialize in taxation, accounting, and business consulting, whereas the other designations work in a variety of finance-related jobs.

Tax lawyers

Tax lawyers often work with accountants; they are called in to study the legality of proposed strategies or to represent a client in tax litigation. They aren't appropriate for most traders, but there may be situations that call for one.

Canada Revenue Agency

The CRA might be a bureaucratic machine, but get them on the phone and they're quite helpful. Their reps have the tax code at their fingertips, so if you're unsure of whether to check a box, or what you can or can't deduct, call them up.

Questions to ask a prospective adviser

After you identify a few prospective candidates to prepare your taxes, talk to them and ask them questions about their experience. Because you're supposed to claim your day trading profits as earned income, there really isn't anything special your tax expert needs to do beyond knowing what to deduct. The main goal is to find someone who can help you determine what you owe in taxes and not one penny more.

You'll feel more comfortable with your tax preparer if *you* have an understanding of the issues at stake. Even if you are hiring someone — and you should — keep reading this chapter and check the appendix for more in-depth references on taxes and trading.

Some things you should ask a potential tax preparer include the following:

>> What investors and traders have you worked with? For how long?

>> Who will be preparing my return? How involved will you be?

>> Do you offer tax analysis of trading strategies?

>> What's your audit record? Why have your clients been audited? What happened on the audit?

>> What are your fees?

It is illegal for tax preparers to base their fees on the size of your tax refund.

You still want to do it yourself?

It's possible for traders to do their own taxes, especially if they're claiming earned income. If you are comfortable with tax forms, you might be able to do this yourself. You need a few things: the proper CRA forms and, if you're not classifying yourself as a full-time trader, tax preparation software that can handle investment income.

Everything you want to know about taxes is at the CRA

The CRA website, www.cra-arc.gc.ca, is a treasure trove of tax information. All the regulations, publications, forms, and explanations are there, and some of it is even in plain English. It's so vast and detailed that you will probably be overwhelmed; get back at the CRA by calling them up and asking them to explain it all to you.

The primary section that covers the tax implications of trading and other investing activities is the Income Tax Interpretation Bulletin IT-479R, "Transactions in Securities." To find this document, go to the CRA's website and type **IT-479R** into the Search bar. Click on the first result, and voilà.

Tax preparation software

Those who do their own taxes know that tax prep software is a godsend, and it's even more valuable for those do-it-yourselfers who trade a lot. The software fills out the forms, automatically adds and subtracts, and even catches typographical errors. In many cases, it can download data straight from your brokerage account, making data entry really simple.

Some of the big brands, such as TurboTax, are set up to import and manage investment data, but if you're making regular and frequent trades you may want to shell out the close to $1,000 it costs to purchase something like TJPS Software, which offers a range of trading-related functions.

What Is Income, Anyway?

Income seems like a straightforward concept, but not much about taxation is straightforward. To the CRA, income falls into different categories, with different tax rates, different allowed deductions, and different forms to fill out. In this section, we cover income definitions you'll run into as a day trader.

Earned income

Earned income includes wages, salaries, bonuses, and tips. It's money that you make on the job. If day trading is your only occupation — and even if it isn't — your earnings could be considered earned income. This means that day traders will have to pay tax based on their current marginal tax rate (also known as personal income tax rate).

Canada has both federal and provincial tax rates — the latter varies by province, but the former is consistent for all Canadians. In the federal system, you're taxed:

» 15 percent on the first $48,535 of taxable income

» 20.5 percent on the next $48,536 of taxable income

» 26 percent on the next $53,404 of taxable income

» 29 percent of taxable income on the next $63,895

» 33 percent of taxable income over $214,368

Got that? To put it another way, if you fall into the highest tax bracket, about half of your yearly earnings will go to the government. (*Note:* These numbers are 2020 amounts; the rates can change from year to year.)

Provincial tax rates vary from province to province. To find out how much you'll be taxed, go to `www.cra-arc.gc.ca/tx/ndvdls/fq/txrts-eng.html`, scroll two-thirds down the page, and find your province.

Most traders are self-employed, which means you can deduct expenses and reduce your income's dollar figure. That could bump you into a lower bracket and therefore you'll pay less tax.

The big benefit of claiming your gains as income is that, if you lose money, you can apply those losses against all sources of income or any profits down the road. So, if you have a part-time job, those losses will help bring down your tax bill leaving more money in your pocket. The CRA allows you to apply losses against income earned for the last three years, or carry them forward indefinitely.

WARNING

Keep your long-term investments separate from your day trading income — if you don't, the CRA could assume all your investing is related to trading. And that is bad news. As we mentioned, the tax treatment for investments is different than work income, so if the CRA thinks all your investing, including that mutual fund you've held for 20 years, is related to day trading, all your gains will be taxed at the marginal tax rate.

TIP

Being a day trader once meant you didn't have access to employment insurance benefits. That's not the case anymore. Traders who pay income tax can apply for maternity, parental, sickness, and compassionate care benefits. You have to opt in to this yourself — and decide whether you want to send even more money to the taxman. Visit CRA's website to find out more.

Capital gains and losses

A *capital gain* is the profit you make when you buy low and sell high, and that's the aim of day trading. The opposite of a capital gain is a *capital loss*, which happens when you sell an asset for less than you paid for it. Investors can offset some of their capital gains with some of their capital losses to reduce their tax burden.

Those who trade frequently and can avoid having their gains classified as earned income will have many capital gains and losses. Day traders get tripped up by capital gain and loss problems all the time, so when designing your trading strategy think long and hard about how to ease the pain taxes might cause.

The financial world is filled with horror stories of people who thought they found a clever angle on making big profits, only to discover at tax time that their tax liability was greater than their profit. That's why properly tracking gains and losses is a must. It's not easy. The price difference of every trade you make needs to be accounted for, so create an Excel spreadsheet or use Write-Up, a comprehensive computer program offered by TJPS Software (www.tjpssoftware.com).

Tax treatment

Day traders want to pay taxes on capital gains, rather than earned income, because only half of a capital gain is taxed. If you make $1,000 on a trade, and it's being taxed as income, the entire gain will be subject to tax. If you're paying capital gains you'd pay only tax — at your marginal tax rate — on $500. See why the CRA wants day trading profits to be taxed as income?

If you lose money on a trade you can claim capital losses. It's similar to applying losses against earned income, but you can only use half of the amount you lose, rather than the entire price tag of the loss. Capital losses would be applied against gains, which can reduce your total tax bill. Capital losses can be carried back three years or used indefinitely in the future.

Now's a good time to remind you, again, that the CRA frowns upon traders who claim capital gains instead of earned income. If you meet the criteria of a trader, which we list earlier in the chapter, you're supposed to claim your earnings as income — just as you would if you worked in a cubicle shuffling papers.

Covering your basis

Capital gains and losses are calculated using a security's *basis,* which may or may not be the same as the price that you paid for it or sold it at. Some expenses, such as commissions, are added to the cost of the security, and that can reduce the amount of your taxable gain or increase the amount of your deductible loss.

For example, if you bought 100 shares of stock at $50 per share and a $0.03 per share commission, your basis would be $5,003 — the $5,000 you paid for the stock and the $3.00 you paid in commission.

The superficial loss problem

Say you love LMNO Company, but the price of the shares is down from what it was when you purchased them. You'd like to get that loss on your taxes, so you sell the stock, and then you buy it back at the lower price. You get your tax deduction and still keep the stock. How excellent is that?

It's too excellent to be true. The CRA does not count the loss. This trick is called a *superficial loss*. The rule was designed to keep long-term investors from playing cute with their taxes, but it has the effect of creating a ruinous tax situation for naïve day traders.

Under the superficial loss rule, you cannot deduct a loss if you have both a gain and a loss in the same security within a 30-day period. (That's calendar days, not trading days, so weekends and holidays count.) However, you *can* add the disallowed loss to the basis of your security.

Consider this example to understand what we mean. On Tuesday, you bought 100 shares of LMNO at $100. LMNO announced terrible earnings, the stock promptly dropped to $80, and you sold all 100 shares for a loss of $2,000. Later in the afternoon, you noticed that the stock had bottomed and looked like it might trend up, so you bought another 100 shares at $60 and resold them an hour later at $70, closing out your position for the day. The second trade had a profit of $1,000. You had a net loss of $1,000 (the $2,000 loss plus the $1,000 profit), but the CRA will disallow the $2,000 loss and let you show only a profit of $1,000. However, the CRA will let you add the $2,000 loss to the basis of your replacement shares, meaning that instead of spending $6,000 (100 shares times $60), for tax purposes, you spent $8,000 ($6,000 plus $2,000; you've essentially bought the stock back at $80 per share). If the price rises back to $100 a share, you only make a profit of $2,000 instead of the $4,000 your buddy made by buying 100 shares at the $60 price.

TIP

Day traders likely won't have to worry about this rule. Technically, the superficial loss rule applies only when you own the share 30 days after the original sale's settlement date. (The settlement date is usually three days after you sell a stock.) Because you're buying and selling shares quickly, it's unlikely you'll own the stock at the end of the month. But keep track. If you sell it and then 30 days later you buy it again for some reason, the rule will kick in.

Tracking Your Investment Expenses

Day traders have expenses. They buy computer equipment, subscribe to research services, pay trading commissions, and hire accountants to prepare their taxes. It adds up, and the tax code recognizes that. That's why day traders who pay personal income tax can deduct many of their costs from their income taxes. In this section, we go through some of what you can deduct.

TIP

You'll make your life much easier if you keep track of your expenses as you incur them. You can do this in a notebook, in a spreadsheet, or through personal finance software such as Quicken or UFile.

REMEMBER

Day traders who try to get around paying personal income tax don't have nearly as many expensing opportunities. That's one of the benefits of treating your day trading activities as a regular job.

Qualified and deductible expenses

You can deduct expenses as long as they are considered to be ordinary, necessary, and used to produce or collect income, manage property held for producing income, and directly related to the taxable income produced.

Clerical, legal, and accounting fees

You might use the services of a lawyer to help you get set up, and you will almost definitely want to use an accountant who understands investment expenses to prepare your income tax returns each year. The good news is you can deduct attorney and accounting fees related to your income. If your trading operation gets big enough that you hire clerical help to keep track of all those trade confirmations, you can deduct that cost, too.

Office expenses

If you do your day trading from an outside office, you can deduct the rent and related expenses. You can deduct the expenses of a home office, too, as long as you use it regularly and for business. Your trading room can be used as the guest room, but you need to figure out how many hours you use it for business. According to the CRA, calculate how many hours in a day you use the room and divide that by 24. Multiply the number by your business-related home expenses. Deduct that number.

You can also deduct certain office expenses for equipment and supplies used in your business; just use the same formula above to determine how much of your computers, desks, chairs, and the like you can write off. (If it's an office chair that's used only for work, you can write off the entire amount. If it's a love seat that doubles as a work chair, you can claim only part of it.)

REMEMBER

To get the deduction you have to spend the money first, and your expenses don't reduce your taxes dollar-for-dollar. If you're in the highest tax bracket, then each dollar you spend on qualified expenses reduces your taxes by around $0.46. (It could be higher in some provinces.) In other words, don't go crazy at the office supply store just because you get a tax deduction. It may be helpful to think of deductible expenses as discounts, because in the end that's more or less what they are.

Investment counsel and advice

The CRA allows you to deduct fees paid for counsel and advice about investments that produce taxable income. This includes books, magazines, newspapers, and research services that help you refine your trading strategy. It also includes anything you might pay for investment advisory services, such as trade coaching or analysis.

Safe deposit box rent

Have a safe deposit box down at the bank? You can deduct the rent on it if you store any investment-related documents. If you also keep jewelry that you inherited and never wear or other personal items in the same box, you can deduct only part of the rent.

Investment interest

If you borrow money as part of your strategy, and most day traders do, you can deduct the interest paid on those loans. In most cases this is *margin interest* (see Chapter 4 for more information on margin), and for most day traders it is relatively small because few day traders borrow money for more than a few hours at a time.

If you borrow money against your account for anything other than income-producing activities, you can't deduct the interest. And yes, most brokerage firms let you take out margin for your own general spending, as a way to let you stay in the market and still get cash.

REMEMBER

You can deduct expenses only if day trading is your day job and you're getting taxed on earned income. Again, paying income tax, rather than capital gains tax, will allow you to claim all that good stuff we mentioned. Sure, you may have to pay more in tax than if you just paid gains, but, as a consolation, you can write off a lot more — and you don't have to worry about being reprimanded by the CRA!

Commissions

If you're a day trader paying income, you can deduct commissions come tax time. However, if you're paying capital gains, you're out of luck. We know, it's disappointing, but that's life. (Well, at least the way CRA wants life to be.) Again, if you really want to deduct those extra fees, claim your profits as income.

Paying Taxes All Year

If you have been an employee for years and years, all of your tax liabilities would have been covered by your payroll tax deductions. The CRA likes it best that way, because then it gets money all year round. And really, the easier it is to pay, the more likely you are to do it.

People who are self-employed don't get the luxury of having their tax bill taken care of by someone else. To ensure you have squirrelled away enough for the CRA, estimate your tax liability for the year, divide it by 12, and put aside a portion of your profits every month. Nothing's worse than having to pay tax and not having the money at the end of the year. (It's tempting, but don't buy a new TV with what's supposed to be the government's money.)

In your first two years as a day trader you won't be forced to pay in installments, but after that, and if you're making over $30,000 annually, the government will require you to send in a cheque four times per year. The CRA bases the amount on what you've made the prior two years; if you end up owing less you'll get money back, and if you owe more your final cheque will make up the difference.

REMEMBER

Estimated taxes are paid via Form INNS3, also known as the Installment Remittance Voucher. Fortunately, they're due on a nice, even, quarterly schedule: the 15th of March, June, September, and December.

Using Your RRSP

Much of the tax hassle associated with day trading is eliminated if you trade through a self-directed *Registered Retirement Savings Plan,* or RRSP. Most brokerage firms can set them up for you and handle the necessary paperwork. You're allowed to contribute 18 percent of your previous year's earned income up to a maximum of $27,830 (for 2021). If you didn't use up all your room the year before, you can carry it forward indefinitely. That means if you haven't used an RRSP before, you could deposit a lot of cash.

When you put money into the registered account, you'll get a tax break, which can be nice if you've made a lot of money that year. However, if you want to take cash out, you'll be taxed at your marginal rate and you won't get any contribution room back. (Refer to the section, "What Is Income, Anyway?" in this chapter for more.) That's why most people wait until they're 71 to withdraw, as the older you are, the lower your earned income is likely to be. So it's not a good idea to use an RRSP if you need immediate access to your money.

What's different about day trading in an RRSP is that capital gains and losses don't apply. You don't have to pay any tax on the investments. You're asked to pay the taxman only on the amount you remove from the account. Again, if you can hang on to the money until you retire (though day trading is not a good retirement strategy) then you'll pay a lot less tax. You're also not allowed to trade on margin in an RRSP, and you can't participate in *naked call options* (when an investor sells a call option without owning the security) or *short selling* (selling a security you don't own and buying the stock back at a lower price). The CRA considers it carrying on a business activity inside an RRSP, which is a no-no.

TIP

Do your bulk of trading in an unregistered account so you can have quick access to money without incurring the withdrawal taxes that come with investing in an RRSP.

Trading within a Tax-Free Savings Account

On January 1, 2009, the federal government introduced a new savings vehicle for Canadians called the *tax-free savings account* (TFSA). The idea is to get more people saving money. You're allowed to put $6,000 into the account each year and remove it tax free at any time, so if you didn't deposit anything in 2009, and were 18 at the time, you could put in $69,500 in 2020. (When the TFSA launched, you could contribute $5,000 per year. One year, you were allowed to put in $10,000, but as of now, room grows by $6,000 per year.) The TFSA is meant for both short- and long-term investors. You might put your cash in a mutual fund or an ETF in the TFSA account and let it grow. But you might also withdraw it if you wanted to buy a car or house, because you can take it out without incurring a tax penalty. The TFSA is similar to an RRSP, except you don't get a tax break when you deposit money into the account, and you don't get taxed when you remove it.

The best part is that neither capital gains nor earned income is taxed on profits made in a TFSA. That's good news for traders who claim gains or income. However, you can't claim losses — not so good if you're losing money. Your initial deposit also can't exceed your contribution room, so this is not the place to make a $100,000 trade. If you do put more in the account than your allotted contribution amount, 100 percent of the profits from the extra cash will go to the taxman.

Like an RRSP, you can't participate in naked call options or short selling and you can't take advantage of margin in a TFSA. Use this as a secondary account, not your primary one.

The Part of Tens

IN THIS PART . . .

Discover ten good reasons to day trade.

Find out about ten common day trading mistakes so you don't make them.

Consider ten different money-management techniques and find one that works for you.

But wait, there's more! Explore the appendix for lots of resources to help you get started in trading.

Chapter **19**

Ten Good Reasons to Day Trade

D ay trading is a great career option for the right person in the right circum-stances. It requires a strong, decisive personality who wants to be running the show every step of the way. And because those profits aren't steady, good day traders have some financial cushion and good personal support systems to get them through the tough times. In this chapter, we list ten really good rea-sons to take up day trading. Think you have what it takes? See how many of these characteristics fit your life right now.

You Love Being Independent

Day trading is like owning any small business. You're the boss and you call the shots. Each day's successes — and failures — are due to you and you alone. The market is irrelevant because you can't control it. Working by yourself all day, you're responsible for everything from the temperature in the office to the func-tioning of the computers to the accounting for trades.

Good day traders are independent. They don't want someone to tell them what to do; they want to figure it out for themselves. They love a challenge, whether it's finding a good bargain on office supplies or developing a profitable way to arbitrage currency prices.

If you would like to work for yourself and control your own destiny, keep reading. Day trading may be for you.

You Want to Work Anywhere You Like

As a day trader, you have the luxury of setting up shop wherever you please. All you need is an account with an online brokerage firm and high-speed Internet access. You don't even need a computer if you have a smartphone. Nowadays you can find these tools almost anywhere: at home, at the library, in a bar, in a big city, in a small town, in the mountains, or in another country. Day trading offers a lot of geographic flexibility, which few other businesses do. You can trade while travelling as easily as you would trade at home — especially with improved mobile services.

You're Comfortable with Technology

The financial-services industry was one of the first to embrace computer technology in a big way, back in the 1960s, and it is still a technology-intensive industry. The people in colored cotton jackets running around the exchange floor, waving their hands and yelling at each other, are anachronisms.

Day traders use software to develop and refine their trading strategies. They trade online using programs to monitor and automate their trades. They track their trades in spreadsheets and other software. They spend their days in front of a screen, communicating online with other traders all over the world. They interact with computers, not human beings, during the trading day. In fact, many successful day traders automate their trading — programming skills can be a big help.

Day traders are also self-employed, and many work from home. That means that if their software crashes, they have to fix it. They have to handle the upgrades, install the firewalls, and back up the data. Sure, you can pay someone to do these tasks, but the tech consultant probably won't be able to drop everything to get you up and trading again immediately. Hence, good day traders are comfortable with technology. If you like to mess around with programs, don't mind maintaining your computer, and understand how to set up your hardware for maximum efficiency, you're in good shape for day trading.

You Want to Eat What You Kill

You don't have to be a self-employed day trader to trade securities. Brokerage firms, hedge funds, and exchange traders employ people to trade for them. In fact, most securities trading takes place through such larger organizations. But maybe you don't want to share your profits with someone else. Maybe you don't want someone dictating your strategy, placing limits on your trades, or determining your bonus based as much on factors such as teamwork and firm profitability as on what you brought in. You want to "eat what you kill," as they say, and day trading is one way you can do that.

When you day trade, you're responsible for your profits and your losses. That means that you reap the rewards and you don't have to share them with anyone else. It's a powerful incentive for independent people.

You Love the Markets

Good day traders have always been fascinated with the markets and how they move. If you watch BNN Bloomberg for fun and have been following the securities business for years, no matter what your day jobs have been, then you may be a good candidate for day trading. Of course, we hope you've picked up more than "some people make a lot of money doing this!" A lengthy immersion in the cycles and systems that drive securities prices can help you develop trading strategies and know what you are up against.

And the markets are amazing, aren't they? All the buyers and sellers with all their different needs come together and find the price that gets the deal done. The prices assimilate all kinds of information about the state of the world, the desires of the people trading, and the future expectations for the economy. It's capitalism in its purest form, and watching how it works is almost magical. If you love how the markets work and want to learn first-hand what they tell you about making money, then by all means keep reading.

You Have Market Experience

If you have never opened an account with a brokerage firm, purchased a stock, or invested in a mutual fund, you may not be suited for day trading. It's not that those activities alone are adequate preparation for day trading, but they're a start. They can help you understand all that can happen to cause you to make or lose money.

If you haven't made any trades before, don't quit your day job to day trade. Instead, flip back to Chapter 12 for some ideas on how you can use short-term trading in an investment portfolio. That way, you can learn more and build up your savings before taking the plunge.

You've Studied Trading Systems and Know What Works for You

Much of the work of day trading takes place long before entering the buy or sell order. You have to define your trading system, see how it would have worked in the past, and test it to see how it works now. The preparatory work isn't as exciting as actually doing the day trading, because you aren't making real money, but you're not losing money, either.

Short-term trading has a huge potential for loss, and many traders are chasing the exact same ideas. The more you know about how your strategy works in different market conditions, the better prepared you will be to act appropriately and profitably.

It can take a long time to find a strategy that works enough of the time to make it worth your while. Many day traders spend months developing, testing, and refining their day trading strategy. You can read more about the process of strategy testing in Chapter 14.

Because backtesting (which lets you test your trading strategy) uses historic prices, you can do much of the work on the side, at night, and on weekends, before you start day trading full time. It's a good way to get prepared for your trading business while you save your money and make other preparations for your new day trading venture.

You're Decisive and Persistent

Short-term traders don't have the luxury of thinking too much about what they're doing. Trading has to become intuitive. They have to be able to act on what they see when they see it. There's no room for second guessing, for hesitation, for choking, or for panic attacks.

Good day traders are also persistent. After they find a strategy they trust, they stick with it no matter how things are going. That's how they're able to buy low and sell high.

REMEMBER

Even great traders go through bad periods, but if they trust their system and continue to stick with it, they usually pull out of the bad period, often with money ahead. If you've been able to stick it out when things went wrong other times in your life, you know what to expect when day trading.

You Can Afford to Lose Money

Obviously, you want to make money. That's the whole idea of day trading. But day trading is difficult. Most traders quit in the first year. Some can't take the stress, some lose all their money, and some simply don't make enough money to make it worth their time.

Like any small business, you're taking a risk when you set up shop as a day trader. That risk is easier if you can afford to lose money. We're not saying you need to have so much money that you won't miss it when it's gone, but you shouldn't be day trading with money you need to live on, any more than you would open a store or start a law practice with money you need to buy groceries and pay the mortgage.

TIP

If your household does not have a second source of income, be sure to set aside enough money to cover your living expenses while you get started. And you should keep a second pot of money, your *walk-away fund* (see Chapter 2), so that you're free to quit day trading and move on to your next adventure if you decide it's not for you.

It's especially important to have a financial cushion when you're day trading for the following reasons:

>> **You can afford to commit to your trading:** Having your living expenses covered, at least at first, isn't just about dealing with losses. It's also about being able to stick with your trading. If you need cash to pay your bills, you may be tempted to take money out of the market whenever you're doing well. Doing so may keep you from reinvesting your profits. Plus, by not sticking to your strategy, your trading capital won't grow as fast. Think of day trading as a way to build a long-term asset, not a way to generate a steady stream of current income.

- >> **You can stay in the market through the rough times:** You know the old saying that the best way to make money is to buy low and sell high, right? Well, this means that the best time to buy is usually when securities prices have been beaten up and you've lost a lot of money. If you can afford some losses, staying in the game will be easier. Plus, you'll be able to stick to your strategy so that you can profit big when the market finally turns.

- >> **You can better handle the stress of losses:** Not all your trades are going to work out. Some days, you're going to lose money. If you have enough money that you don't fear loss, you can make better decisions. And you're less likely to panic if you know that you'll still be able to eat, pay your electric bill, and have a roof to sleep under at night. With sufficient funds, you're better able to view the markets clearly and follow a winning strategy.

Trading is very much a game of psychology. Give yourself an edge by waiting to do it until you can afford to.

You Have a Support System

Trading is stressful. The markets gyrate from events that no one can foresee. Things just happen, and no one else who's trading cares how these events affect you. It's enough to make you crazy some days, and unfortunately, some traders do get crazy. Alcoholism, depression, divorce, and suicide seem to be occupational hazards for those traders who have trouble separating what's happening in the market with who they are as people.

REMEMBER

The securities markets are wonderful mechanisms for bringing together diverse buyers and sellers. They are not wonderful for propping up your ego, helping you through a rough time in your life, or slipping you a little extra money when you most need it. The markets are not human. They are ruthless machines designed to generate the best price for the aggregate of the buyers and sellers participating that day. Some days, the markets will be in your favour, and some days, they will go against you.

Good day traders are psychologically strong. They understand how their weaknesses come out when they are stressed. They have people (good friends and supportive families) and activities (from exercise routines to hobbies) that help give their brains a break from trading.

Chapter 2 talks about managing the stress of day trading, and in many ways, we think it's the most important chapter in this book.

Chapter **20**

Ten Common Day Trading Mistakes

D ay trading is tough. Many popular markets are *zero-sum games*, meaning that for every winner, there's a loser. Other markets, such as the stock market, are *positive-sum* games, meaning they have a tendency to increase in value over time, but you may rarely see big moves in any one day. And the whole point of day trading is to close your positions each night. Most day traders lose money, in part because they make obvious, avoidable mistakes.

This list of ten mistakes can help you avoid the most serious ones. Avoiding these mistakes is no guarantee that you'll make money trading, but it can certainly reduce your risk and improve your odds. And that's half the battle.

Starting with Unrealistic Expectations

Most day traders lose money. Some research shows that 80 percent of day traders wash out in the first year. Brokerage firms that deal with day traders are constantly figuring out ways to attract new customers, because it is so hard to retain the ones they have for the long term.

Yes, some traders make money. A few make a lot of money. But they are the exception. Making money day trading is tough, making enough money to cover the value of your time is even tougher. If you go into trading knowing that it's hard, that you should only risk money that you can afford to lose, and that you need to think about it as a business, you'll have a leg up on those who think that they've found an easy way to make millions from the comfort of their own home — and who are then stunned to discover they are broke.

Beginning without a Business and Trading Plan

Trading is a business. When you decide to day trade, you are committing capital to an entrepreneurial business with a high risk of failure. You are no different from your brother-in-law who decided to open a sandwich shop franchise, your neighbour who joined a startup company for little salary and lots of equity, or your university buddy who has been trying to make a go of it as a full-commission life insurance salesman. You are all out on your own, risking your capital in the hope of great success but knowing that many others doing the same thing fail.

Successful businesses have business plans, and your trading business is no different. You need to specify what you are going to trade, when you're going to trade, how you're going to trade, and with how much money — *before* you get started. You need to determine what equipment you need, what services and training you want, and how you will measure your success. Chapter 2 can help you with a business plan, and the rest of the book can help you fill in the appropriate sections of it. Having the plan will keep your expectations in line and create a professional starting point for your new trading venture.

You also need to supplement your business plan with a plan for your trading. How are you going to trade? What signals will you watch for? Under what conditions will you enter a position, and under what conditions will you close it? That's your trading plan. Good traders have trading plans so that they know exactly what they want to do when they see opportunities in the market. This plan reduces the fear and doubt that can unsettle most traders, and it heads off the panic that destroys more than a few. Read Part 2 of this book for ideas on trade strategies.

In addition, good trading plans have to be tested and evaluated. Chapter 14 has good information on testing and evaluation so that you have enough confidence in your system to follow it, even when the market gets squirrelly on you.

REMEMBER

Failing to plan is planning to fail, as the cliché goes. You are risking too much of your hard-earned money to skip careful upfront planning. Take responsibility for your trading.

Ignoring Cash Management

Because financial markets can be volatile, you can easily get wiped out. Good cash management can help you stay in the game. Because you never commit all of your capital to any one trade, no one trade can shut you down. At times — like when you know you've got a great idea — holding back some cash may not seem right, but if you plan to trade for the long run, you need to follow your money-management strategy. Otherwise, you'll never be able to get a winning trade that can offset your losses.

You need to have your wits about you to day trade, but you also need to have capital. Chapter 7 has some great information on cash management, so don't skip it!

Failing to Manage Risk

Day trading is risky business, and most day traders quit because of losses. (Have we told you that already?) Even traders who stick with it have many losing trades. That's why they have risk-management systems in place. Their trading plans include *stops*, which automatically execute buy or sell orders when securities reach predetermined levels.

The day trader looking for trouble places orders without thinking about how much of a security to buy or sell at any one time, and she thinks that she'll just know when to sell. And then she second-guesses herself and finds herself with bigger losses than she intended.

If you're going to day trade, be safe. You know what the risks are (that's why you picked up this book), so use the protection offered by stops and sound money management.

WARNING

Most day traders lose money. Don't risk money you can't afford to lose, and plan for the risks that you take.

Not Committing the Time and Money to Do It Right

Day trading is a job. It's a small-business endeavour that requires research and training well in advance of the first trade. It's not something you can squeeze into an hour a day as a hobby. To do well, you need to set regular hours and have enough money to generate reasonable returns without unreasonable risks.

Many people think day trading is something that they can easily enter into and that they can generate profits while their kids are napping. That thinking is a mistake. If you can't dedicate the time necessary to study the markets and understand how you react to them, you will have trouble staying in the trading business.

Day trading is a business of frequent trades with small percentage gains and a high potential for loss. If you have days of losses, a small account will quickly end up with too little money to meet minimum order sizes. Therefore, successful traders start with enough money to last through periods of drawdown and are still able to generate meaningful dollar returns. Consider this: A 1 percent return on $1,000 is equal to $10, but a 1 percent return on $100,000 is $1,000.

If you have more money to begin with, the dollars you make from day trading will seem more real to you. If you have, say, $25,000 you can afford to lose, you are more likely to be a successful day trader than if you have only $2,500 — and you'll be considered to be a day trader, not a dilettante.

REMEMBER

You are going to lose money. All day traders have bad days, and they are more likely to lose money early in their trading careers before they get a feel for the markets and their own reactions to it. If you have enough money when you begin, you can consider these losses to be part of your apprenticeship.

Chasing the Herd

Everyone in the market is looking at the same data and the same technical indicators (like those we discuss in Chapter 9). Good day traders follow market trends but with the goal of being early or on time. Those who get in late get crushed: They buy too high, or they sell too low. Chasing the herd is tempting, because it's so hard to watch the market move away from you.

Day trading requires quick reactions. It's video games and psychology, some people joke, because the trader who can figure out what others in the market are doing and then click on the mouse button fastest has a huge advantage. The trader who hesitates or goes along for the ride is likely to be ruined.

There's no easy solution for this. It helps if you know that you are psychologically cut out for day trading and have confidence in the long-term performance of your trading system (refer to Chapter 14). But to a big extent, you just have to have some experience in the markets to know how your trading system matches what's in your head.

Switching between Research Systems

Day traders lose money, at least part of the time. And losing money can cause a day trader to lose trust in his trading system. And many do what seems logical, which is move to a trading system that seems to be working. The problem is that no system works all the time; if one did, everyone would use it. And sometimes things look their worst before they turn. By switching systems whenever things look bad, the trader never learns the nuances of how a given system works for him. And he's likely to get stuck on another downtrend, picking up the new system right when the old one starts to work again.

REMEMBER

Markets go in cycles. No system works all the time, but if you panic and start trying new things without doing a lot of upfront work, you're likely to make things worse. Chapter 14 covers performance evaluation and system testing in great detail. The more you understand your system and how it works, the less likely you are to be brought down by floundering around for new systems all the time.

Bottom line: Anyone who has a magic trading system that works in all markets is retired and living on a beach in Maui. Everyone else has to live through a few rough stretches.

Overtrading

Because day traders don't hold positions for long periods of time, they rarely enjoy big and profitable price moves. Instead, they make money from lots of transactions with small profits. They are crazy people, moving in and out for short periods. But believe it or not, the day trader who trades *too* much loses out. She won't be in the market for large intra-day moves, and she'll get killed on commissions and other transactions costs.

As paradoxical as it seems, many day traders do better by making fewer trades each day. That way, commissions and fees take a smaller bite of the profit. One way to profit from fewer trades is with better money management, discussed in Chapter 7. A trader who puts money to work appropriately can often make more money than one who trades frenetically.

Sticking Too Long with Losing Trades

Day traders are often overcome with fear, doubt, greed, and hope. They are afraid to recognize a loss. They wonder whether they're good traders. They don't want to pay the commission to get out of the loser. And if the security was a good buy at the higher price, it's surely a better buy now that the price has gone down. These traders think that if they just keep a positive mental attitude, everything will work out all right in the end.

Good traders have systems in place to limit their losses. They use stop orders to force themselves out of bad trades. They would rather put the money to work on a good trade than stick out a bad one.

REMEMBER

The market doesn't know your position; even if it did, it wouldn't care. Therefore, no amount of wishing and hoping will cause the market to reward you for your patience. If a trade isn't working, get out. As the man in the musical sings, tomorrow is a latter day.

Getting Too Emotionally Involved

Trading is a stressful business. You're up against an impersonal market that moves seemingly at random (and many academics would say that it moves truly at random). It involves money, which to some people is a way to keep score in life and to others is their primary source of security. Losing trades mean a loss of status and a loss of safety. It's no wonder that so many traders are head cases when the entire market sometimes seems to be conspiring against you — you specifically.

The best traders are almost Zen-like in their lack of attachment to the market. They are able to remove themselves from the frenzy of the trading day so that they're not susceptible to fear, doubt, greed, and hope. Chapter 2 has some advice that can help you approach the trading day in a calmer manner. Only you know whether you are capable of that.

Chapter **21**

Almost Ten Alternatives to Day Trading

Maybe you like the idea of trading, but after reading this book you've decided that working for yourself making large numbers of short-term trades isn't exactly what you want to do. But then what options are there? In this chapter, we put forward several ideas for alternative activities that might match your interests better than day trading. These include other career options, different ways to invest your money, and entertainment that gives you the excitement of trading without the same amount of risk.

Proprietary Trading for an Investment Company or Hedge Fund

Day trading is a solitary pursuit, and not everyone who wants to trade also wants to run his own business and work by himself all day. Good thing many companies need people to trade for them. Investment companies, brokerage firms, and hedge funds hire traders. These people are often known as prop traders, short for *proprietary*, and their job is to trade money for the firm's account. These traders may have to follow a set style, or they may be free to trade as they see fit. Prop traders don't keep all their profits, but they get a small salary, benefits, and a bonus that represents a generous cut of the money they make.

Proprietary trading lets you combine the safety net and camaraderie of a job with the excitement and potential huge returns of trading. It's a good option for those who want to spend their days with other people.

Trading for an Agricultural, Energy, or Commodities Company

The options and futures markets were developed to help commodity companies manage their income and expenses better. That's why the traditional products on those exchanges almost seem funny in the era of modern finance: pork bellies, soybeans, and orange juice.

But you know what? Those traditional customers for those traditional products are still active, and they need people to help them. Energy companies, growers, food processors, and metals companies need someone to trade barrels of oil, bushels of corn, live cattle, and silver futures. They are often more interested in *hedging* — using trading to reduce risk rather than increase return — than in trading to maximize return, but depending on market conditions and firm philosophies, they may be open to traders who want to take on risk.

Joining a Market Making Firm

In the olden days, day trading was impossible because individuals could not afford to get a data feed, let alone execute orders. People who wanted to trade for themselves had to move to a city with an exchange, submit their membership application, pay their fees, and go to work on the floor. Times have changed, though, at least in Canada where the exchanges are virtual. You won't be able to join the TSX and buy and sell on the floor, but you can be part of a market maker firm that trades stocks in order to keep the markets liquid. Market makers maintain activity in the markets, service odd lots, help keep the markets two sided, and also do a whole lot more.

Becoming a trader at a firm requires experience and hard work. First you have to get hired by a TSX market maker companies, then work junior jobs and prove to your boss that you have the chops to trade. It's a good idea to have an MBA or another financial degree, experience in the industry, and — most importantly — a strong knack for numbers and markets.

Traditional Investing for Your Own Account

Some people who buy this book probably don't want to day trade. Instead, they want to manage their own investment accounts during the day rather than having a regular job. You can manage your money yourself without making a high volume of short-term trades, and given the huge numbers of day traders who wash out (80 percent, according to some studies) you might be better off. True, you won't have the drama of day trading, and you won't need to focus your attention for hours on end. Instead, you'll be researching stocks and mutual funds, allocating your portfolio among several different assets, and tracking your tax liabilities. If you aren't sure where to start, consider picking up a copy of *Investing For Canadians For Dummies* by Eric Tyson and Tony Martin (Wiley). In addition, Chapter 12 has some ideas for ways that you can use day trading techniques for long-term accounts.

Taking a Swing at Swing Trading

Swing trading is a cross between day trading and longer-term investing. Instead of closing out their positions at the end of each day, swing traders may hold their positions for a few days or even weeks. It's a way to change the risk and return profile. Price changes can happen overnight when you're away from your computer monitors, but the luxury of time means more opportunities for your position to work out. Swing trading favours traders who have a little bit of patience, who can handle the risk of holding open positions overnight, and who have some interest in industry news and fundamental information. We discuss it a little bit in Chapter 8.

Gambling for the Fun of It

Sloppy day traders are often gamblers: They aren't following a strategy; they just like the rush and the expectation of the positive return. This means that they aren't always paying attention to the market, nor are they ready to commit to the discipline of spending days in front of a screen and evenings reviewing market activities. If you are more of a gambler than a trader, why not just admit it?

Assuming you're not a problem gambler (see www.gamblersanonymous.org), keep your day job, contribute to your retirement plan, and set aside a portion of your spending money to take to the casino. And don't gamble more money than you bring. When you gamble, the odds always favour the house, so you'll probably lose money. When you day trade, the odds on each particular trade are even or slightly in your favour, at least before considering commissions, but not so much that you're guaranteed an easy return. So if it's the rush and not the return you want, admit it and book a flight to Las Vegas.

Playing Day Trading Video Games

Want the excitement of day trading without the risk of losing your money, either to the markets or to the casino owner? Think you can figure out the markets, but don't want to put real money or your job on the line to find out? Then why not play a day trading video game?

Well, okay, it's not exactly a game; it's a simulator designed to teach you to day trade. The RapidSP Day Trading Simulator, available at www.rapidsp.com, gives you all the excitement of day trading without risk to your capital and without the sales pitch. It's a low-cost, low-risk way to enjoy the day trading experience.

Trading in Demo Accounts

Simulators are a good way to learn day trading, but they cost money. If you're looking for a free way to try day trading in general, or if you're a day trader thinking of adding new securities to your repertoire, you can trade in demo accounts. Many brokerage firms (see Chapter 15 for a list of some that deal with day traders) allow prospective customers to start with a demonstration account, both to check out the broker's capabilities and to see whether day trading is right for you.

These demo accounts will let you try out everything the broker offers, but they do come with trial periods. Your free account may be locked out after 30 days; you'll have to open a real one if you want to continue trading at that particular broker. If you've got the day trading bug, but aren't yet ready to trade real dollars, open a demo account at another brokerage firm. It's a good idea to test more than one out anyway, just to see what each company has to offer. In any case, you owe it to yourself to do some simulation to work through your trading system. And if you just like the idea of playing around with trading, paper trading in a demonstration account can help you have fun without risking your hard-earned money.

Participating in a Trading Contest

Each year, some prominent companies offer trading contests. People can sign up for them, manage a paper portfolio (investing or day trading, as they please), and the participant with the greatest return wins a cash prize.

One popular Canadian contest these days is the Horizon ETFs and National Bank Direct Brokerage's Biggest Winner trading competition: `https://horizonsetfs.com`.

These contests offer all the fun of trading with none of the risk — although past cheating scandals have scuttled many of the more popular contests. Consider also that they offer all the fun of trading with none of the oversight of the provincial securities commissions or the SEC.

Chapter **22**

Ten Tested Money-Management Techniques

The key to success in day trading is discipline. That starts with good money management: determining how much money you will trade, when you will cut your losses, and when you will walk away with money in your pocket. If you don't manage your money, you won't be trading long.

Here, you get an overview of the key money-management techniques that you should consider as well as one that is a very bad idea. Some of these techniques are simple; no calculation is required, and you can use them right away. Others involve a little workout with your calculator. A few of these techniques need your performance history to work, so you can't use them right away, but you can experiment with them as you build your trade data. (And yes, this is one of the many reasons that traders should keep records of trading activity.)

TIP

These days, many brokers include money-management calculators and apps in their trading systems, so you can enter the parameters that reflect your trading style and your account balance to get the right amount to trade, right away. These calculators remove the guesswork and mystery associated with some of these techniques — if you use them.

Taking Money off the Table

Here's the simplest form of money management: When you're up, take the profit rather than waiting to make even more money. Fight the greed, take the cash, and call it a day.

If you have a week, month, or year with particularly strong profits, take a little money out of your trading account and put it in a retirement fund, use it to pay off a debt, or move it into a low-risk investment to help diversify your high-risk trading activities.

Even if you do nothing else, taking profits when you have them can help keep you in the game longer.

Using Stops

Unless you're a machine, staying disciplined all the time can be difficult. Humans do goofy things. That's why there's a simple way to force discipline on your trading to keep your losses from destroying your trading account: a stop order.

A *stop order*, also called a *stop-loss order*, is an order to buy or sell a security as soon as it hits a given price, known as a *stop price*. The order sits dormant in the broker's computer until the market price hits the stop, and then the order is executed. This automated action helps you lock in a profit or cut a loss. Some traders don't like stops because on occasion one will be executed on a one-time down trade or while a stock is shooting up at price, causing them to leave some money on the table. However, stops are an easy way to force discipline into trading. They can help you manage your money with very little extra effort.

Yes, some brokers charge an extra commission for a stop order. But it may be worth it.

Applying Gann's 10 Percent Rule

The Gann money-management system is part of a complicated system of technical analysis used to identify good securities trades. The chart system is complex, but the money-management system is simple. The core of it is a limit on the money placed on any one trade to 10 percent of the account value, never more. The dollar value of that 10 percent goes up or down as the account value changes, but the 10 percent limit ensures that you always have some powder dry to stay in the market.

Most traders who follow Gann's 10 percent rule combine it with stops to limit losses.

You can't take advantage of a profitable opportunity if you have no money to trade. You can lose everything in your account if you let your losses run.

Limiting Your Losses with the Fixed Fractional System

The fixed fractional system is misnamed; it's actually a range of fractions that determine how much of your trade capital to risk on any one trade. A larger fraction is allocated to less risky trades; a smaller fraction to more risky ones. The calculation can be found in Chapter 7.

To do the calculation, you need to know how much money you can lose on any one trade. The study needed to determine that amount can go a long way toward improving your trading without getting into the math. Fixed fractional takes the stop a step further; it helps you limit your losses and pick up more from your wins by considering how much to trade along with the potential value of losses and gains.

Increasing Returns with the Fixed-Ratio System

The fixed-ratio system of money management is related to fixed fractional trade sizing. The key difference is that it looks at accumulated profit rather than total account size. (Accumulated profit is the value of the account less the capital that you put into it when you started trading.)

This system was specifically designed for options and futures trading by Ryan Jones, a trader himself. The goal is to increase returns from winning trades and protect profits from losing ones. The basic calculation is in Chapter 7.

Following the Kelly Criterion Formula

The Kelly criterion is based on some statistical work by mathematicians working at Bell Labs in the 1950s. They realized that it had applications to gambling, so they went to Las Vegas and made a lot of money at blackjack. We kid you not. The casinos changed the rules so that it no longer works at Vegas, but it does work in securities markets.

What this formula does is ensure that you will never run out of money, so you will always be able to place yet one more trade. In the real world, of course, you can reach a point where you still have money but don't have enough to place a trade.

$$\text{Kelly \%} = W - \left(\frac{1-W}{R} \right)$$

The equation looks at the percentage of trades that are expected to make money (W), the return from a winning trade, and the ratio of the average gain from a winning trade relative to the average loss of a losing trade (R). You may not be able to use the Kelly criterion until you have been trading long enough to amass data to use in the equation, but that's okay — you have other choices here!

The Kelly criterion often generates a trade size larger than many traders are willing to use. One alternative is a *half Kelly* trade, using half of the amount recommended by the equation.

Figuring the Amount to Trade with Optimal F

Optimal F is another money-management system that needs performance figures to generate an ideal trade size. It was developed by Ralph Vince, a trader, and it comes up with the ideal fraction of your account to trade based on your past performance. The calculation changes with every trade, so it's usually done through a spreadsheet or an app.

Measuring Risk and Sizing Trades with Monte Carlo Simulation

The Monte Carlo simulation is another money-management system drawn from gambling. It's used for risk management in many different businesses, including trading. You enter risk and return parameters into a computer program, and it tells you the likelihood of total loss and the optimal trade size.

The system can't account for every possible thing that can go wrong, and it requires a lot of computer power — even nowadays. That being said, many trading and brokerage platforms have Monte Carlo applications that can be used to help you measure risk and size trades.

Taking a Risk with the Martingale System

Martingale is another simple money-management system, no calculator required. It's popular with gamblers and traders alike. You start with a small amount per trade — you get to pick it yourself, but it should probably be less than 5 percent of your account value. If the trade works, your next trade should be the same amount. If the trade does not work, then you close it out and place double the amount (*double down*, as they say) on the next trade so that you win back the loss. That doesn't work? Double again. After you have a winning trade, go back to the initial amount for your next trade.

WARNING

If you have to double down for a long series of trades, the money involved quickly grows: from $2,000, for example, to $4,000, $8,000, $16,000, $32,000, $64,000, and even $128,000 if you have six losing trades in a row. This is the problem. If you have an infinite amount of money, you will come out ahead using martingale. Of course, if you had an infinite amount of money, you probably wouldn't be reading this book.

With martingale, you can run out of money before you have a trade that works. The method works best for aggressive traders with large accounts who start with small initial trades. It's a risky money-management strategy, but it's also far preferable to having no strategy at all.

Throwing It to the Fates

Many traders have a logical problem with money management. If you have a sure thing, why shouldn't you put all your money on it? If you know the next trade is going to be great, why should you close out the day with a balance decline? Ah, but your logic is coloured green with greed.

WARNING

Few sure things are as sure as they seem. Lose on the sure thing, and you won't be around for the next trade. Exceed your daily loss limit, and you'll have even greater losses.

The wise sage Bart Simpson once said that years of watching television taught him that miracles always happen to poor children on Christmas Eve. Knowledge of money management is more of a sure thing than believing that you will be the beneficiary of a miracle today.

Appendix

Additional Resources for Day Traders

As much as we hate to admit it, *Day Trading For Canadians For Dummies*, 2nd Edition, doesn't tell you absolutely everything there is to know to get started in day trading. This appendix lists books, websites, periodicals, and other resources offering trading strategies and techniques and ideas on managing risk, taxes, and stress.

Great Books for Great Trading

Have a shelf that looks a little bare? Fill it up with a few of the beauties we list in the following sections.

Basic trading guides

The following books offer nuts-and-bolts information on day trading:

>> *The Bible of Options Strategies: The Definitive Guide for Practical Trading Strategies* **by Gary Cohen (FT Press):** Many traders prefer options to stocks, and this book covers the main strategies as well as some of the more esoteric ones that may work for you.

>> *Currency Trading For Dummies* **by Kathleen Brooks and Brian Dolan (John Wiley & Sons, Inc.):** *For Dummies* writers are happy to recommend each other. If your interest is currency trading, this book covers the conventions and tools that can increase your chances for success. It covers the economic and psychological factors that affect currency values, looks at the major pairs, and helps you identify the factors that matter in this market.

- » *Mastering the Trade,* 2nd Edition, by John F. Carter (McGraw-Hill): The author, an experienced trader, walks day traders and swing traders through the ins and outs of the markets, offering specific advice on different trading opportunities. He includes charts and data that explain when to place a trade and when to close it out. This book is practical, useful, and detailed.

- » *The New Money Management: A Framework for Asset Allocation* by Ralph Vince (John Wiley & Sons, Inc.): Money management can keep traders in the game longer while maximizing potential returns. It's a key discipline that can mean the difference between long-run success and failure. Unfortunately, many day traders completely overlook money management. This book reviews Vince's money-management system in great detail.

- » *Trading Rules That Work: The 28 Lessons Every Trader Must Master* by Jason Jankovsky (John Wiley & Sons, Inc.): If it were possible to get rich from knowing just a handful of specific trading indicators, every trader would retire and run huge charitable foundations. But it's not that easy. Instead, a disciplined, professional approach to the market makes a difference over the long run. This book is a useful overview of different trading rules, why they work, and how traders should apply them.

- » *Trading Systems and Methods,* 5th Edition, by Perry J. Kaufman (John Wiley & Sons, Inc.): This textbook on trading systems provides a detailed analysis of the popular and the obscure alike. What makes it especially nice is the book has a companion website with actual trading programs on it. You can use them as a starting point for developing your own trading systems.

Technical analysis guides

Technical analysis is a system of looking at price and volume trends to determine supply and demand levels in the market. Supply and demand, of course, drive price changes, so understanding the dynamics is pretty darn useful. Here are a few books that cover technical analysis in detail:

- » *Candlestick Charting For Dummies* by Russell Rhoads (John Wiley & Sons, Inc.): Candlestick charts were developed in Japan and are the basis of a system of technical analysis that's popular with short-term traders, including day traders. This book explains how to identify and use candlestick patterns.

- » *Charting and Technical Analysis* by Fred McAllen (CreateSpace): This guide covers technical patterns in great depth, with advice for day traders, swing traders, and investors. It gives a good explanation of what you're looking for and why it matters, which can help you set up signals and trading algorithms.

» ***Mind Over Markets: Power Trading with Market Generated Information*** **by James Dalton, Eric Jones, and Robert Bevan Dalton (Wiley Trading):** Don't let the title fool you. This book is not about trading psychology. Instead, it covers a price-charting and technical-analysis system in great depth, especially the relationships between price changes and volume changes. The system, called *market profile,* is especially useful for day traders working in futures markets.

» ***Tape Reading and Market Tactics*** **by Humphrey B. Neill (Marketplace Books):** In the early part of the 20th century, traders looked at price and volume information that came across ticker tapes. Traders still rely on an analysis of price and volume information, just with different tools. This book was originally written in 1931, but many day traders find that Neill's advice on what to look for and what to avoid when looking at price data still holds true.

» ***Technical Analysis For Dummies*** **by Barbara Rockefeller (John Wiley & Sons, Inc.):** Day traders use technical analysis to help gauge market activity, and this book is a detailed guide on reading charts and applying the information to trading in an intelligent way. What else would a *For Dummies* book offer?

» ***Trend Following, 5th Edition: How to Make a Fortune in Bull, Bear and Black Swan Markets*** **by Michael W. Covel (Wiley Trading):** The trend is your friend, right? Many day traders live by this maxim, and this book breaks out some trend-following strategies, as well as information on how and when to deviate from the general direction of the market.

Schools of price theory

Most day traders take an eclectic approach to the markets. They find a few indicators that help them and then apply those indicators to the situation in the market. Over time, they refine their systems. Some traders, however, rely on specific theories for how prices should move. Here are some basic texts on the different theories:

» ***Elliott Wave Principle: Key to Market Behavior*** **by A.J. Frost and Robert R. Prechter, Jr. (Wiley):** The Elliott Wave theory is a strange animal. It looks for really long-term patterns in the markets — over decades and even centuries — based on the *Fibonacci series,* a number series found in nature. It's not widely used, but some traders swear by it.

- >> *How to Make Profits in Commodities* **by W.D. Gann (Lambert Gann):** This book isn't exactly an easy read, but many analysts believe that Gann's system can help them figure out how prices change over time. The original text dates from the 1940s. Some people find it dated; others think it's timeless.

- >> *How to Make Money in Stocks: Your Ultimate Guide to Winning in Good Times and Bad* **by William J. O'Neill (McGraw-Hill):** William O'Neill's system is of most interest to people who are swing trading or investing in common stock, but it may help day traders understand what other participants in the market are looking at when they place orders. The book explains *momentum* investing, which looks for stocks of companies with improving business trends and performance.

Trading psychology

Good traders are mentally tough. They need the confidence to face the market, the decisiveness to place orders, and the fortitude to take losses —and do it against a faceless mix of everyone else trading that day. Several books address trading psychology specifically; others on mental strength are also popular with traders because their lessons can be applied to the markets:

- >> *The Art of War* **by Sun Tzu:** It seems like every trader we've ever met has a copy of *The Art of War*. It's a Chinese text describing military strategy, including the importance of mental toughness and strict discipline. First translated into a European language in 1782, several different versions and translations are in print.

- >> *Awaken the Giant Within* **by Anthony Robbins (Pocket Books):** This basic self-help book is popular with all sorts of folks. Many traders find that Robbins's methods give them confidence and help them control their minds when they're trading. *Tip:* Avoid his advice on the markets and stick to his work on psychology.

- >> *The Crowd: A Study of the Popular Mind* **by Gustave LeBon (Dover Books):** In the 19th century, Gustave LeBon wrote this treatise on crowd psychology. He didn't think much of his fellow human beings, but many traders have found that his insights explain some short-term irrational behaviour in the markets. Understanding why traders make mistakes can help you make profits.

- >> *Principles: Life and Work* **by Ray Dalio (Simon & Schuster):** Ray Dalio has built a great track record at his hedge fund, Bridgewater Associates. This book is partly his memoir, but it includes his approach to trading strategy and psychology. Given his well-documented success, there's much to think about and discover in the 500 or so pages of this book.

>> *Trading in the Zone* **by Mark Douglas (Prentice Hall):** This book covers the mental discipline of trading, emphasizing the practices and routines that take the emotion out of it. A trader has a short time to make a profit, and some panic at the idea. This book has helped many traders focus on the key elements of trading rather than the fear, doubt, and greed that can undo the best of them.

History and memoir

We're not willing to accept the Elliott Wave and say that all market movements are part of overarching trends, but market history — like all history — tends to repeat. Why? Because people are people, and no matter how commerce and the economy change, people do the same things over and over again:

>> *Flash Boys: A Wall Street Revolt* **by Michael Lewis (W.W. Norton & Company):** High-speed trading has changed the way that the market works, and it has certainly affected traditional strategies for day trading. This book is a detailed discussion of the traders who worked to expose the system, leading to some changes in regulation. Michael Lewis has also written other good books about Wall Street and money.

>> *Fortune's Formula: The Untold Story of the Scientific Betting System that Beat the Casinos and Wall Street* **by William Poundstone (Hill and Wang):** Claude Shannon and John Kelly were Bell Labs scientists working on queuing theories for long-distance calls when they stumbled on what is known as the Kelly criterion: The ideal proportion of money to bet can be found by the ratio of your edge in the market divided by the odds of winning. Day traders can use this *edge/odds formula* to figure out how much money to allocate to a trade. This book explains how the system works, though it never quite proves that it works when applied to legitimate casinos or to trading.

>> *Reminiscences of a Stock Operator* **by Edwin LeFevre (John Wiley & Sons, Inc.):** This classic, written before the 1929 market crash, tells of the adventures of Jesse Livermore, one of the most successful traders of his time. It's a disguised memoir of speculation, with a character named Larry Livingston standing in for Livermore. Some traders like it for the lessons they can learn from Livermore; others are just amused by how unchanged the art of day trading is despite dramatic changes in technology.

The Trader's Internet

Day trading was made possible by the Internet. When high-speed connectivity to market data became affordable, almost anyone could trade with the same speed as folks working on the exchange floor or a brokerage trading desk. And yet the Internet can be a terrible distraction to a day trader or to anyone else working alone. Here are some good websites for day traders, but you may want to limit your use of them to before and after trading hours:

>> **Elite Trader:** Elite Trader, www.elitetrader.com, is one of the big trader communities online, with forums, book and software reviews, and broker ratings. The participants can be passionate, but the information is often great.

>> **IndexArb.com:** Interested in trading futures on the market indexes? This site, https://indexarb.com, has useful information. It lists the premiums on different contracts, offers strategies for different market conditions, and gives you some good background information to help you make your own decisions.

>> **Reddit:** Reddit, with its forums on just about everything imaginable, has plenty of discussions for day traders at www.reddit.com/r/daytrading/. There's some great information here, but watch out for trading tips of dubious quality.

>> **TraderInterviews.com:** Looking for something educational and inspirational to listen to? TraderInterviews.com (www.traderinterviews.com) features discussions with different traders.

>> **Trader Mike:** Every day, Michael Seneadza, a day trader, updates his blog at www.tradermike.net. It includes his trading journal, thoughts on the markets, and advice on day trading, which he admits is not definitive. This blog is often thought-provoking.

>> **Trade2Win:** Are you looking for forums about trading? Want to find out what other traders think about a service or a strategy? Looking to learn more? Check out Trade2Win, www.trade2win.com, one of the most comprehensive trader sites in cyberspace.

>> **Traders Laboratory:** If you are interested in meeting other day traders online, finding web-based seminars, reading traders' blogs, or checking out economic release calendars, then Traders Laboratory, www.traders laboratory.com, is the site for you.

Other Mainstream Media

Even though traders are hooked to real-time market data through the Internet, they still look to some old-style sources for information. Believe it or not!

>> **Barron's:** *Barron's* (www.barrons.com) is a weekly financial newspaper published by Dow Jones & Company. The primary emphasis is on long-term investing, but it carries in-depth market analysis and often interviews outstanding traders. In addition, the regular "Electronic Trader" column carries news and ratings of online brokerage firms, many of which specialize in services for day traders.

>> **BNN Bloomberg:** BNN Bloomberg (www.bloomberg.ca) is a cable channel and website that carries news and information about the markets. (In 2018, Bell Media's BNN and Bloomberg joined forced to create BNN Bloomberg.) Some traders keep it running in the background while they trade. Others watch the shows before and after market hours.

>> **Financial Post** (www.financialpost.com): Canada's other national newspaper also has a robust business section that traders may find useful, at least to keep them abreast of the many macro economic issues that could influence the company they're interested in buying and selling.

>> **Investor's Business Daily:** This newspaper, www.investors.com, is published by the William O'Neill Company, which also publishes charts and technical analysis systems used by stock investors. Every morning, *IBD* has new trade ideas and market analysis for active traders, especially those in the stock market.

>> **Report on Business:** The "Report on Business" section of the *Globe and Mail* (www.theglobeandmail.com/business), which is what paper calls its daily business section and its magazine, is the go-to resource for business and investing news in Canada. Its "Globe Investor" section has a lot of great market-related sotries and information to sift through.

Index

A

Abbey, Boris, 22
Aequitas NEO Exchange (NEO), 71
agricultural producers, 9, 326
AIG, 119
algorithms, 7–8, 197. *See also* trading algorithms
alpha, 57, 250
alternative trading systems (ATS), 69, 71–72
AmiBroker software package, 252
Andrews, Alan, 171
anger, 38–39
anomalies, 193–196
anxiety, 38, 40
Apple Mac computer, 30, 252
arbitrage. *See also* risk arbitrage
  discussion, 59, 96
  high-frequency trading and, 99
  market efficiency and, 96–97, 204–205
  price discrepancies in, 98
  in program trading
    ETF, 211–212
    fixed income, 212–213
    index arbitrage, 213
    interest-rate, 212–213
    market efficiency, 204–205
    merger arbitrage, 213–214
    options markets, 215
    overview, 203
    price discrepancies, 205–206
    risk arbitrage, 207–210
    transaction costs, 215–216
  synthetic securities and, 97–98
Art of War, The (Sun Tzu), 42, 340
assets, 61–62, 81–82. *See also specific assets*
ATS (alternative trading systems), 69, 71–72
Australian dollar, 26
automated trades, 17, 38. *See also* trading algorithms

average true range, 185–186
Awaken the Giant Within (Robbins), 340

B

backtesting
  building confidence via, 38, 316
  discussion, 17, 56–57, 139, 200
  for performance measuring
    hypothesis, 248
    market comparison, 249–250
    overview, 248, 316
    running test, 248–249
    software, 251–253
  program trading and, 201, 316
  trading algorithms, 201
Bank of Montreal (BMO) InvestorLine, 275
Barber, Brad, 22–23
basis point, 140
bear market
  discussion, 160, 169, 174
  maxims/clichés on, 148–149
  VIX and, 186–187
Bear Stearns, 119
bear traps, 194–195
behavioral finance, 37
Bell Laboratories, 126–127, 334
Berkshire Hathaway, 17–18
beta, 57, 186, 250
Bible of Options Strategies, The (Cohen), 337
bid-ask spread
  discussion, 68–69, 221
  Level I quotes and, 271
  scalping and, 206
Biggest Winner trading competition, 329
bills, 75. *See also* bonds
Bitcoin, 87–88
Black Monday, 196

Robbins, Anthony, 340

Rockefeller, Barbara, 339

round lots, 65

Royal Bank of Canada, 71

RRIF (Registered Retirement Income Fund), 291, 294

RRSP (Registered Retirement Savings Plan), 15, 26, 291–293, 298

S

S&P 500, 51

S&P/TSX 60 futures contract, 91–92

S&P/TSX Composite Index. *See* TSX/S&P Composite Index

saving, 19

scalping, 206–207

scams
  avoiding brokerage, 279–280
  pump and dump, 74, 89, 207

schedule, 31–32

School of Gann, 242

Scotia iTrade, 277–278

ScotiaMcleod, 241

SEC (Securities and Exchange Commission), 88, 244, 282–283

securities, 61–62, 66, 191

Securities Act, 283

self-regulatory organization (SRO), 284–285

September 22, 2001 attacks, 287

share prices, 10

Shopify, 69–70

short and distort campaign, 107

short selling
  choosing stocks for, 108
  discussion, 105–107
  risks and returns from, 109, 115–116
  short interest ratios, 189–190

short squeeze, 108

sick leave, 31

simulation trading, 200, 250–253

sleep, 32

Small Order Entry System (SOES), 282

smart money, 184

smartphones, 37

Smith, Adam, 46

software packages. See also specific software packages
  for performance measuring, 251–253
  for tax preparation, 302
  for technical analysis, 158–159

software-based platforms, 274

speculating, 9, 19

speed, 17, 31

spreads, 49, 206

SRO (self-regulatory organization), 284–285

standard deviation calculation
  discussion, 56–57, 64
  for measuring volatility, 64–65, 122
  risk and, 65, 263–265

stock callback, 108–109

stock index futures, 35

stock market, 10, 14, 52. *See also* financial markets

stock market crash of 1929, 66, 282

stock market crash of 1987, 282

Stockaholics.net, 43

stocks. *See also* Canadian stocks; U.S. stocks
  brokerage firms for, 275–278
  budget needed for, 65
  discussion, 67
  leverage with, 109–110
  margin requirements for, 66

StockTwits service, 240

stop and limit orders
  decisiveness and, 17
  discussion, 9, 14, 21, 52, 324
  for quick close out, 123

stop orders, 141, 202, 220, 332

stop-limit orders, 142

stop-loss exit points, 29

strategies. *See* program trading; trading plan

strategy ETFs, 84, 86

stress
  advice on, 28–29
  discussion, 14–15, 22
  managing, 32, 53
  planning to minimize, 25

strike price, 110

strips, 76. *See also* bonds

subpennying, 98, 206

About the Authors

Annie Logue, MBA, is the author of *Hedge Funds For Dummies, Socially Responsible Investing For Dummies,* and *Emerging Markets For Dummies* (all published by John Wiley & Sons, Inc.). She has written for *Barron's, The New York Times, Newsweek Japan, USA Today,* and the International Monetary Fund. She is a lecturer at the Liautaud Graduate School of Business at the University of Illinois at Chicago. Her current career follows 12 years of experience as an investment analyst. She has a BA from Northwestern University and an MBA from the University of Chicago, and she holds the Chartered Financial Analyst (CFA) designation.

Bryan Borzykowski is an award-winning journalist who focuses on business, investing, personal finance, and technology. He's coauthored three previous *For Dummies* books: the first edition of *Day Trading For Canadians For Dummies, Exchange-Traded Funds For Canadians For Dummies,* and *Building Wealth For Canadians For Dummies* (all published by John Wiley & Sons, Inc.). He's also written for the *New York Times,* CNBC, BBC, *Wired, Washington Post, MoneySense, Globe and Mail, Financial Post, Report on Business,* and many other publications. He now spends most of his days as the founder and editorial director of ALLCAPS Content, a content agency that works with businesses and organizations in the finance, consulting, technology and healthcare sectors, among others, to create editorial-style content across a variety of mediums. Bryan also appears weekly on CTV News Channel and SiriusXM Radio to discuss the latest business news.

Dedication

Bryan: To Lainie, Molly, Shae, and Romi, for their constant love, support, laughter and, most importantly, patience. None of this would be possible without all of you.

Authors' Acknowledgments

Ann: So many wonderful people helped me on the different editions of this book. I talked to many day traders, brokers, and others in the investment business, including Jack Alogna and Beth Cotner; Michael Browne of DTN Inc.; Nihar Dalil, Glenda Dowie, Greg Gocek, and Robert Cohen of the CFA Society of Chicago; Mary Haffenberg and Curt Zuckert at the Chicago Mercantile Exchange; John T. Hoagland, Conor Meegan, and Michael Patak at TopstepTrader; Anil Joshi of NuFact; Karen H. at Gamblers Anonymous; James Kupfer of Waterston Financial; James Lee of TradersLaboratory.com; Wayne Lee of Nasdaq; Michael Lindsay, Khurram Naik, and James Cagnina at Infinity Brokerage Services; Kristy Gercken, Casey Nicholson, Erika Olson, Don Padou, Karina Rubel, Mario Sant Singh, Chris Tabaka, Elizabeth Tabaka, and Allen Ward. I also talked to several other traders who asked to remain anonymous; they know who they are, and I hope they also know how much I appreciate their help. As for the mechanics of putting together the book, Tim Gallan and Tracy Boggier of Wiley were great to work with this time around. Finally, my agent, Marilyn Allen, made it all happen.

Bryan: Day trading is a complicated topic and while this book will help you figure out how to get started and possibly even make a few bucks, it take years of practise to really understand how it all works. Fortunately, I was able to speak to a lot of differen people — for the first edition Canadianized 10 years ago and for the new one — who helped me understand all the ins and outs. First off, I must thank Ann, who wrote the original *Day Trading For Dummies* and the subsequent U.S. editions. She researched and wrote the bulk of this book, so if it weren't for her hard work, I may not have had the opportunity to put the Canadian editions together. I also want to thank Bruce Seago, who now runs a strategic consulting business, but gave me a lot of information for the first edition of this book while he was president and CEO of CMC Markets Canada. I want to thank Wally Trenholm; Jeff Waite, product manager of self-directed investing at Questrade; Susan Willemsen, president and founder of The Siren Group; Jamie Golombek, manager of tax and estate planning at CIBC; Benny Osher, a CA with Toronto's Kopstick Osher; and people from the IIROC, the OSC, TMX Group who helped answer my seemingly random questions about day trading. I also want to thank Duncan Hood, business editor at the *Toronto Star*, who worked with me at *Canadian Business* magazine on the original day trading story that ended up getting the *For Dummies* ball rolling.

Last, but certaintly not least, a big thank you to Tracy Boggier at Wiley, who asked me to create a second editon of this book, and to Tim Gallan for the edits and for keeping things on track. Feel free to send me a note on Twitter @bborzyko.

Thanks, and enjoy the book.

Publisher's Acknowledgments

Senior Acquisitions Editor: Tracy Boggier

Project Editor: Tim Gallan

Senior Editorial Assistant: Elizabeth Stilwell

Technical Editor: Rick Stambaugh (previous edition)

Proofreader: Debbye Butler

Production Editor: Siddique Shaik

Cover Images: © ismagilov/ Getty Images, © alexsl/Getty Images

Leverage the power

Dummies is the global leader in the reference category and one of the most trusted and highly regarded brands in the world. No longer just focused on books, customers now have access to the dummies content they need in the format they want. Together we'll craft a solution that engages your customers, stands out from the competition, and helps you meet your goals.

Advertising & Sponsorships

Connect with an engaged audience on a powerful multimedia site, and position your message alongside expert how-to content. Dummies.com is a one-stop shop for free, online information and know-how curated by a team of experts.

- Targeted ads
- Video
- Email Marketing

- Microsites
- Sweepstakes sponsorship

20 **MILLION** PAGE VIEWS EVERY SINGLE MONTH

15 MILLION **UNIQUE** VISITORS PER MONTH

43% OF ALL VISITORS ACCESS THE SITE VIA THEIR MOBILE DEVICES

700,000 NEWSLETTER SUBSCRIPTIONS TO THE INBOXES OF *300,000* UNIQUE INDIVIDUALS EVERY WEEK